Managing the Public's Business

MANAGING THE PUBLIC'S BUSINESS

The Job of the Government Executive

Laurence E. Lynn, Jr.

Basic Books, Inc., Publishers

New York

021287

Library of Congress Cataloging in Publication Data

Lynn, Laurence E   1937–
   Managing the public's business.

   Includes bibliographical references and index.
   1. Government executives—United States.
I. Title.
JK723.E9L96   353'.074   80–68176
   ISBN: 0–465–04378–X

To Pat

CONTENTS

PREFACE

THE ORIGINS of this book go back well over fifteen years to when I was first offered a job in government by then Deputy Assistant Secretary of Defense Alain C. Enthoven. (The rewards of beginning one's professional career working in government for a first-rate public official were such that I continue to urge this course for my students.) Since than I have been fortunate to have had as mentors men whom I believe history will judge to have been gifted—and, not incidentally, controversial—public servants; Robert S. McNamara, Henry A. Kissinger, and Elliot L. Richardson. Their intellect, energy, and vision exemplify those characteristics we should hope to discover in our senior public officials. Also influential were numerous other associates and colleagues who inspired those with whom they worked by their intelligence, resourcefulness, sensitivity, and dedication to the public interest. From serving with them on the staff of the National Security Council and in the Departments of Defense, of Health, Education, and Welfare, and of the Interior, I acquired the convictions which have inspired this book.

The first of these convictions is that managing the public's business, that is, serving in a senior executive position in a government department or agency, is a high calling. The most effective public officials have been those who have brought not only a degree of idealism to the opportunity to hold public office but also an abiding respect for the importance of their work. The failures have been those who served reluctantly, with purely self-serving motives, or without real understanding of why such jobs were both important and difficult enough to demand their best efforts.

A second conviction is that top federal executive posts are the most difficult jobs to do well in our society. The actions, or failures to act, of the men and women in these positions have an almost limitless range of social consequences. These jobs must be performed, moreover, under constant critical scrutiny from outsiders, in the face of conflict at every hand, and at times with the most meager managerial discretion.

The third conviction is that, despite the difficulties, the government is manageable. With wit, skill, and insight, qualified men and women can perform effectively in directing and overseeing government organizations. Good public management, however, is not what it is often thought to be: a matter of applying the latest techniques of business administration to government, such as Management by Objectives or Zero Base Budgeting. Nor is it a matter of harnessing, whipping, and cajoling recalcitrant bureaucrats into action. Career civil servants are not recalcitrant; neither are they eager to respond to management techniques which presume that they are. Good executive management occurs when capable executives recognize the unique combination of demands—political, bureaucratic, and substantive—that they face and then cope with them successfully by taking the time to manage, that is to learn, to motivate, to supervise, to communicate, to follow up.

When I left government service in 1974, I had no plans to write a book of this kind. I was subsequently motivated to do so by two sets of influences. The first stems from continued observation of the attempts by recent presidents and their advisers to improve the management of the federal government. Not only have these attempts made little difference, but federal executives, from the president on down, continue to make costly mistakes while working on the most elementary of management tasks and problems.

The second influence has been the environment of the Kennedy School of Government at Harvard University, where I have taught for the last six years. Year after year, bright, highly motivated graduate students come to the school to prepare for service in government. In their courses, they are repeatedly confronted with tangible problems that a department or government executive has faced, and they are asked to discuss how they would deal with the situations. Could the problems in these cases have been better handled or avoided altogether? One cannot help but learn a great deal from participating in, and from guiding, such discussions.

These influences have stimulated my desire to develop a coherent account of how government organizations could be effectively managed, an account which would capture the feel for public management that I acquired during nearly a decade of service with people whom I believe were good managers and also from my additional years of reflection, research, and observation of other public managers.

This book has been made possible by the help of many friends and colleagues. Martin Kessler of Basic Books helped enlarge my original, more modest vision for the book and provided constant encouragement and editorial advice. Graham T. Allison, Dean of the Kennedy School of Government, ensured that I had sufficient time to write. Graham Allison, Chris Argyris, Dan Fenn, Mark Iwry, Valerie Nelson, Dick Neustadt, and Don Price provided valuable comments on drafts of the manuscript, and they have my deepest thanks. My administrative assistant Alicia McFall aided in the production of this book in every possible way, from typing to proofreading to trouble shooting. Christopher Allen Edward Lawlor assisted with the research and brought keen personal interest and excellent critical judgment to the task. Eddie Lawlor also helped draft chapter 6. Finally, my wife Pat provided the encouragement, forbearance, assistance, and faith that I needed to start and to finish this book.

Managing the Public's Business

CHAPTER 1

Management Without Managers

AMERICANS in large numbers distrust and resent their government. They have become convinced that government, especially the federal government, is wasteful, oppressive, and insensitive, and they have come to doubt that public officials act in the public interest or in accordance with commonly held values. Reflecting this dissatisfaction, David A. Stockman, a former congressman (R-Mich.) who became Ronald Reagan's director of the Office of Management and Budget (OMB), has criticized

the excesses of the American superstate—the vast accumulation, at the top of our society, of too much governmental machinery; too much control over the incomes of households and firms and the daily commerce of the marketplace; too much usurpation of the institutions of family, neighborhood and local government; too vast an outpouring of state-manufactured rights, entitlements and remedies; and too much activism and advantage among society's elites at the expense of diminished choice for the citizen of ordinary rank.[1]

The state of affairs that has brought about this collapse of popular confidence in government has been termed "a crisis of competence."[2] Weary of governmental ineptitude, people willingly respond to candidates and officeholders with ideas that promise solutions.

Such ideas are not lacking. As with other crises in American life, the crisis of confidence in the competence of government officials has produced an outpouring of remedies, from the notion that "outsiders" should be elected or appointed to high office to the adoption of procedural solutions such as zero base budgeting, sunset laws, and paperwork budgets to increased oversight of executive agencies by congressional committees. Making government work better has become a central theme of presidential campaigns and a leitmotif of American political discussion everywhere from barrooms to academe.

Yet an examination of the problem of governmental performance and the many ideas for improving it reveals a paradox. The executives of those government agencies we depend on to conduct the public's business, especially those two hundred or so officials appointed to head the cabinet-level departments and key subordinate and independent agencies, have been given responsibilities of immense importance, complexity, and difficulty by Congress, the president, and the courts. Each year, moreover, hundreds of new legislative enactments, executive orders, and court decisions expand and diversify these responsibilities. At the same time, the political and judicial processes that create these responsibilities generate centrifugal forces that tear away at executive authority and force the manager to share control. The result is that top executive jobs, of great importance in principle, are very hard to perform with distinction. Indeed, distinguished performance by appointed executives is sufficiently rare that these persons are often regarded as vestigial to a government in which the president and his most intimate advisers in the White House are seen as the only figures of real significance in the executive branch.

Sharpening the sense of paradox is the absence of serious proposals to improve governmental competence by strengthening the capacities of the political executives to direct the activities of their departments and agencies. Indeed, most ideas for reform would place additional constraints on the discretion of executives and expect them to conform even more closely to standard operating procedures and protocols. We want better management and greater competence in the federal government, but we do not want to rely on strong, competent executives to help achieve it.

The illumination of this paradoxical situation and its implications for governmental competence is a central purpose of this book. We shall seek to provide insights into the nature of the responsibilities appointed executives must bear and the centrifugal forces that extinguish the capacity of these officials to perform with distinction on behalf of the prized objective of governmental competence. In the concluding chapter, we shall explore the possibilities for modifying these forces sufficiently to increase the political executive's prospects for effective performance.

As background for the discussion to follow, it is useful to review those features of the American political system that account for the political executive's jeopardized and diminished status within it.

Centrifugal Forces

Ours is a government of large, complex organizations created to carry out public purposes. "The orders and statutes in our big democracy do not invest persons with power," wrote Paul Appleby, "they invest organizations with responsibility." In 1978 alone, for example, Congress assigned the following additional responsibilities to the already sprawling U.S. Department of Health and Human Services (then the Department of Health, Education and Welfare):

- "to make improvements in the end stage renal disease program" presently authorized under Medicare (Public Law 95-292);
- "to promote the healthy development of children who would benefit from adoption by facilitating their placement in adoptive homes" and "to improve the provisions of the Child Abuse Prevention and Treatment Act" (Public Law 95-266);
- "to provide for improved programs for older persons" (Public Law 95-478);
- "to revise and extend the program of assistance . . . for health maintenance organizations" (Public Law 95-559);
- "to increase the availability of assistance to middle-income students" (Public Law 95-566);
- "to establish a community service employment program for handicapped individuals, and to provide comprehensive services for independent living for handicapped individuals" (Public Law 95-602);
- "to establish a National Center for Health Care Technology" (Public Law 95-6232); and
- "to meet obligations under the Convention of Psychotropic Substances relating to regulatory controls on the manufacture, distribution, importation, and exportation of psychotropic substances" (Public Law 95-633).

In the same year, the administrator of the U.S. Environmental Protection Agency was directed to "develop and disseminate information and educational materials to all segments of the public on the public health and other effects of noise," to "administer a nationwide Quiet Communities Program," and to "develop and implement a national noise environmental assessment program to identify trends in noise exposure and response, ambient levels, and compliance data" (Public Law 95-609). The secretary of commerce was directed to "initiate and carry out research, technology development, technology transfer, and demonstration projects to test and demonstrate the economic feasibility of the manufacture and commercialization of natural rubber from Parthenium or other hydrocarbon-containing plants" (Public Law 95-592). The secretary of labor was authorized to establish and carry out a black lung insurance program which could enable operators of coal mines to purchase insurance, and he was directed to prescribe the premium rates and the terms or conditions of such insurance.

These federal departments were directed, in other words, to create new industries, technologies, and lines of business, to improve their existing programs, and to start from scratch to tackle social problems of unknown scope and complexity with methods that had not yet been developed.

Some of these added responsibilities were sought by the executive branch, while others originated in the committees and subcommittees of the U.S. Congress or in congressional staffs. What did Congress have in mind by voting to authorize these new responsibilities? How was it expected that the necessary tasks would be performed? Who was to be held accountable for the results?

The actual performance of the work would have to depend heavily, of course, on the "bureaucracy," that is, on already existing subordinate agencies—the Rehabilitative Services Administration, the Food and Drug Administration, the Health Resources Administration, or the Administration on Children, Youth and Families—and their professional staffs. Given the scope of these new demands and the burden of existing responsibilities, it could not be otherwise. But the political executives in charge of these departments are the president's agents for taking care that the laws pertaining to their organizations are faithfully executed, a presidential responsibility under Article II, Section 3, of the Constitution. In other words, the government's senior executives have an important constitutional function, ratified by Supreme Court opinions holding that administrative acts of heads of departments are acts of the president. As if there were any doubt about this delegation of responsibility, the new statutes reiterated it in concrete terms, directing the heads of the departments and occasionally even subordinate officials to perform specific tasks necessary to executing the law. It is the political executives, and not their subordinate agents, who are held accountable by the oversight committees of Congress, by the General Accounting Office, by the department's inspector general, by the courts, and by the president if serious problems or controversies arise.

What the law gives in the way of specific responsibilities, the law can later take away, however, and therein lies the key to understanding the circumstances facing departmental executives. They are not only agents of the president; they are also agents of Congress, particularly of the committees that authorize and oversee the activities of their departments and appropriate the funds to carry them out. Contests for control over government organizations—for the power to create, reorganize, or extinguish them and to establish their directions, design their programs, and provide them with resources—are at the heart of American politics, and political executives are in the middle of these contests, their discretion steadily narrowed by the determination of the contestants to leave nothing to chance. The framework for this competition is to be found in the Constitution.

The president was made the chief military and political officer of the United States, but the Constitution made little direct provision for the exercise of administrative power.[3] Article II, Section 1, vests the "executive power" in the president, and Section 2 of that article gives the president the power to "require the opinion, in writing, of the principal officer in each of the executive departments, upon any subject relating to the duties of their respective offices." This latter provision is the only power of administrative direction given the president in the Constitution. The president is also empowered to appoint, subject to authorization by law and the advice and consent of the U.S. Senate, "officers of the United States" not provided for elsewhere in the Constitution, though Congress "may by law vest the appointment of such inferior officers, as they think proper in the President alone . . . or in the heads of departments." But the Constitution says little about the executive departments of government and nothing about the number, power, responsibilities, or duties of the heads of executive departments. They are mentioned in the Constitution only in references to "officers of the government" and "heads of departments."

The vesting of the executive power in the president and the "take care" provision have subsequently been interpreted by Congress and the courts in a way that permits the conferring of substantial *legislative* authority on the president and on the heads of the executive departments. Congress may delegate to the president or the heads of departments acting on behalf

7

of the president the power to issue regulations concerning how the law is to be carried out, regulations which have the force of law. Thus, the Constitution guarantees that departmental executives will be thrust into the center of what is fundamentally a legislative process.

At the same time, important administrative powers are vested in Congress. Article I, Section 9, empowers Congress "to make all laws which shall be necessary and proper for carrying into execution . . . all . . . powers vested by this Constitution in the Government of the United States, or in any department or officer thereof." In particular, "no money shall be drawn from the treasury, but in consequence of appropriations made by law."[4] By insuring that executive actions shall be in accordance with law, that expenditures shall be in accordance with lawful appropriations, and that the U.S. Senate shall authorize and consent to the appointment of key presidential subordinates, the Constitution places Congress at the center of departmental administration. In appropriating funds for departmental budgets, for example, Congress is engaging in what is fundamentally an administrative function.

It is hardly surprising, therefore, that American politics has been punctuated by competition between the president and Congress concerning their overlapping prerogatives. Because of their relative silence concerning departmental administration, constitutional arrangements guarantee that the departments and independent agencies will provide terrain to be fought for as the president and Congress seek to maximize their authority to determine how the public interest shall be defined and carried out. At any given moment, the departmental executive's actual authority reflects the precarious balance of power between Congress and the president. If the committees of Congress have specific ideas as to how a mandate shall be carried out, or if the executive branch desires authorization to execute the laws in particular ways, the language of the statutes will reflect them. Though the legislation cited earlier implied a general assignment of responsibility to the secretary of health and human services to carry out the several new duties, that official was given specific directions as to *how* these responsibilities were to be carried out. The secretary was directed to

- determine the standards for "ethical medical practice in this country . . . on the basis of a consensus of the views of the American medical and scientific community";
- "prescribe requirements to be met by providers of services and renal dialysis facilities, . . . transplantation services, [and] self-care home dialysis support services which are furnished by the provider or facility," including "requirements for a minimum utilization rate for covered procedures and for self-dialysis training programs";

- "establish in accordance with such criteria as he finds appropriate, renal disease network areas";
- prescribe regulations governing the determination of findings that a child has been sexually abused;
- establish a National Health Maintenance Organization Intern Program and approve all awards of grants and internships following submission of applications in a form he or she prescribes;
- prescribe regulations which designate who is a "health professional" and which govern the submission by health maintenance organizations of information demonstrating that they are fiscally sound;
- submit to Congress a report on the extent and nature of drug abuse in rural areas, the special needs and circumstances which must be addressed in order to provide drug abuse prevention facilities to these areas, and specific recommendations respecting such facilities in these areas;
- prescribe those specialized services for the mental health of children and of the elderly that are to be offered by community mental health centers.

These same laws also spelled out the secretary's continuing responsibilities for program administration. He or she must, for example, establish requirements for the maintenance of records and information, approve payments to those eligible for federal grants, establish cost reimbursement rates, rule on all exceptions or waivers to conditions prescribed in regulations, make periodic reports to Congress, determine compliance with specific legislative provisions, and formulate criteria for program design.

Thus the secretary of health and human services and all other department and agency heads operating under the authority of law are in many respects less executives with general grants of authority to manage their organizations than contractors obligated to produce specific programmatic outcomes in defined ways, with the terms of the contract subject to unilateral alteration. Under the best of circumstances, it is a precarious existence.

Complexity and Constraints

Declining faith in governmental competence is largely a result of major changes in governmental activity over several decades that have strongly reinforced these centrifugal forces and further eroded the possibilities of effective public management.

The first of these changes is the transformation of governmental tasks. Prior to the early decades of this century, government at all levels was engaged primarily in providing services directly to the general population or to specific client groups. By far the largest government agency was the Post Office. The public's business also included the administration of patents, customs, public lands, Indian affairs, and the taking and publication of the census as well as the activities associated with defense, foreign affairs, and revenue collection. The growth of government for over a century took the form of expansion in the kinds of services offered, such as the gathering and publication of statistics and the conduct of research, and in the creation of direct service agencies: the National Park Service, the Weather Bureau, the Public Health Service, the Bureau of Public Roads, the Coast and Geodetic Survey, and the Bureau of Mines. The Progressive era's response to the emerging social and economic problems of the late nineteenth and early twentieth centuries and the Depression era reaction to economic disaster permanently altered this pattern of governmental activity in two significant ways.

First, people began to expect and allow government to assume responsibility for the social welfare of Americans in need. The new welfare and social insurance programs greatly changed the character of federal executive responsibilities. Such programs are characterized by vague or uncertain technologies, strong ideological and value commitments on the part of staffs and organized interest groups, the dominance of trained professionals, and the near impossibility of defining measures of effectiveness and standards of efficiency.[5] The politics of social welfare tend, moreover, to be colored by their redistributive character; grants to the needy financed by tax proceeds may provoke strong resentment. Thus senior executives began to be drawn into new kinds of ideological conflicts in which the classic tools of political accommodation were less effective.[6] The typical executive in the newly created agencies could expect to be embroiled almost continuously in ill-defined and hard-to-resolve controversies arising both inside and outside his or her department.

A second shift of far-reaching importance was the increased use of the grant-in-aid mechanism:[7] payments to states, municipalities, or other eligible recipients for a specific public purpose, such as the promotion of child welfare, the provision of vocational education, or the construction of housing. Grants-in-aid to state and local governments have grown to account for well over 20 percent of both total federal outlays for domestic programs and total state and local expenditures. Virtually all federal departments administer intergovernmental grants of some type. This development, too, has had significant implications for executive practice. For the most part, the federal government, not the state or localities, defines the purposes of the grants, thus provoking conflicts with state and local officials who want greater latitude in determining the uses of grant funds. Political executives are thus regularly drawn into conflicts with governors, mayors, and county executives, and they have become the president's agents in dealing not only with Congress and interest groups in the traditional sense but also with officials at other levels of government and, through them, with their constituencies.

A second major change has been growth in the scope of departmental and agency responsibilities as existing organizations have assimilated ever-growing numbers of functions and programs.

The consolidation of federal activities in large conglomerate departments under the watchful eye of staff officials gathered in the White House was given impetus by President Franklin D. Roosevelt following the advice of his Committee on Administrative Management, headed by Louis Brownlow. The Brownlow Committee stated in its 1937 report that efficient administration required "the establishment of a responsible and effective chief executive as the center of energy, direction, and administrative management [aided by] appropriate managerial and staff agencies."[8] The Executive Office of the President was created under authority of the Reorganization Act of 1939. Transferred to it were the Bureau of the Budget (from treasury), the National Resources Planning Board (from Interior), and the Federal Employment Stabilization Board, the forerunner of the Council of Economic Advisers (from commerce). The same reorganization also created the first modern conglomerate agency, the Federal Security Agency, comprising the Social Security Board, the Public Health Service (from treasury), the Office of Education (from interior), and allied activities.

The spirit of administrative reform and consolidation was revived after, and further stimulated by, World War II. The initial finding of the first Hoover Commission in 1949 was that

the executive branch is not organized into a workable number of major departments and agencies which the President can effectively direct, but is cut up into a large number of agencies, which divide responsibility and which are too great in number for effective direction from the top.[9]

During the next fifteen years, some of the largest agencies of government were created: the Defense Department in 1949, the Department of Health, Education and Welfare in 1953, the Departments of Housing and Urban Development in 1965 and Transportation in 1966. At the same time, the formal authority of cabinet officers to organize and direct the activities of their departments was expanded. The force of this consolidation movement has ebbed and flowed, reaching its high point with Richard Nixon's proposals to create four "super agencies" and its low point with Jimmy Carter's opposite inclination to disassemble existing agencies, as reflected by his support for the creation of the Departments of Energy and Education.

However, because of their diversity, federal programs, which now exceed 1,200 in number, cannot be readily sorted into natural administrative clusters. One could imagine administration by target group (children, the handicapped), by the character of the service provided (education, income security), by social institution (families, communities, health maintenance organizations), by the end sought (economic development, delinquency prevention), by facility (hospitals, prisons, highways), or by hybrid schemes of various sorts (children, youth, and families; education for the handicapped). Small, self-contained, relatively autonomous bureaus have given way to sprawling agglomerations of loosely related categorical programs. Inevitably, the scope of larger administrative units tends to be both arbitrary and overlapping, making the task of general management that much more difficult.

A third major change has been the coming to maturity of the career civil service.[10] As civil service coverage was extended outward, downward, and especially upward from its inception in 1887, an important issue arose: Where should the line be drawn between career service and noncareer political supervision? This issue had first arisen at the conclusion of President Grover Cleveland's second term, when he added 30,000 positions to the covered service in one executive order. "Incoming secretaries and bureau chiefs began to complain that they were administratively handicapped in controlling their agencies because they could not appoint or easily move their subordinates."[11] It later became an insistent question as the New Deal wore on, bringing a realization of the difficulties facing political executives in supervising highly specialized and experienced civil servants. After World War II, the personnel issue broadly conceived became the principal concern of the second Hoover Commission, which undertook the first systematic study of the relationships between career executives and political executives. Among its principal recommendations was the creation of a Senior Civil Service of neutral, mobile, generalist career executives, the existence of which would insure flexibility and competence in the management appointments of succeeding administrations.

The enactment of civil service reform in 1978, incorporating the second Hoover Commission's recommendation, cannot alter the reality of the situation now facing the political executive, analyzed in depth by Hugh Heclo in *A Government of Strangers.* The lines between political and career officials have become complex and vague. Satisfactory patterns of mutual influence and communication take patience and skill to create. The necessity of doing so is just one more difficulty facing the political executive.[12]

Perhaps the most consequential changes in recent decades have been those affecting the two other branches of government: Congress and the courts.

Since the earliest days of the national government, Congress has asserted its prerogative to engage in investigations pursuant to its constitutional grant of "all legislative powers."[13] Its exercise of that role has been uneven and, for the most part, ineffective, often amounting to no more than harassment of the executive. That it has retained its determination to engage in oversight and investigations, however, has proved an important constraint on freedom of executive action.[14]

Congress has employed a variety of methods to control and influence executive activity, principally statutory language, appropriations, and investigations. Though statutes often authorize considerable discretion by administrators, "Congress has avoided broad general grants of authority whenever it was feasible to do so."[15] To an increasing extent, Congress has especially prescribed the internal organization and administration processes of executive agencies. The federal executive who wishes to exercise initiative must become preoccupied with ducking around generalized, unworkable procedural requirements.

From the congressional perspective, the nearly thirty years prior to the enactment of the Budget Reform and Impoundment Control Act of 1974 involved a frustrating and unequal struggle with the executive branch over the "power of the purse." Many legislators were alarmed at their own irresponsible tendencies to authorize high levels of spending, or to use subterfuges such as "tax expenditures" and "backdoor financing," and then to hold the president accountable for fiscal responsibility. Nixon's resort to impoundments to hold down spending seemed an affront, yet many legislators believed that Congress had only itself to blame.

Political executives saw the same years from a somewhat different perspective. "Until 1975," said Elliot L. Richardson, "the process of Congressional choice was impulsive, random, and fragmented."[16] Federal executives could expect to be drawn into and even become preoccupied with the trench warfare between congressional committees and the executive branch, to have their daily schedules held hostage to the congressional "compulsion to legislate."[17] They were often caught in the middle between the committees, on the one hand, and the Office of Management and Budget and the White House, on the other. Richardson noted that the "imbalance from which the Congress suffers most is a matter not of power but of capacity for coherent action—the ability to weigh competing claims, formulate a consistent strategy, and arrive at a sound consensus."[18] Congressional oversight activities were not systematic. "Much of [congressional oversight] is ad hoc and temporary, reactive to immediate issues and scandals."[19] As Alan L. Otten wrote in the *Wall Street Journal:*

. . . oversight has been infrequent and slipshod. It's usually dull, thankless work; there are more reelection brownie points in running errands for the folks back home, and more satisfaction in passing new laws. Tough oversight can make enemies among congressional colleagues or powerful interest groups. Committees supposed to exercise oversight are often the ones that created the programs in the first place, and thus not overly anxious to spotlight flaws.

"Everyone recognizes the need for oversight," says former Sen. Edmund Muskie, one of its most effective practitioners, "but other things come along, and it gets pushed farther and farther down the ladder until it disappears."[20]

With the growth of federal programs and of the intergovernmental grant system, Congress faced increased pressures to exercise oversight, compounded in the 1970s by the determination of congressional leaders to impose more checks on the power of the executive in reaction to Lyndon Johnson's dominance of the legislature's deliberations and Richard Nixon's determination to substitute his priorities for those of Congress. Attempting to restore the balance, the Legislative Reorganization Act of 1970 authorized increased staffing for committees and funds for outside experts. It also increased the resources and program evaluation authority of the General Accounting Office (GAO). In general, the congressional enthusiasm for programmatic innovation of the 1960s gave way to a concern for evaluating the efficiency and effectiveness of programs.[21] Congress began requiring more evaluations and reports, instituting legislative vetoes, controlling impoundments, analyzing programs, and requiring periodic reauthorizations of programs, during which congressional inquiry into program operations was possible. The 1974 Committee Reform Amendments required each House committee to establish a separate oversight subcommittee.

But the major congressional attempt to restore the balance of power in its favor was the Budget Reform and Impoundment Control Act of 1974. This act created budget committees in both houses and procedures whereby these committees would assume responsibility for creating a legislative budget that would be binding on the appropriations committees. The act also created the Congressional Budget Office to provide cost information and policy analysis for legislative proposals. Unlike its reception of the Legislative Reorganization Act of 1946, Congress has, albeit with much fretting and grumbling, adhered to the 1974 act, a measure of its value. Congress is undoubtedly better informed now concerning the relationships among the economy, specific legislative proposals, and the budget. Moreover, competition among the Congressional Budget Office, the GAO, the Congressional Research Service, and the Joint Economic Committee, and between these entities and analytical organizations such as the Brookings Institution, the American Enterprise Institute for Public Policy Research, the Urban Institute, and other policy "think tanks," has increased the amount and general quality of policy analysis oriented to decision makers' needs. There are now far larger and better-trained congressional staffs to translate this material into forms immediately useful to legislators.

As congressional interest in effective oversight has grown, the authority and capabilities of the GAO have been broadened and expanded to the point where, under Comptroller General Elmer B. Staats, the GAO has adopted the mission of improving the performance of government.[22] Thus, beyond its traditional function of auditing the financial management of federal agencies, the GAO, either on its own initiative or at the request of elements in Congress, systematically reviews federal agency program management and, on the basis of its studies, makes proposals concerning the improvement of management. These studies go directly to Congress and the media and are available to the public. Thus they can and do spark critical debate about agency activities.

Yet, there are limits to how far Congress will go to concentrate its power to confront the executive branch. Proposals from inside and outside Congress to centralize the oversight function in a single standing committee, in the budget committees, or even in a subcommittee of each standing committee have been rejected out of reluctance on the part of the hundreds of subcommittees to yield potentially important power. Moreover, not all measures to maintain congressional power over the executive branch have been fully effective. Of necessity, for example, the GAO, like Congress, is selective in what it undertakes. The impact on executive branch officials has been less than overwhelming:

... there are a good many in the executive branch who know little about the GAO, or if they are aware of it, share the common misconception that it is only an external financial auditing agency like public accounting firms in the private sector.[23]

Executives complain of the GAO's accounting mentality, lack of concern for the problems of management and policy making, and unfamiliarity with professional activities.

15

021287

Though the Budget Reform and Impoundment Control Act may have introduced somewhat more order into the budget process, an advantage to the executive branch, it has also greatly increased the pressures on political executives. Hearings are more frequent, and legislators explore issues and controversies in more detail. Legislators do not hesitate to confront top officials with questions and arguments based on the work of their staffs and staff organizations and on the research findings of the many policy studies organizations. Expert witnesses of all kinds are regularly brought into the legislative process and often serve as consultants to congressional committees and staffs. Thus political executives who wish to appear as credible leaders of their organizations must know more and be better prepared if they are to maintain satisfactory relations with Congress.

Perhaps the most far-reaching change in governmental practice affecting executive procedure in this century is the most recent (or the most recently identified): the changing character of judicial review of administrative decisions, manifested in the dramatically higher number of lawsuits over executive actions and in the character of the judicial decrees that result from these suits.

The process of judicial review of legislative and administrative acts is, of course, virtually as old as the Republic. For nearly a century, a series of court decisions gradually established a body of administrative law which clarified and defined the formal powers and obligations of executive authorities. Indeed, the study of public administration was initially based on the study of administrative law. The extension and refinement of this body of law accelerated as the federal government increased its regulation of private activities, especially business, to prevent private parties from harming one another. From 1880 to 1960 there emerged what Prof. Richard B. Stewart has called the "traditional model" of administrative law.[24] The objective of judicial review was "to reconcile the competing claims of governmental authority and private autonomy by prohibiting official intrusions on private liberty or property unless authorized by legislative directives."[25] In other words, in reviewing administrative actions, the courts were presuming that policy was to be made by the legislature. The executive agency was merely to follow directions.

To an increasing extent during this period, however, Congress, as noted above, was acting not only to control harmful private actions but also to create public benefits, such as research findings, hydroelectric facilities, income supports, and child health clinics. Furthermore, it was allowing the executive substantial discretion in carrying out congressional intent. The programs thereby produced also created troublesome new issues. Programs reflected or created group interests, not just individual interests. Moreover, conferring benefits on one group might simultaneously impose costs on other groups, and the magnitude and balance of benefits and costs would depend on exactly how governmental executives used the discretion delegated by Congress. Whereas Congress often acted to rein in executive branch officials, the courts were inevitably drawn into adjudicating the complicated disputes involving group interests that arose in connection with the widening array of government programs. By accepting responsibility to adjudicate such disputes, the courtroom, in Abram Chayes's view, became "an explicitly political forum and the court a visible arm of the political process."[26] Legislative history, for example, is often confusing and contradictory. By making authoritative determinations of what Congress intended, when such intent is in dispute, judges take on a legislative function.

Trial judges in federal courts now frequently issue decrees which compel government executives to provide equitable relief to an injured group by foregoing a planned activity, by revising or redesigning programs, or by carrying out a specific course of action prescribed by the judge. More often they prescribe the decision-making process an executive must follow to ensure that all affected interests are properly represented. Judges, in other words, have assumed a significant managerial role. Though Congress can theoretically adjust any perceived imbalance of authority between the courts and the executive agency, it often fails to do so because the politics are too divisive.

Thus federal executives have had to adjust to the reality of significant judicial sharing of executive responsibility. Perhaps more than any other factor, the importance of litigation has frustrated officials with a penchant for decisive action and a distaste for procedural delays and the tedious detail that the requirements of legal sufficiency often entail.

Educating Handicapped Children: A Case Study

The interplay of these forces, and their implications for executive performance, have been evident in the evaluation of federal programs concerning the education of handicapped children.

The Education for All Handicapped Children Act of 1975, originated in

Congress, passed relatively quickly, and was approved by the president on November 29, 1975. The purpose of the act is

to assure that all handicapped children have available to them . . . a free appropriate public education which emphasizes special education and related services designed to meet their unique needs, to assure that the rights of handicapped children and their parents or guardians are protected, to assist States and localities to provide for the education of all handicapped children, and to assess and assure the effectiveness of efforts to educate handicapped children.

Congress was not the first policymaker with respect to educational opportunity for handicapped children. In 1972 a U.S. district court judge ruled that handicapped and emotionally disturbed children have a constitutional right to a public education. Several state legislatures, usually in reaction to litigation, passed statutes with a similar intent. The Nixon administration's Education Special Revenue Sharing proposals had included special funds earmarked for the handicapped. Thus all three branches and both federal and state levels of government were attempting to make policy for the education of handicapped children. Doing the decent thing for a dependent, neglected, and unquestionably deserving group, especially when federal judges were already moving into a national policy vacuum, constituted a political opportunity Congress could not resist.

The congressional declaration of purpose was an admirable and in most respects adequate statement of national policy. Why not simply turn the matter of implementation over to officials in the executive branch, with adequate provisions for continuing oversight of executive performance? The reason is that the committees that authored the legislation were as much concerned with how their purpose was to be achieved as with the purpose itself. Thus, the law continues for twenty-two more pages. (Among other things, it contained definitions of handicapped children and of the educational services they are to receive. These were at variance with definitions of handicapped persons and of the education to which they are entitled under the Rehabilitation Act of 1973, which was a product of the same congressional committees and which provides for equal opportunities for all handicapped persons.)

The term "related services," for example, was defined to include

transportation, and such developmental, corrective, and other supportive services (including speech pathology and audiology, psychological services, physical and occupational therapy, recreation, and medical and counseling services

except that such medical services shall be for diagnostic and evaluation purposes only) as may be required to assist a handicapped child to benefit from
special education. . . .

Further, the local educational agency was directed to establish an Individual Educational Program for each handicapped child at the beginning of
each school year; this program was to be in the form of a written statement
containing five specific types of information. States were directed to submit plans which, among other things, set forth procedures to assure that
all personnel necessary to carry out the purposes of the act are "appropriately and adequately prepared and trained," as well as procedures for
adopting, where appropriate, promising educational practices and materials development. The commissioner of education, at the time a subordinate
of both the secretary of health, education and welfare and the assistant
secretary for education, was directed to propose various implementing
regulations and to submit them for review and comment to the House
Committee on Education and Labor and the Senate Committee on Labor
and Public Welfare. The commissioner was also authorized to hire twenty
people for data collection and program evaluation outside of regular civil
service procedures and pay scales.

Clearly Congress was interested in far more than articulating a national
policy. It was interested in far more than monitoring implementation of
that policy. Included in the statute were detailed instructions concerning
precisely *how* the implementing agencies and officials were to carry out
their mandates. These instructions, moreover, greatly complicated the task
of the responsible political executives by interposing congressional supervision of subordinates' actions and by dictating how their staffs were to
be organized. Who is responsible for managing this complex program? The
law has left it quite unclear.

Enactment of the statute was not the end of congressional involvement
in program execution. The implementing regulations promulgated by the
executive branch covered more than 130 pages of the *Code of Federal Regulations.*[27] In the course of their preparation, numerous issues arose. Among
them were the following:

· The regulations had to include numerous definitions of key terms in
the act so that its provisions could be uniformly carried out. Comments on
the preliminary draft led the Office of Education to revise them so that
they would better conform to current definitions and uses employed by
professional associations, which collectively represented an influential political force. For example, the definition of "related services" was changed

19

from the one appearing in the statute to one which enumerates the specialists who are to provide the services. The definition now reads:

Each annual program plan must include . . . the number of other additional personnel needed [to meet the goal of providing full educational opportunity for all handicapped children], including school psychologists, school social workers, occupational therapists, physical therapists, home-hospital teachers, speech-language pathologists, audiologists, teacher aides, vocational education teachers, work-study coordinators, physical education teachers, therapeutic recreation specialists, diagnostic personnel, supervisors, and other instructional and non-instructional staff.

Commenters on the draft regulations also wanted them to list the specific service areas they represented as among those to be provided in the Individual Educational Program. However, federal officials, having already made a substantial concession to the professional associations, chose not to include such a list.

· How much data should be required in the annual program plans? Some of those commenting on the preliminary regulations felt more data were needed for effective monitoring, while others wanted data requirements substantially reduced as unnecessary and fulfilling no useful purpose. The Office of Education responded to this conflicting advice by increasing each state's monitoring and enforcement obligations.

· Who shall be judged qualified to provide services to handicapped children? The act used the phrase "appropriately and adequately prepared and trained" in reference to service workers. The proposed regulations interpreted this to mean, again in conformity to the wishes of professional associations, formal certification, registration, or licensing by regulatory agencies of the state or the professions. Several commenters objected to this kind of change, stating that formal certification should not be required or that competency should be determined in some other way, but the Office of Education stuck to its guns.

Not surprisingly, a variety of additional issues emerged as the law and the regulations were put into effect. The competence of the government began to be called into question. Parents and interest groups complained, for example, that local educational agencies mass-produced Individual Educational Programs instead of specifying appropriate services for each child's needs, as the law required. The related services required by law often were not adequately provided because of confusion among state agencies over how they were to be paid for. Moreover, federal definitions of related services were thought to be too narrow. Why limit medical services to those for diagnostic and evaluation purposes only? Why not include treatment? As these and other problems materialized, Congressman John Brademas (D-Ind.), chairman of the House Education and Labor Committee, which had jurisdiction over the law, advised the commissioner of education that he would "work hard with State and local authorities and others affected by the laws we have written to help them implement responsibly, sensitively, and effectively the authorizing statutes."[28] At no time did he ask federal officials appearing before him what assistance Congress could give to help *them* manage this program effectively.

This case illustrates the extent to which the interrelationships and declarations of congressional intent, definitions contained in the agencies' regulations, and local decisions concerning the design of individual educational programs are seamless. It is impossible to tell where policy leaves off and administration begins or where the dividing line is between the role of Congress and that of the executive branch and its responsible officials, or even between the role of the federal government, the state, and local education agencies. As far as the handicapped child and his or her parents are concerned, moreover, such distinctions are irrelevant. They want their public schools to deliver on a federal mandate, and they could not care less about the niceties of administrative theory when seeking remedies for their complaints.[29] They will go to whomever they believe will help them.

The implications for the political executive are ominous. The secretary of education, who has overall management responsibility, must operate through his or her commissioner of education, who has also been independently instructed by Congress, then through state and local education agencies to achieve a goal of extraordinary complexity. The congressional committees are deeply involved in the details of administering the program and will not hesitate to change the language of the act if displeased with executive actions. Litigation has brought the federal courts and many state courts into the picture. Suppose the secretary of education questioned the commissioner's definition of related services and its effect on program costs and administrability. Would it be worth the time and political controversy to intervene and change it or to ask for a study on the issues raised by the definition? A conscientious executive might well want to do so, but a politically savvy one might leave well enough alone.

Surmounting the obstacles to the diligent performance of these types of responsibilities is an extraordinary achievement for any political executive. No other group of executives in American life, if they are to be effective, must combine the political sensibilities and leadership qualities of elected officials, the general management skills and strategic judgment of business executives, the technical grasp of program managers, and the sensitivity to human needs and capacities of service workers in the field.

Popular dissatisfaction with government cannot, of course, be solely attributed to mismanagement or to failures of execution by the government's senior officials. Capable administration of federal programs such as a Quiet Communities Program or a program to assure a free, appropriate education for handicapped children will not mollify those critics who object to the very existence of the programs. The careful rationing of scarce fiscal resources or the efficient redistribution of income from one group to another via taxes and transfer payments will hardly silence the complaints of those who perceive that they are losers in the process. In such contentious circumstances, however, where both the ends and the means of government are in question, an effective executive can be most valuable: in accurately identifying problems, in explaining complex issues so that they are widely understood, in describing the costs and consequences of different policies, in seeing to it that official actions are skillfully designed so as to reflect the diverse interests at stake, in maintaining organizational morale and productivity, and in earning the respect, if not the outright approval, of Congress and of influential constituencies. Whatever one's philosophy of government, in other words, the performance of the government's political executives is an important issue.

Can direction of governmental activity by the government's senior executives become more intelligent and purposeful given the centrifugal forces of American politics? Should the president or Congress exercise enough self-restraint to create the conditions for effective management performance in government organizations? How should the performance of political executives be judged? How should they judge themselves? These questions become all the more urgent as dissatisfaction with government combines with underlying trends in governmental structure and practice to further divide and limit power and disperse the capacity to manage, thus making effective executive leadership even less likely. They are the questions that are the preoccupation of this book.

The first question we address is: What is the essential nature of the work that senior federal executives are called upon to perform?

CHAPTER 2

The Tyranny of
the Task

IN 1971, William D. Ruckelshaus, administrator of the Environmental Protection Agency (EPA), promulgated two sets of regulations to govern how provisions of the Clean Air Act Amendments of 1970 would be carried out.[1] The first, concerning the establishment of national air quality standards required by the act, provided that:

the promulgation of national primary and secondary air quality standards shall not be considered in any manner to allow significant deterioration of existing air quality in any portion of any state.

The second, concerning EPA approval of the State Implementation Plans (SIPs) each state was required by the act to submit, provided that

in any region where measured or estimated ambient levels of a pollutant are below the levels specified by an applicable secondary standard, the State implementation plan shall set forth a control strategy which shall be adequate to prevent such ambient pollution levels from exceeding such secondary standard.

This second regulation, which permitted the deterioration of air quality to the level of the federal ambient air quality standards, appeared to contradict the first, which seemed to permit no deterioration of existing air quality.

Inevitably, EPA administrators were questioned concerning the apparent contradiction in the regulations. Ruckelshaus's official position was that this issue was strictly a matter of determining what the law required. Unfortunately, both the act and its legislative history were ambiguous; the Senate appeared to have intended to establish a policy of nondegradation, but the House had not addressed the issue. Thus, an interpretation by EPA lawyers was needed. The Clean Air Act, in the lawyers' view, did not permit the EPA administrator to impose a nondegradation requirement on the states; all the EPA could do was enforce the federal standards, and this is what the second regulation was intended to do. A state could, however, on its own initiative, adopt air quality standards more stringent than the federal standards; this is what the language of the first regulation meant. Environmentalists, led by the Sierra Club, offered a different interpretation: Ruckelshaus had bowed to pressure from the Office of Management and Budget (OMB) and made a concession to industry in issuing the second regulation, thus backing away from his initial position and permitting the deterioration of air quality. They sued Ruckelshaus and, despite the explanations of the EPA's lawyers, won a court order from Federal District Judge John H. Pratt (later upheld by the Supreme Court) restraining the EPA administrator from approving any SIP which did not contain a nondegradation requirement and, incidentally, requiring him to revise his regulations accordingly. In this way Ruckelshaus was forced to start over.

What were Ruckelshaus's responsibilities in this case? What was his job? His job could not be adequately described as "promulgating regulations"; he had done that, and now he had to do it again. Nor was it a matter of carrying out the president's wishes; President Nixon probably had been content with Ruckelshaus's second set of regulations, but the wishes of Judge Pratt and the Sierra Club proved to matter at least as much. It was clearly not simply a matter of carrying out the statute as intended by Congress, either; Congress had not spoken clearly, and the federal courts had stepped into the vacuum. Nor, finally, was it a matter of following Judge Pratt's order. Judge Pratt had not worked out the details of how the law was to be administered. That task remained undone. A strict interpretation of the court's order, moreover, while it might satisfy the environmentalists, would have virtually halted economic development in much of the country and inhibited urban redevelopment elsewhere. Neither the states nor, unfortunately, Congress would have stood for that kind of policy, Judge Pratt notwithstanding.

Deprived of an easy way out, the EPA administrator was faced with the necessity of devising a policy that would prevent significant deterioration of the nation's air quality in areas where air quality was already higher than required by the law—that is, where there was little or no pollution from industry, shopping centers, or automobiles. There was no way he could conscientiously avoid coming to grips with this substantive issue. Doing so proved to be an arduous task, made more so because it had to be carried out under the ever-present threat of more litigation. The EPA administrator would have to determine precisely on what bases each approval of a state implementation plan was to be made so as to recognize the principle of nondegradation, yet also somehow to avoid crippling the process of economic growth and change.[2]

Ruckelshaus was long gone and his successor, Russel Train, was the responsible official when the EPA, under a new court order to get on with it, promulgated "final" regulations concerning the prevention of significant deterioration on December 5, 1974. After considering four different approaches to dealing with significant deterioration, the EPA chose one of them, the "area classification plan," as a basis for controlling air quality. According to this plan, each state would be required to establish air quality "zones" with separate pollutant emissions limits for each. Subject to certain restrictions, areas of each state were to be designated as either Class I, Class II, or Class III, in ascending order of the maximum allowable increases above baseline concentrations of sulfur dioxide and particulate matter that would be permitted. Certain areas, such as national parks, were automatically to be included in the zone of purest air, but the states were given some discretion in classifying other areas.

Another round of litigation was initiated by the still dissatisfied Sierra Club, which opposed any concessions made in the interests of economic development, but this time, in August 1976, the federal courts upheld the EPA administrator. The following year, in response to EPA appeals to clarify its intent with respect to nondegradation, Congress substantially amended the Clean Air Act to incorporate the EPA regulations as the law of the land. In more than eleven pages, the amended Clean Air Act provided detailed directions as to how the federal government was to prevent the significant deterioration of air quality.

At the heart of Ruckelshaus's (and later Train's) management responsibilities was the process of working out the complex substantive problems of maintaining air quality in a highly charged political environment, within the framework of unworkable legislation. It was a process, however, that was obscured by the routines, conflicts, and emergencies of bureaucratic life.

From the day a senior executive shows up for work, there is work to do. For the public's business to continue, the official's formal authority must be invoked. Signatures are needed on documents, regulations must be issued, vacancies filled, legislative and budgetary tactics chosen, disputes mediated, and testimony prepared and given. The official's job is quickly defined by events and circumstances. The job may be what the executive is doing, and no underlying pattern or purpose may be apparent. Caught up in the frustrating experience of issuing regulations, many of which he can neither understand nor take the time to question, and responding to the environmentalists' lawsuits, an EPA administrator might not perceive the vexing and highly interesting problem that was generating the bureaucratic and political pressure he was feeling.

There are methods in the bureaucratic madness that seems to surround the senior executive. Much of the pressure he or she feels is in reality a product of the organization's attempts to grapple with substantive tasks originating in legislation, court orders, or presidential directives. Understanding the character of these substantive tasks and the pressures they exert on the political executive is essential to understanding the nature of the executive's responsibilities.

Working the Problem

The tasks that underlie bureaucratic activity vary greatly in their apparent complexity. Some appear straightforward, whereas others are vague and perplexing. Even those that seem simple, however, are usually enormously complicated in practice.

WHO IS BLIND?

There is widespread agreement, for example, that the federal government should provide income assistance to poor people who are blind, and Congress created a program to do so. But who shall be considered blind and therefore eligible for benefits? The answer might seem obvious: someone who cannot see. But what if an individual can "see"—that is, perceive light, shadow, and even shape—but not well enough to work? The proper answer might still seem clear enough: include such people in the blind category, too. But are we speaking of the ability to see with or without corrective lenses? With corrective lenses, of course.

We are not done yet. Precisely how weak must a person's corrected vision be before we say that he or she is blind? What instructions shall we give to the government worker who is determining eligibility? Let us say, using the standard measure of visual acuity, 20/200. (An eye examination by a reputable individual is required; bring a note from your doctor.) In both eyes? No, in the better eye. What if an individual has tunnel vision, that is, better than 20/200 corrected vision but covering only a small part of the visual field? Perhaps we can resolve all these questions by saying that an individual shall be considered blind if he or she has a central visual acuity of 20/200 or less in the better eye with corrective glasses, or a limitation in the visual field such that its widest diameter subtends an angle of no more than 20 degrees, or if he or she meets the definition of blindness under the aid-to-the-blind plan in the state of residence and was receiving benefits in December 1973.[3] Instead of one word—"blind"—we now have nearly eighty words, the product of an attempt to be precise about whom a program providing aid to the blind will serve, a level of precision sought by client groups who will later complain that government is too bureaucratic.

How shall we determine if a blind person is poor? First, find out his or her income. From all sources? Well, yes. Alimony? Yes. Inheritance? Yes. Royalties from inventions or publications? Yes, income from all sources, earned or not. What if the blind person is a college student with a scholarship? Are the scholarship proceeds counted as income? Well, no, not if the scholarship is for the payment of tuition and fees. Only the excess above that needed for tuition and fees should be treated as income. What if the blind person is a child living with parents who work? Income in such cases shall mean the parents' income. What if the parents are poor and there are brothers and sisters? Make exceptions for those situations. Some poor families own their own homes. Should their blind children get the same aid as poor families that own nothing and have to pay rent? Well, that depends on how much the home is worth.

Again, a seemingly straightforward term such as "poor" is translated into thickets of words that appear impenetrable to the uninitiated. They conceal choices with enormous social, budgetary, and political consequences, however. A health and human services secretary who sees merely another turgid set of regulations to be issued and fails to comprehend their significance misunderstands the real importance of his or her job.

Grasping the underlying issue may not be enough, however. Consider another apparently straightforward but in fact more difficult task: providing social security benefits to the disabled. In 1978, state government employees who were paid by the federal government and who operated under federal rules and regulations made 1,239,700 individual determinations concerning entitlement to social security disability benefits. In recent years, the costs of the program have risen dramatically, from just over $3 billion in 1970 to well over $18 billion a dozen years later. In the late 1970s, there were widespread political demands that something be done to improve the management and reduce the costs of this program. This was a high-priority task facing the top executives of the federal human services agency.

Among the statutory bases for disability determinations is the requirement that the claimant be able to demonstrate that inability to work is a result of "medically determinable" illness or injury or of a combination of medical and nonmedical factors—age, schooling, work experience—which prevent the individual from holding a job.[4] The intent of the law is to distinguish between *voluntary* unemployment, which Congress does not intend to subsidize and therefore encourage, and *involuntary* unemployment due to disability, for which income protection shall be provided.[5] The actual provision of benefits depends first on decisions on the individual applications by disability officials acting in the name of the secretary of the Department of Health and Human Services. Invariably, subjective judgments are necessary to making such determinations. If individuals A and B have similar ailments, for example, but A works despite the ailment while B does not, B is likely to be denied benefits on the grounds that B may be voluntarily withdrawing from the labor force. A works, doesn't she? B had better, too, since B's disability is apparently not medical. Some observers believed that the rising costs of the disability program reflected increasing generosity on the part of disability officials, especially in view of the difficulty applicants were having finding jobs. Others argued that the problem lay in the intrinsically difficult nature of the cases to be decided. Said Gerry L. Mashaw, professor of law at Yale University:

The difficult problem in the cases I've seen concerns the people with multiple problems, none of which is clearly disabling and all of which are controllable. You see a lot of cases like that. The question is, how do you evaluate them? Are they really worn out or is it only temporary? It's a very difficult judgment and has a lot to do with pain. There's no way to measure pain.[6]

Whatever could be said of service worker motives, nearly 70 percent of the disability determinations made by the Department of Health, Education and Welfare (HEW) were that benefits should be denied.[7] Approximately 250,000 of those who were denied benefits asked for reconsideration, which they are entitled by law to do; 200,000 of these were once again denied benefits. More than half of those denied benefits a second time, 103,881, appealed their cases to administrative law judges. Indeed, there were more administrative law judges in HEW hearing social security disability cases in 1978 than there were judges in the entire federal judicial system. These administrative law judges reversed the administrative denial of benefits in 54,000 cases. Many of those still denied benefits, that is, denied benefits a third time, appealed to the federal courts; in 1978, 18,000 disability cases were awaiting decision there. In such cases, judges, who, not being part of the executive branch do not have to consider the program as a whole or its annual budget, are likely to find in favor of the individual claimant on the grounds that the secretary has produced insufficient evidence to support a finding that the disability is not medical.[8]

Secretary of HEW, Joseph A. Califano, Jr., reacting to criticism that there was too much delay in the appeals process, attempted to address the problem by urging the administrative law judges to decide cases more quickly. The judges sued the secretary on the grounds that he was exerting improper pressure on them and threatening their independence and the due process of clients. Califano also sought changes in the far-flung system by which the original determinations were made. A GAO study had concluded that the department had failed to provide clear and precise guidance to field workers on how the disability definition in the law should be interpreted. The department began devising new regulations instructing field workers on how to evaluate applications.

Intelligent and purposeful management of programs such as the federal disability program requires an extensive understanding of the program and of the reasons for its various features. Acts that appear simple and correct, such as speeding up the appeals process, may easily backfire, and furthermore, may not get at the source of the problem. A conscientious federal executive can hardly avoid becoming immersed in the issues and complexities of program administration in sufficient depth to insure that decisions are made with one eye to their likely effects.

UNCERTAIN MANDATES

Complexity is compounded when the mandate to be carried out is unclear or controversial or when possible methods for doing so are uncertain.

The Education Amendments of 1972, for example, established the basic structure of federal aid to higher education. The final act was a product of intense controversy. The Senate, led by Senator Claiborne Pell (D-R.I.), wanted the centerpiece of federal assistance to higher education to be a program of grants awarded directly to students in demonstrable financial need. The goal of this approach was to strengthen the access to educational opportunities and freedom of choice of low-income students. In contrast, the House of Representatives, led by Congresswoman Edith Green (D-Ore.), wanted to continue the existing grant program, under which assistance was channeled to students through financial aid officers of institutions of higher education. Further, the House wanted to permit these officers greater flexibility in determining eligibility so that more middle-income students would be helped. The goals of this approach were to augment college financial resources as well as to relieve the financial strains of paying for college felt by both middle-income and low-income families.

The compromise reached in the conference between the House and the Senate was to enact both programs, with their conflicting philosophies: a Basic Educational Opportunity Grant (BEOG) program giving eligible undergraduate students a basic entitlement to a grant, and a Supplemental Educational Opportunity Grant (SEOG) program, the existing grant program with its low-income restriction removed. In a last-minute compromise, the House succeeded in including in the statute a provision by which a minimum amount had to be appropriated and spent on the SEOG program *before* the BEOG program could even be funded. The resulting confusion in the administration of federal aid to postsecondary education ultimately was traceable directly to this congressional hedging of a significant philosophical conflict.

A similar instance is that of the Employee Retirement and Income Security Act of 1974, which was intended to protect the pension rights of American workers. The Education and Labor Committee and the House Ways and Means Committee produced rival bills calling for implementation by the Department of Labor and the Internal Revenue Service, respectively. In the end, one bill became Title I of the new act, while the other became Title II.

When the Senate and the House, or powerful factions within either chamber, disagree on goals or priorities, the solution is often to accept both, conflicts notwithstanding, and to let the executive agencies cope with the confusion. The top officials of the agencies must somehow untangle the knots and devise a program that is workable.

The difficulties of doing so are illustrated by the case discussed at the beginning of this chapter. Should air quality ever be allowed to deteriorate? Should a state, for example, be permitted to accommodate economic growth by shifting new industry and commercial activity from regions with dirty air to regions with clean air so long as air quality in the latter is not degraded below federal statutory standards? The problem was that the Clean Air Act Amendments failed to address the question clearly, and the legislative history of the act indicated that views in Congress were divided. The result was the time-consuming, litigious process described above.

Disagreements often center on *how* results are to be achieved rather than on the general character of the results. Everyone agrees in principle that any program should be achieved in a manner that is equitable, efficient, and effective. In practice, these objectives are often in conflict, and the degree of emphasis placed on each differs widely among participants in policymaking. These participants seek to ensure through legislation, regulations, and budget allocations that appropriate emphasis is placed on the objective they care most about. Political executives are at the center of the resulting controversies.

In 1975, for example, without even holding public hearings, Congress passed the Age Discrimination Act (ADA) (89 Stat 713) as a floor amendment to the Older Americans Act. This amendment, though nominally assisting all age groups, was in fact designed to aid the elderly population. "The ADA was premised upon a fundamental analogy between race discrimination and age discrimination."[9] As a result of the ADA, both types of discrimination are now prohibited by law in virtually identical language. But, argued Peter Libassi, the HEW general counsel responsible for drafting implementing regulations, "age is a classification so different from race. It is difficult to justify any distinction based on race, but we can all think of many distinctions based on age which are appropriate and sensible."[10] Peter H. Schuck, who was involved in the act's implementation, notes that Congress inadvertently combined two quite different approaches to the elimination of age discrimination, thereby generating "distinctive tendencies and implications that are at war with one another."[11] The act, among other things, prohibits discrimination on the basis of age in all federally assisted programs and activities, but at the same time it excludes from coverage programs or activities established under the authority of any other law which prescribes age criteria for conditioning benefits of participation.

Thus, the act sought not only to prohibit discrimination based on age but to encourage increased expenditures on programs that benefit the older population. The former involves the determination of legal rights and the application of rules based on those rights. The latter involves the exercise of managerial discretion concerning the balance of social benefits and social costs to be obtained from different ways of allocating resources. The burden of straightening out the confusion falls first on the executives charged with carrying out the law. The issues they face are exquisitely difficult. Asked the *National Journal:*

Is it discriminatory to give flu shots only to the very young and the very old? Can states set a minimum age for driver's licenses and require older people to be reexamined to retain their licenses? Can local Head Start programs limit admissions to children three years or older?[12]

Or, asked HEW regulation writers:

To what extent (if any) does the existence of a federally funded senior citizen legal aid program relieve the neighborhood legal services program of the obligation to serve the elderly? Does a general program fulfill its obligation by referring applications to the age specific program?[13]

Further, no matter how much care and wisdom executives use in interpreting congressional intent, the act is an open invitation to the courts to arbitrate disagreements over whether the human services secretary's socially beneficial allocations of resources violate someone's rights. Observes Schuck, "for Congress to enact a law based largely upon conflicting premises and then to refuse to define or even guide its policy except through broad intimations of sentiment is to require other institutions to fill this void."

Faced with the task of carrying out the intent of the act, HEW Secretary Califano ordered a review of all federal laws that contain age distinctions in order to determine if any discriminate against the elderly in negative and harmful ways. Said Califano:

We intend to subject to rigorous and skeptical analysis those laws, policies, and practices that seek to fall within these exceptions [permitted by the law]. They must meet not only the legal standards explicit in the statute but the imperatives of common sense and congressional intent.[14]

But this was only the beginning of a long, continuous process that would make heavy demands on the political executives responsible for eliminating age discrimination in the United States.

VAGUE TECHNOLOGY

The technology for achieving governmental purposes is often vague or nonexistent, thus compounding the difficulties of designing policies and programs. By technology is meant the use of available know-how to transform raw material into the desired output. The raw materials in government are not equipment, technology, and skilled personnel. Rather, they are firms that are polluting the environment; unemployed teenagers; state and local agencies providing educational services to the handicapped; and banks which offer credit in urban neighborhoods. These raw materials are to be transformed into desired outputs: cleaner air; employment opportunities for young people; a free, appropriate education for handicapped children; and the availability of residential and commercial loans to qualified borrowers in deteriorating communities. The task facing the public executive is discovering and applying available know-how to accomplish these transformations.

In assessing his tenure as administrator of New York City's Health Services Administration, the late Gordon Chase analyzed the difficulties encountered while making these kinds of transformations. He had been charged, at one time or another, with pursuing three different objectives: reforming the health system in the city's prisons, establishing a lead poison control program, and creating a large-scale methadone maintenance program. To accomplish any programmatic goal, Chase argued on the basis of his experience with these three, the public manager must consider beforehand the following sources of potential problems:

- the operational demands implied by a particular program concept;
- the nature and availability of the resources required to run the program;
- the program manager's need to share his authority with or retain the support of other bureaucratic and political actors while assembling the necessary resources and managing the program.[15]

Chase goes on to identify specific cases and questions that the public executive must consider: How easy will it be to reach, that is, identify and contact, the client population with the service? (Reaching a population of prisoners or polluting firms is relatively easy; reaching abused children, drug addicts, or banks engaged in illegal credit discrimination is relatively difficult.) How many discrete functions will the program require? What numbers, kinds, and quality of personnel will be needed? How dependent are program officials on favorable actions by overhead agencies or other line agencies? Are powerfully placed politicians likely to support or attack the program? How badly will the program manager need private sector providers? Are there dimensions of the program that predictably will produce bad press? Answering such questions is a time-consuming, intellectually demanding, bureaucratically and politically contentious process.

The difficulties of determining how to achieve a desirable public purpose are further illustrated by the problem of controlling inflation in the costs of obtaining health care. Contributing to the rising cost of medical care has been the spreading use of expensive medical technology. On August 11, 1977, HEW Under Secretary Hale Champion directed the office of the assistant secretary for health to develop standards on which health planning agencies could base their decisions regarding the purchases by hospitals of expensive medical technology such as open heart surgery units and computerized axial tomography (CAT) scanners.[16] He was acting pursuant to goals enunciated by Congress in the National Health Planning and Resources Act of 1974, which directed HEW to regulate the spread of expensive medical technologies, and the Carter administration's objective of controlling the rapid increase in health care costs by limiting spending on the capital outlay expenditures of hospitals.

How should a senior government executive carry out his or her task? Consider the substantive difficulties. The proposition that the proliferation of expensive medical technology has contributed to an undesirable increase in the costs of health care does not go unchallenged. Americans have been educated to prefer medical treatment by the best available specialists using the most advanced methods of diagnosis and treatment if they can get it, and the medical care system caters to these preferences. CAT scanners and open heart surgery are well-known cases in point, but Dr. Steven A. Schroeder points as an example to the field of gastroenterology and the development of flexible fiberoptic endoscopy, which

has led to an explosive increase in the incidence and indications for upper gastrointestinal endoscopy. . . . This procedure now merits its own society, the American Society for Gastrointestinal Endoscopy, and its own journal, *Gastrointestinal Endoscopy.* [17]

How can the actions of government executives affect such developments? As an assistant secretary of health once put it in response to the proposition that Americans would be influenced by economic incentives when choosing medical care, "they will except when they're sick." Moreover, the same president who sought to limit the spread of expensive medical technology was simultaneously supporting increased outlays to the biomedical research community that creates the technology and promotes its adoption.

Even if the patterns of use of expensive technology are regarded as essentially wasteful, what should be done about it? Congress has directed the establishment of a planning and regulatory network of Health Resource Agencies to impose order on the disorderly diffusion of medical technology. However, numerous experts believe that such regulatory approaches will not work, that the only effective approach is to change the way the government pays for health care and subsidizes the training of physicians. Others doubt that the rising cost of medical technology is a primary reason for health care cost inflation. Recent research into the utilization of health care indicates that a relatively small number of patients accounts for a disproportionately large share of the expenditures for health care. Even more significantly, "the most expensive illnesses were less likely to be those that required intensive, short-term, technologically complex care than those involving repeated hospitalizations for the same disease over many months or years."[18] Unhealthy personal habits and unexpected complications during treatment may be of more significance in raising medical costs than technology. In creating a medical care system that is less inflationary, in other words, it is not even clear what behavior or what institutions must be changed or transformed, let alone whether or not any set of governmental actions will accomplish the desired alterations.

Conscientious political executives almost invariably discover that their management responsibilities are complicated by the complex nature of the tasks to be performed, uncertain or conflicting mandates, and vague or nonexistent technology for accomplishing the desired purpose. They also discover that information and ideas on what to do almost never come in neutral, disembodied forms. Information and ideas, packaged in various staff documents, usually come from the bureaucracy. Because it is hard to get the whole story from bureaucratic sources, political executives may think that the bureaucracy is the problem, *their* problem. This is a fundamental error.

The Inevitable Bureaucracy[19]

In addition to illustrating the complexity of the tasks senior executives must confront, the examples in the preceding section illustrate the most misunderstood aspect of government: the extent to which its acts and the consequences that flow from them—the bureaucracy, the regulations that envelop everything in their path like kudzu, the increasing volume of litigation, the rising costs of programs—are the products of perfectly well-intentioned efforts to perform tasks and achieve results in a manner that is accountable to the variety of interests that have a stake in the result. The oft-heard notion that the job of the political executive is to control the bureaucracy is a misconception. The executive who ferrets out and becomes involved in the substantive tasks of the organization becomes a participant in fashioning and overseeing the employment of bureaucratic means to achieve socially useful ends, as mandated by the president, Congress, and the courts.

However much Max Weber believed bureaucracy to be the most efficient form of social organization, with the bureaucratic specialist a natural successor to the unqualified amateur, in American political life bureaucracy is perceived as a problem, even a danger. "For me," writes Charles Peters, editor-in-chief of the influential *Washington Monthly*, "the enemy is not communism or capitalism. It is bureaucracy."[20] Why is government so bureaucratic? Why do government bureaucracies appear to perform so poorly? Why do we observe so much inefficiency, undue delay and unnecessary expense, prejudgment of controversial issues, failure to anticipate or plan, failure to promulgate clear rules, susceptibility to *ex parte* influence, cooptation by special interests, lack of expertise, excessive authority possessed by nonaccountable staffs, inadequate personnel, corruption, and arbitrary and capricious acts? Why do the leaders of government seem unable to prevent these excesses? Why can't accountable officials control these seemingly uncontrollable bureaucracies?

The bureaucratic phenomenon can be better understood if it is recognized that governmental or governmentally supported activity comprises countless individual transactions—with clients, contractors, grantees, applicants, offenders, patients, and the like. Approving a SIP, making a social security payment, and negotiating an individual education plan with the parents of a handicapped child are examples of such transactions. To complete any transaction, certain discrete functions of varying complexity must be performed. As Gordon Chase's analysis suggests, some of these functions are mechanical, while others require subjective judgment.

As governmental transactions and the discrete functions necessary to complete them increase in number and complexity, they can no longer be conducted in an informal, face-to-face manner. They must be administered impersonally by individuals performing specialized, routinized functions. At that point, bureaucratic organizations come into existence. These organizations are characterized by jurisdictions defined formally by statutes and regulations, hierarchical authority, the conduct of internal operations via written communications, and specialization and professionalization of both function and administrative process.[21] That is how the work gets organized and done.

Bureaucracy grows because of pressure to have every transaction, and the steps leading up to it, conform to someone's expectations of how they should be performed: with legislative intent, with the public interest as defined by interest groups, with the values and norms of bureau professionals and service workers, or with concepts of equity and fairness as defined by the courts. An effective way to ensure that expectations are fulfilled is to specify the procedures to be followed in designing and conducting the transactions. "More than any other country," Walter Gellhorn observes,

the United States has attempted to achieve administrative justice by prescribing the steps administrators are to take along the way. Administrative power has been given extensively, but administrators have been commanded to observe procedural regularities before formulating conclusions.[22]

Who is poor? What is an oil field? What is a learning disability? Who is a middle-income student? What is clean air? Determinations of this kind, which are required in the administration of public programs, cannot be left to whim or chance.

Aiding poor blind people, for example, requires bureaucracy, people who specialize in deciding who is blind and how much assistance they are eligible to receive—if not at the federal level, then in the states—and regulations that spell out terms and conditions of their decisions in tedious detail. How else can the government help such people? A nonbureaucratic alternative would be for Congress to permit anyone who can convince the local postmaster that he or she is blind to receive $1,000 each year by presenting a special card, issued by the postmaster, to the local bank, which would in turn send the cards to the federal Treasury for immediate reimbursement. Such a simple, low-overhead solution would, unfortunately, produce howls of protest, and the process of inventing bureaucracy —to prevent the postmaster from giving away money to people who didn't need it and to ensure fairness—would begin in earnest.

For a time, the fashion in academic organizational studies was the search for nonbureaucratic forms of management.[23] Yet many advocates of organizational humanism were forced to concede, as did Warren Bennis, that "bureaucracy is the inevitable—and therefore necessary—form for governing large and complex organizations."[24]

To understand the pervasive and functional character of bureaucracy, consider President Jimmy Carter's pledge with regard to welfare administration "to reverse the bureaucratic mechanism to one of support and compassion and concern and enthusiasm."[25] The intake workers in a local welfare office are responsible for receiving and evaluating applications for welfare assistance, determining eligibility for aid, establishing the amount of payment, and making referrals to other services the client may need. The president evidently wanted these people to be fair, accurate, efficient, publicly accountable, humane, and sympathetic when performing their tasks. The responsibility for carrying out this intent presumably fell on the secretary of health and human services.

An investigation of what goes on in local welfare offices would reveal that the intake process, that is, the point at which an applicant first encounters a public official, often falls short of the president's intent. But why? A number of factors account for the actual performance of intake workers. The wide variations in the observed behavior of intake clerks during initial screening of applicants suggest that both employee attitudes and applicant behavior are in part responsible. Few if any rules govern the initial screening of applicants; intake worker discretion is considerable. Much more consistency is observed in the formal determination of eligibility and the setting of benefit levels, both of which are governed by departmental rules, regulations, and forms and are subject to supervisory review and external audit. Referrals to services for which appropriateness could be easily determined by information on the form filled out for each applicant were more consistent than referrals, such as for counseling, which required a more personal encounter in the offering of advice and information and which are not easy for supervisors to monitor. "Intake workers appeared to prefer to offer their services as a representative of the Welfare Department rather than as a private person."[26] Supervisors' attitudes can influence observable behavior of intake workers, such as whether they take late applicants, the manner in which applicants are summoned for an interview, whether the privacy of the interviewee is respected, general accessibility of the intake worker, and so on.

How can departmental managers reach down through the many reporting levels within the department, through state welfare departments, into local welfare offices, and directly to the intake workers to increase their compassion and enthusiasm? Measures that might succeed, if the above evidence is to be believed, include subjecting as many intake tasks as feasible to departmental rules and regulations and to formal reporting; altering the recruitment of intake workers and supervisors to increase emphasis on desired personal qualities; placing increased responsibilities on supervisors to monitor performance of discretionary but observable tasks; and increasing the training required of personnel. Clearly, these measures, taken in the name of compassion and fairness, add up to more bureaucracy, which the president said he did not want. Even if we insisted that the proper approach was to hire compassionate people and let them follow their instincts in administering the program, society, because of the internal conflicts noted before, would also insist on hiring guidelines, enforcement machinery, grievance procedures, and the like. We cannot get away from bureaucracy.

In December 1978, the president somewhat reversed himself when he directed his OMB director and HEW secretary to streamline federal eligibility requirements for public assistance programs with the aim, also labeled as compassionate, of eliminating fraud and waste.

The American people will not accept callousness toward those among us who are aged or sick or jobless or lacking in education or opportunity. But neither will the American people accept a massive bureaucracy that is too clumsy or too poorly managed to do the job.[27]

How could this revised goal be accomplished? The service worker was again the key, but now, instead of compassion and enthusiasm, workers were presumably to be skeptical and vigilant (or to show, perhaps, compassionate skepticism and enthusiastic vigilance). But could this possibly be accomplished with less bureaucracy? The president complained that in one case a woman had to spend 300 hours in one year filling out paperwork documenting her need. Is it conceivable that eliminating waste and fraud will require less documentation of need?

That those who are distrustful of bureaucratic means eventually come to rely on them is a notion nourished by the results of efforts to purge cheaters from the ranks of applicants for federal BEOGs. "Not a single [BEOG] application had been checked for accuracy," explained Joseph Califano of the effort he mounted while HEW secretary to improve the management of the program. "So we hired Leo Kornfeld [to be deputy commissioner of education for student financial assistance], then found a group of young computer experts and got them to form a consulting firm and offer their services."[28] The result of Kornfeld's efforts, as Califano reported at the time, was a 13 percent rejection rate for BEOG applications: "a major achievement." It was not achieved by simply going to an individual and asking, "Did you cheat?" however. Applicants were required to fill out a detailed form—two pages, with seven pages of instructions—and its accuracy was checked by the computer. The press reported on what the process was like:

Marilyn Nixon, 24, of Kansas City, Mo., was one of the early rejects, even though she had received a $481 BEOG grant to study business and fashion at Penn Valley Community College in Kansas City the previous semester.

"They sent the form back in March and said I hadn't checked a little box on the back," she said in a telephone interview. The box authorizes release of application information to other aid agencies and was one of 100 "edit checks" and changes newly programmed into the computer. . . .

Nixon then got the form back again, along with a letter naming half a dozen errors she had made in listing her taxable, nontaxable and adjusted gross income. . . . There are seven pages of instructions for the two-page form, many in prose reminiscent of income tax regulations.

"The wording wasn't very clear. . . . I didn't really understand what they wanted for adjusted gross income," Nixon said. But she sent it off again. Back it came a third time.

"This time there was a letter with a long list of things that might possibly be wrong, but it wasn't specific about my form. I redid it again, and it was wrong again." By now school had started, so Nixon borrowed money, got two months behind in her rent and let the utility bills go in order to stay in school.

Finally she appealed for help to Penn Valley and was given the toll-free number of the BEOG processing center, where an official helped her fill out the form yet again, line by line. Last week she was finally accepted for another $481 grant.[29]

Of the process, Jerold Roschwalb, director of government relations for the National Association of State Universities and Land Grant Colleges, said: "It's the least sophisticated kids who are getting kicked out. We're reasonably certain that at least 50 percent of the rejects were really eligible." Califano apparently ordered the form simplified, but not at the expense of accuracy of the data. Do you want efficiency and frugality? Red tape may be the best answer.

Consider still another example. The federal government enters into a wide variety of relationships with individuals and organizations. A large number can be classified as "grant and cooperative agreement" relationships, while others, apparently similar, are classified as "procurement" relationships. In Public Law 95-224, the Federal Grant and Cooperative Agreement Act of 1977, enacted February 3, 1978, Congress found that "there is a need to distinguish Federal assistance relationships from Federal procurement relationships and thereby to standardize usage and clarify the meaning of the legal instruments which reflect such relationships" and that "uncertainty as to the meaning of such terms as 'contract,' 'grant,' and 'cooperative agreement' and the relationships they reflect causes operational inconsistencies, confusion, inefficiency, and waste for recipients of awards as well as for executive agencies. . . ."[30] The act directed that a series of measures be undertaken to remedy this situation, and it directed OMB to monitor implementation and study the results. OMB reacted by issuing "implementing guidance." As the act did not expressly define either "procurement" or "assistance," OMB inferred the definitions to be as follows: Procurement is the acquisition, by purchase, lease, or barter, of property or services for the direct benefit or use of the federal government; assistance is the transfer of money, property, services, or anything of value to a recipient in order to accomplish a public purpose of support or stimulation authorized by federal statute. Making accurate distinctions is crucial, because altogether different sets of federal rules apply to procurement and to assistance.

Now, then, when the federal government obtains the services of an "intermediary" such as a private insurance company to provide services to the public, such as the processing of Medicare claims, is it assistance or procurement? Does the support of research constitute assistance or procurement—or both? What if the recipient of assistance funds, such as a prime sponsor for training, insists on earning a profit or fee, which is permitted only in the case of procurements? If profit is allowed under assistance awards, then what is the practical distinction between procurements and assistance? In view of these classification problems, OMB found that different agencies were interpreting the act differently. In attempting to resolve this problem of inconsistent agency behavior, an appealing answer is to include more factors in the procurement/assistance distinction than just the government's principal purpose for engaging in the transaction.[31] Complexity grows.

This is only the beginning of the list of difficult questions posed by an act designed to clarify and reduce uncertainty. Murphy's Law of Legislative Effects applies: "An act designed to eliminate confusion will compound it." The answer toward which reasonable officials are inexorably led is more elaborate and detailed definitions, rules, and guidelines and therefore closer monitoring and enforcement. Do you want to simplify and clarify governmental operations? Try more bureaucracy.

But why not simply leave matters up to individuals and organizations? The reason is that we want protection from human error and avarice. Much of the bureaucracy we observe comprises, in the words of Walter Gellhorn, "protection mechanisms against official mistake, malice, or stupidity."[32] Following the nuclear power accident at Three Mile Island, for example, a Nuclear Regulatory Commission (NRC) task force revealed an incredible, nearly comical series of misadventures:

- An operator inadvertently blocked with his body the view of indicators that would have told him two crucial feedwater pump valves were closed. NRC sources explained after the meeting that the operator was "a big man with a large belly that hung over the instrument panel."
- Listening through an amplifier system to gurgles and thumps within a steam generator, operators decided the noises meant there was water inside, when in fact the generator was boiling dry.

· The computer printout of events during the crisis, similar to an airline flight recorder, jammed for nearly 90 minutes at the height of events. It was running two hours behind and eventually much of its data was lost altogether.

· After operators were ordered to don respirators and face-masks to guard against radiation, they were unable to talk to each other.

· Ordered to evacuate the control room of Unit 2 for the adjacent control room of Unit 1, only a few operators did so, and those who went left the door open.

· In the middle of the crisis, when fuel damage was occurring for lack of cooling water, operators kept the pumps off from fear that vibrations would damage the pumps. "There was a general feeling that there must be something wrong with the [temperature gauges], that the temperature couldn't possibly be that high," reported chief investigator Robert Martin.

· The NRC's regional headquarters did not learn of the accident until 36 minutes after Three Mile Island officials called, because the headquarters director was stuck in a traffic jam and could not respond to the answering service beeper.[33]

Concurrently the GAO said that the prevalence of human error in nuclear plant control rooms increased the desirability of stiffening qualifying examinations, increased reports concerning and monitoring operator competence, and better procedures for dealing with mishaps. Do you want greater protection from potentially disastrous human mistakes? Red tape and bureaucracy are the answer.

The pressures for bureaucratic solutions, and for expanding the bureaucracy, more often than not arise outside the bureaucracy, not inside it. As Herbert Kaufman puts it, "Every restraint and requirement originates in somebody's demand for it."[34] Its sources are, as the examples just cited illustrate, Congress, the GAO, interest groups with a stake in its effects, and the courts. All other things equal, bureaucrats would probably prefer to have discretion when engaging in the individual transactions that compose government activity. "Careerists want statutory language giving them authority and discretion, expanding their jurisdiction, and funding more missions."[35] But we do not want these careerists to have much discretion, especially after we observe the results of its exercise. In a study of how 1,500 adults in a national random sample evaluated their periodic encounters with bureaucracy, for example, one group of investigators found that there is less dissatisfaction with government when services are based on a clear set of eligibility requirements and the same treatment of people with the same entitlement. On the basis of this finding, the investigators recommended

a standardization of service, which in turn implies federal guidelines, well publicized eligibility criteria, and separate agencies for various services. . . . [If] the social worker has to make decisions on benefits and services as he evaluates the merits of each case, we open the way to all kinds of preferential and prejudiced treatment.[36]

We impart this concern for certainty, equity, and "zero defects" administration to the people in government agencies, who are as anxious to avoid criticism as we are to avoid having something to criticize. We want the countless individual transactions to be completed with equity and consistency. We want proof of neutrality. This urge is rooted deep in our history and our institutions. In *The American Commonwealth* (1897) Lord Bryce wrote:

Since the people, being numerous, cannot directly manage their affairs, but must commit them to agents, they have resolved to prevent abuse by trusting each agent as little as possible. . . . There is no reliance on ethical forces to help the government to work. . . . The aim of the Constitution seems to be not so much to attain great common ends by securing a good government, as to avert the evils which will flow, not merely from bad government, but from any government strong enough to threaten the pre-existing communities or the individual citizens.[37]

The bureaucracy problem is then, in reality, the accountability problem. It arises not so much because bureaucrats arbitrarily and deliberately decide to impose their will on the rest of us but because bureaucrats are seeking invulnerability to criticism from the powerful constituencies that are the source of their creation and sustenance by trying to be fair to all of them.

The solution to the bureaucracy problem does not lie in coercing or persuading bureaucracies to be less bureaucratic. Political executives who believe bureaucracy to be a metastasizing, uncontrollable, inimical force are unable to grasp the essential nature of their jobs. Rather than oppose bureaucracy, political executives must instead reformulate the bureaucracy problem as an accountability problem, as a problem of policy analysis and design in which appropriate bureaucratic means must be chosen to achieve public purposes, and then they must solve that problem.

Falling Off the Wire

What if the senior executive has neither the time nor the inclination to work the problem and satisfy the dictates of accountability? It might seem easy and even wise for an EPA administrator or a secretary of health and human services to navigate a path of least resistance through the problems of preventing air quality deterioration or educating handicapped children. They might be warned away from such a course, however, by the history of welfare reform, which is studded with examples of executive inattention and its consequences.

A key feature of President Richard M. Nixon's Family Assistance Plan (FAP), proposed to Congress in 1970, was that working would always be more remunerative than not working; welfare benefits would be phased out gradually as the recipient's earnings increased, so that there would never be a sudden drop in a recipient's spendable income. During the course of Senate hearings on the proposal, Senator John J. Williams, (R-Del.) ranking Republican on the Senate Finance Committee, asked HEW Secretary Robert H. Finch and his assistants to show on a chart how a welfare recipient's total spendable income from all sources—food stamps, Medicaid, and public housing benefits, as well as cash payments from FAP—would be affected by increased earnings from taking a part-time or full-time job. As Williams triumphantly pointed out when the HEW officials returned with the results, the chart revealed a crucial detail. A welfare recipient might well be made worse off by going to work full-time because once earnings reached a certain level, the individual would become ineligible for lucrative public subsidies for food, health care, and housing, as well as for supplementary cash payments from the state. Moreover, the earnings would be subject to taxation, providing a further disincentive to work. This feature of the benefit structure was called a "notch" because on charts showing total spendable income from all sources, there was a sharp drop at the point where the recipient became ineligible for valuable public welfare subsidies. Always on shaky ground, FAP was virtually dead once Williams mounted his attack on the notches it apparently contained.

The political significance of the revelation in these charts appeared to catch HEW executives off guard. They did not seem to the legislators to understand their own program; they had not done their homework. Policy analysts in the executive branch had been aware of notch problems in public assistance programs, but these programs were administered by several different agencies. Even though these agencies were planning to restructure their programs in order to eliminate some of the benefit notches, the executive leadership needed to pull these agencies together in a coordinated presentation to the Senate Finance Committee had clearly not been exerted. The administration and its executives appeared incompetent, and crucial momentum for welfare reform was irrevocably lost.

Would a greater mastery of the substantive task of program design by senior administration officials have led to a different outcome? Would the

Senate then have approved FAP? Probably not. The issue of welfare reform provoked powerful ideological responses from both liberals and conservatives. Executive mistakes and political problems of a more conventional kind had their effect. For example, though he was the ranking Republican on the Senate Finance Committee, Senator Williams had not been consulted while the FAP proposal was being developed, and he had not even been invited to a White House meeting at which plans for the Senate hearing were discussed.[38] Moreover, when Elliot Richardson, who succeeded Finch as HEW secretary, later attempted to discuss the complex substantive issues of FAP with the same committee, he made no headway. Apparently he had failed to establish a personal relationship with any senator on the committee, and its chairman, Russell Long, was quoted as saying that he was "disgusted" with Richardson and that "I'll get that guy if it's the last thing I do."

What the incident does reveal is that if top executives fail either to master the substance of complex issues or to satisfy themselves that their key subordinates have done so, they are vulnerable to sharp and even fatal political setbacks. Furthermore, this mastery must be achieved in the context of all the usual obstacles to executive success: ideological and political rivalries, fragmentation of authority between departments and agencies, the difficulties of communications within bureaucracies, and incompatible styles and personalities among the people who must do business with each other. Without such mastery, a shaky cause can become a losing cause.

The subsequent evolution of the welfare reform issue has continued to demonstrate the problems that arise when top executives fail to immerse themselves in the substantive demands of their agencies.[39] On August 6, 1977, President Jimmy Carter announced his Program for Better Jobs and Income, a comprehensive welfare reform proposal. It would add, he said, only $2.8 billion to the federal budget. That figure was the result of an almost wholly nonanalytic calculation in which the overriding objective of the administration's senior officials was political: Keep that number as low as possible. Doing so proved to be singularly bad politics, however. Critics from every part of the political spectrum jeered at the administration's cost estimate. The Congressional Budget Office (CBO), for example, said that the increase would be $14.0 billion, later revised to $17.4 billion. In debating the Carter proposal, Congress adopted the CBO estimate of its cost; it appeared more honest. Indeed, many congressmen believed that the administration had intentionally placed a deceptively low price tag on the program.

How could this happen? Was it a wholly understandable political miscalculation? Problems with Congress over the cost estimates had not been entirely unanticipated, but early warnings on the subject had been largely ignored by senior management at HEW. For example, in May 1977, after a working proposal had been drafted, HEW Secretary Joseph Califano requested information on the political history of welfare reform from his policy analysis staff. The resulting paper, which was forwarded to him by Assistant Secretary for Planning and Evaluation Henry Aaron, stated:

Pay attention to details. The FAP opponents were able to use the analytic failings within the Administration's case against the very idea of comprehensive case coverage. Welfare reform expenditures are held to a higher level of analysis and detailed justification than any other government program. Compare, for example, the relative inattention to the large expenditures involved in both long-term and short-term financing issues of Social Security as opposed to the very detailed attention paid to relatively small net expenditures involved in welfare reform. This suggests that a few months in 1977 will pay dividends in 1978–80. *It also suggests that HEW cost estimates should be checked with the Governors, Mayors, CBO, Hill staffs, etc.* [40]

Similar warnings to circulate cost estimates were being sounded at that time by Jeff Peterson,the HEW legislative coordinator for welfare reform. In a memorandum to his boss, Assistant Secretary for Legislation Richard Warden, Peterson summarized congressional prospects for welfare reform and closed with this counsel:

Whatever HEW welfare reform package is sent to the Hill should contain not only its own cost estimates but also the cost estimates of other groups such as the Congressional Budget Office, the Ways and Means Committee and the Finance Committee. *It is better to have these alternative cost data submitted at the outset than to have alternative data thrown in HEW's face later.* [41]

History vindicates those who sounded the warnings. The argument over the budgetary cost of welfare reform degenerated into mean-spirited carping. A White House source who "leaked" a story to the *New York Times* did his best to portray President Carter as a conscientious (though somewhat naive) budget balancer who had been deliberately deceived by the "big spenders" at HEW and on the White House Domestic Policy Staff. According to the May 15, 1978, op-ed piece:

Why the original $2.8 billion figure? Mr. Carter's subordinates on the domestic policy staff and in the Department of Health, Education and Welfare wanted welfare reform. Mr. Carter said he wouldn't go for it unless the cost was held down. So they apparently misled Mr. Carter to get the program past him originally. Once he found out what had happened, according to a White House source, he did not feel he could admit the true dimensions of the error without seeming incompetent, so in the budget he raised the cost to only $8.8 billion [actually the difference between 1978 and 1982 dollars], or less than a third to a half of what it will turn out to be.

The key "sinners" in this story, the source said, were two of the abler people in the Carter Administration, Joseph A. Califano, Jr. . . . and Bert Carp. . . . Suzanne Woolsey of the Office of Management and Budget knew what was going on but she is a kind and gentle soul with little taste for the bureaucratic hardball that blowing-the-whistle would have required.[42]

In a subsequent letter to the *New York Times,* however, Aaron objected to this interpretation of events:

Charles Peters [editor of the *Washington Monthly*] asserts that a small group of President Carter's advisors deliberately misled the President about the cost of welfare reform. That is false. The estimates were discussed in detail among all the Cabinet officers involved, with all the appropriate members of the President's staff and, finally, at some length with the President himself.[43]

However extensive the discussions may have been, a complex substantive issue—what will the program cost?—had been mishandled. It is possible to sense in the history of this issue that many political executives failed to understand it. In retrospect, none of the participants believed that the disagreement over the costs of welfare reform was the reason the Carter welfare reform proposal failed to gain congressional approval. However, Califano did say that "I think if we have to do it again, we should have come to some kind of agreement with the Congressional Budget Office going in. . . . [That] was just one of those things which slipped through the cracks."[44]

The political executive who intends to lead his or her agency in achieving high standards of performance simply cannot afford to let too many matters of importance "slip through the cracks." He or she must achieve a threshold awareness of the nature and complexity of the tasks that must be performed and the issues that must be resolved. This means more than getting briefed on the eve of a congressional hearing or meeting with White House officials or reading and checking off options on an issues paper that an executive assistant includes in morning or evening reading. It means some degree of immersion in the problem: informal conversations with advisers and subordinate officials, active direction of staff effort, reading, thinking out loud, paying attention to the details, and learning how the bureaucratic world works and thinks. It means developing an ear and eye for substantive nuance and subtlety. It means conscious effort to create and nurture an advisory system that supports substantive decision making, and it means an active leadership role in policy making and program management.

This type of involvement in policy making and administration, moreover, requires more, not less, political acumen. Ruckelshaus's initial decision not to enforce a nondegradation policy might have seemed good politics to many senior Nixon administration officials at the time. Had he chosen initially to become more substantively involved with nondegradation, he would have had to develop an understanding of more than how to define and make complicated trade-offs between economic development and cleaner air. He would have had to understand the congressional politics that produced a vague and confusing statute and legislative history; the likely reactions of legislators, state officials, and environmental groups to different actions he could take; and the legal consequences of those same actions, all of which were eventually necessary.

In the same way, it seemed to be a relatively straightforward political judgment to keep the announced cost of welfare reform as low as possible to satisfy the president's wishes to present a low-cost program. To deal with the more sophisticated problem of producing a believable proposal that anticipated opposing arguments would have been a more delicate and time-consuming political task. In both instances, moreover, taking a more complex view of the problem would have exacerbated already strained relations with White House officials—including the president—who expected actions that were, above all, loyal to the president's interests as they perceived them. Indeed, Califano clearly chafed under the restraint of having to minimize costs above all else and ended up with the worst of both worlds: a suspicious White House and an incredulous Congress.

Failure to work the problem can, therefore, carry embarrassing and costly penalties for the senior executive. The official who fails to get a feel for important issues of substance and to gain an understanding of substantive reasons for bureaucratic activity—who habitually seeks easy or expedient courses of action—may become dissociated from program realities and be placed irrevocably on the defensive in political debates.

But what of the converse proposition? Are executives who become immersed in the problem solving of the department more likely to enjoy trouble-free tenure in office? Are they supported in their efforts by superiors, peers, and subordinates with a stake in what they do? The unfortunate answer is that the activist, problem-solving, independent-minded, visibly competent executive encounters a different set of difficulties that can be even more risky to tenure and reputation than taking the path of least resistance. Passivity may be a more satisfying management approach, all things considered, than activity, as we shall see in the following chapter.

CHAPTER 3

The Problem of Incentives

IN THE PERIOD from September 1978 to September 1979, three senior executives in the Carter administration left their posts under adverse circumstances. Their fates exemplify those that may await political executives who seek leadership within their agencies or departments.

· Robert A. Derzon came into the government from the position of director of hospitals and clinics at the University of California in San Francisco, where he was said to have built the institutions he directed into financially stable operations. He was appointed in June 1977 by HEW Secretary Joseph Califano to be administrator of the newly created Health Care Financing Administration (HCFA). His mandate was to integrate the administration of Medicaid and Medicare programs and to design and execute cost controls, tasks for which his experience seemed ideal. He was said to have strong views on the sources and cures for health cost inflation, believing in the need to balance cost containment with the assurance of reasonable economic stability within the hospital industry. Fifteen months later Califano fired him, claiming privately that he was not tough enough.[1] In the intervening months, reported the *National Journal,* Derzon, new to Washington, had become the victim of the trends described in chapter 1.

49

He felt he had been forced to make appointments on the basis of applicants' civil service standing rather than their demonstrated competence to do the work that would be expected of them, and he had to cope with the lack of good managers in his agency and with constraints stemming from the statutory delegation of administrative authority to the states.[2] At the same time, his boss appeared to be consumed by impatience. Califano, it was said, "beats on Derzon's head at every turn, demanding to know why HCFA cannot move faster to integrate Medicare and Medicaid than it has done until now."[3] Said one official, "At some meetings, Califano was really yelling at Derzon."[4] Said a Derzon aide later, "I think it was a difference in personality."[5]

· John O'Leary was named deputy secretary in the new Department of Energy on the basis of an impressive background for the job. He had been deputy assistant secretary in the Department of the Interior for mineral resources, chief of the Bureau of Natural Gas at the Federal Power Commission, director of the Bureau of Mines (a post from which he had been fired by President Nixon apparently for an excess of zeal on behalf of safety), director of licensing for the Atomic Energy Commission, chief energy administrator for the state of New Mexico, and administrator of the Federal Energy Administration, predecessor agency to the Department of Energy. "He was opinionated and outspoken," reported the *National Journal,* "well-versed in the technical jargon of many disciplines and, from his words, 'convinced that the United States must mount a crash program of energy development and conservation.' "[6] In July 1979, the *U.S. News and World Report* related:

White House aides are trying to curb [Secretary of Energy James] Schlesinger's authority by pressing for resignation of his handpicked deputy, John O'Leary, a career bureaucrat. They argue that the agency's No. 2 job should be filled by someone possessing political influence.[7]

In September 1979 O'Leary resigned—some say he was forced out by the White House staff—and an aide confided, "The political infighting, the long hours, the constant verbal battles with Congressmen, heads of interest groups and officials here in the department were just too much."[8]

· Joel W. "Jay" Solomon became head of the General Services Administration (GSA) on May 13, 1977.[9] He was vice president of the Arlen Realty and Development Corporation, one of the largest real estate development firms in the country, and had been chairman of the board of the Chattanooga, Tennessee, Housing Authority. He and members of his family had been early Carter supporters and had been involved in Carter's presidential campaign. On March 31, 1979, under intense pressure from the Carter White House, he resigned. In the intervening months, he had earned a reputation in the press for vigorously and honestly pursuing the unfolding problems of corruption and maladministration in GSA. Behind the scenes it was another matter. Agency veterans claimed he was blowing ordinary management problems out of all proportion to their significance. And he made at least one major mistake. He obtained the president's approval to dismiss his own choice for deputy administrator, the politically well-connected Robert T. Griffin, saying that he had been unable to control the agency effectively because its employees were unsure of who was in charge. Solomon apparently began to feel that Griffin, a career GSA official, and his staff wanted him to be largely a ceremonial leader and to stay out of the internal operations of the agency.[10] Griffin's powerful patron, Speaker of the House Thomas P. "Tip" O'Neill, Jr., immediately and publicly protested the ouster of a "competent and loyal" official and friend. Though the firing was allowed to stand by the White House, Solomon's days were numbered. The White House subsequently overruled Solomon's recommendation concerning an important senior position within GSA, and stories began appearing in the newspapers concerning White House un-happiness with Solomon's leadership style and loyalty. Publicly but anonymously repudiated by the president who had appointed him and apparently on the brink of dismissal, Solomon finally quit. The *Washington Post* later eulogized him as "a do-gooder businessman—'straight-arrow' is an oft-used phrase—who came here as a reward for backing Carter, and got ground up in the sausage grinder of professional politics."[11]

The stories of these executives conclude with ironies. The successor to twice-fired O'Leary was John C. Sawhill, who had "resigned" as President Gerald R. Ford's head of the Federal Energy Administration, a post held later by O'Leary. Press accounts of Sawhill's departure described it as "a classic case of Washington politics—a petty and silent infighting, political inexperience up against political acuteness, and outspoken independence against team play."[12] He was regarded as an oddball for voluntarily releasing his own financial statement and for vowing not to defect to the oil industry when he left government. Califano and Schlesinger were themselves fired by President Carter, the former for a reputed inability to work with the White House staff, the latter for having alienated important members of Congress and the public. Less than a year from the date of Solomon's dismissal, the man who cost him his job, Robert T. Griffin, whom Carter had moved to another position in the administration, also left the government.

Top officials who exhibit ideas, an independent sense of purpose, or a determination to manage their agencies soon discover that they may have inadvertently invited their own execution. History reveals few examples —Carl Schurz, William G. McAdoo, Herbert Hoover (as secretary of commerce), and Robert S. McNamara are among a handful of candidates—of government executives who were judged outstanding by virtue of their executive ability and managerial accomplishments.[13] Many vigorous, self-initiating cabinet officers of recent years—Elliot Richardson, John T. Dunlop, James Schlesinger, and Joseph Califano, for example—quit or were fired, some more than once, amid controversy and recriminations. Others, such as Nixon's Commerce Secretary Peter G. Peterson, were "promoted" or moved away from positions of influence because they upstaged the president. Of the departure of Schlesinger and Califano from President Carter's cabinet, the *National Journal* observed, "The personalities that have departed from the Administration have tended to be the strong-minded, less flexible officials with ideas—and constituencies—of their own."[14] Of Peterson, presidential aides were said to complain "about favorable publicity in the national media (describing Peterson as the most powerful Secretary of Commerce since Herbert Hoover), violating their concept of the faceless, anonymous, perfect servant."[15]

How could ostensibly competent executives fail in administrations that had promised the kind of management they appeared to practice? Why do results-oriented behavior or visible displays of professional competence and integrity so often lead to dismissal from office?

The reason relates to the structure of the centrifugal forces bearing on the government's political executives. No matter what their styles, goals, or expectations, government executives inevitably discover that there is little in their political environment that systematically pushes them toward conscientious, aggressive, results-oriented performance. Virtually the opposite is the case. From the day they assume office, senior executives are made aware of the limitations on what they can do. They are reminded of their many masters: the president, Congress, the courts, the career bureaucracy, interest groups, state and local officials. These executives of necessity become involved in the intense struggle for influence over the actions of the government. The dismaying reality senior executives face is that they are surrounded by those who desire to restrict their power to act decisively. Whereas the logic of problem solving draws conscientious executives into a central role in departmental affairs, the politics of problem solving may confine them to limited roles or may push them out of the picture altogether.

The Imperial Presidency

The first major discovery senior executives are likely to make is that their relationship to the official who appointed them is almost certainly not a personal one of informal meetings, regular phone conversations, and casual access. Even long-time friends and political associates of Richard Nixon soon discovered, for example, that as cabinet officers, their relationship would be with the institutional presidency, not with the increasingly aloof president. The apparent exceptions only prove the rule. "When I wake up," Lyndon B. Johnson said in 1965, "the first one I call is McNamara."[16] Secretary of State Dean Rusk and Secretary of the Interior Stewart L. Udall also were said to be influential with Johnson, "but this had nothing to do with their position in the Cabinet and only slightly more to do with their status as secretaries."[17] Said Charles Schultze, Johnson's director of the budget: "On matters of substance, Johnson hardly ever talked to Cabinet members."[18] President Carter's early relationship with his cabinet became increasingly awkward. "I don't think the President has become overly close with any of them," said one White House aide six months into Carter's term.[19]

The distance separating the president from the cabinet officers and other agency heads is a product of the differing roles they play. The remark of Charles G. Dawes, first director of the Bureau of the Budget, has not diminished in salience: "Cabinet members are vice-presidents in charge of spending, and as such they are the natural enemies of the President."[20] The chairman of the committee whose 1937 report led to the creation of the Executive Office of the President, Louis Brownlow, noted that

the detailed departmental organization of the Executive is controlled by the Congress, and the appropriations for the operation of the departments are made in detail by the Congress. Therefore, in these jurisdictional disputes and departmental feuds the President all too frequently finds the Cabinet, which is deemed to be his principal help, actually operating as the principal hindrance to him in carrying out his task of overall coordination and management.[21]

In the same vein, Doris Kearns quotes Lyndon Johnson:

When I looked out at the heads of my departments, I realized that while all of them had been appointed by me, not a single one was really mine. I could never fully depend on them to put my priorities first. All too often they responded to their constituencies instead of mine. . . . I was determined to turn those lordly men into good soldiers. I was determined to make them more dependent on me than I was on them.[22]

Jimmy Carter began his presidency, like every modern president, with a determination to rely on his cabinet. Though his attempt to do so was more sustained than Nixon's, he too ended up in an adversarial posture, periodically bullying them, ordering them to toe the line, and dismissing those who evidently failed. At a meeting at Camp David in April 1978, Carter was reported to have cited cases in every department where he felt his policies had been undercut. "The President must have gone to some pains to collect all the examples," an aide is reported to have said.[23]

As their distance from the president grows, political executives find that relationships with the people who serve the president and who collectively comprise the Executive Office increase in frequency and importance. Those relationships are likely to be perplexing and frustrating. Executives appointed by the president are likely to view themselves as important aides and advisers; the prospect of playing such a role has probably been among the inducements to accept the position. They soon realize, however, that they are regarded with increasing suspicion by the White House staff. The president's staff, many of whom have been with him for years, grow closer to their chief, learning his thinking, acquiring self-confidence, developing a proprietary sense of the presidential office. Departmental executives, in contrast, grow closer to their departments, to departmental constituencies, and to relevant congressional leaders and committees. Both see themselves as the president's men and women, but they increasingly see each other as antagonists. Richard P. Nathan, who was a senior member of Richard Nixon's OMB staff, describes how the departmental executive's evolving role appears to the White House staff.

Both Nixon's Cabinet and sub-Cabinet appointees, particularly if they were new to the programs or agency that they had been named to head, entered on their appointment into an almost ritualistic courting and mating process with the bureaucracy. They were closeted for long hours in orientation sessions with career program officials, the purpose being for these career officials to explain to them program goals and accomplishments and to warn them about the need for support from powerful outside interests. It soon became clear to new appointees, if it was not already at the outset, that these experts would be needed close at hand to supply the necessary facts about program complexities and to help shape in specific terms the proposals they would want to put forward for Administration approval as new policy initiatives. Thereafter, in many obvious and subtle ways, the praise and respect of the agency's permanent staff was increasingly made a function of the performance of these presidentially appointed officials as spokesmen and advocates for the agency's interests.[24]

HEW Secretary Robert Finch, HUD Secretary George Romney, Secretary of Defense Melvin Laird, and Secretary of State William P. Rogers, for example, were all perceived by Nixon aides as rapidly "going native." A Carter White House aide observed in February 1978:

We learned that you can't pick that many fights. No one has that much time for it, and the Cabinet agencies won't stick with you. The Secretary will at first, and then will walk away from your position under questioning by a Congressional Committee. The assistant secretaries will stay further away, and the bureau chiefs will pull the rug out from under you.[25]

The executives come to realize that they are not part of the White House culture; they do not belong to the inner circle. Instead, they are viewed as special pleaders and little more than extensions of the bureaucracy. By the end of Johnson's administration, Joseph Califano, the chief domestic aide, had come to symbolize the subordination of departmental policy makers to the White House staff. "Time and time again," reports Patrick Anderson, "in developing and implementing the President's program, Califano fought to impose Johnson's interests over the narrower interests of the departments of government."[26] "On occasion," Richard Nathan said of the Nixon administration, "Cabinet members were completely left out of White House deliberations, as with special revenue sharing in 1971, until plans were fully formed."[27] Of Brock Adams, who was deposed as President Carter's secretary of transportation, it was said that he was "preempted on presidential regulatory initiatives [on airlines and trucking], originally ignored on energy policy and caught in the middle on mass transit funding."[28] Secretary of Agriculture Bob Bergland was reported to have told aides that he "might as well go home" if his credibility with Congress continued to erode as a result of unclear guidelines from the White House on farm policy.[29]

Thus, members of the chief executive's staff acquire considerable power at the expense of subordinate political executives. Said a former under secretary of commerce:

Although legally the appointee is answerable to the President, it is now generally conceded that the typical Cabinet officer's immediate supervisor is one or more members of the White House staff. To those incoming Secretaries who are not aware of this shift in relationships, the new system can be and is a source of conflict and continuing problems, particularly since the typical Cabinet head, a former elected official as often as not, has a different view of his responsibilities and constituency than the President's resident surrogates.[30]

Joseph Califano noted that

> White House aides tend to be bright, mostly young, energetic, and aggressive. Whether they serve in a conservative, socially *laissez-faire* administration or a liberal, interventionist one, their instinctive tendency will be to involve themselves in as much detail in as many matters as time permits. When they discover that most department and agency officials will follow their decisions on minor matters, they tend to become seduced by the allure of power and they revel in its exercise.[31]

As President Carter was replacing Energy Secretary James Schlesinger with Charles W. Duncan, Jr., rumors appeared in various national publications concerning the rise to power of the thirty-three-year-old White House and OMB aide Elliot R. Cutler. Aides to the departing energy official suggested that Cutler had consistently undercut their former boss. Of Cutler, Vice President Walter F. Mondale said, "He personally decides where billions of dollars will be spent."[32] Cutler himself said, "I don't apologize for one moment for having some strong views of my own. I think I was relatively well informed about them, and that it was my duty to make as strong a case as I could in behalf of them."[33] HUD Secretary Patricia R. Harris, who decided that conservative Republican Oakley Hunter, chairman of the Federal National Mortgage Association, a subordinate agency of her department, had to be dismissed, was blocked by the White House. According to newspaper accounts, the recommendation that Harris be overruled came from a thirty-two-year-old White House domestic policy aide named Orin Kramer, who was termed at HUD "that little creep." Kramer reportedly told friends, "I'm not going to let this turn into another Marston affair [referring to an incident in which a departmental subordinate's actions had created problems for the White House]. My job is to protect the President."[34]

Departmental officials often become the objects of complicated White House plots to coopt them or their subordinates. Throughout the Nixon years, for example, a favorite device for neutralizing cabinet departments was the working group. Under the auspices of a cabinet-level body such as the National Security Council (NSC) or the Urban Affairs or Domestic Councils, the president would authorize creation of a working group chaired by a White House staff member, staffed by White House aides or by people detailed from the agencies to the White House, and comprising assistant secretary-level officials from the agencies. These groups would become the forums for staff discussions of key policy issues such as strategic arms limitation or welfare reform. More importantly, however, they permitted the White House to take over direction of agency staff work. Senior departmental officials were often in the frustrating position of being on the outside looking in at activities involving their own staff aides. The practice continued under Carter. An important decision memorandum on farm policy was forwarded to the president by economic adviser Charles L. Schultze, Presidential Assistant Stuart Eizenstadt, Budget Director James T. McIntyre, and Frank Moore, the president's special assistant for congressional liaison. The secretary of agriculture's name was not on the memo.[35]

Deeply impressed by the success of Henry A. Kissinger's NSC in protecting him from direct confrontations with the national security bureaucracy, Richard Nixon went so far as to create a parallel Domestic Council to serve as a "counter bureaucracy" with respect to the domestic agencies.[36] Whereas Kissinger had staffed his NSC with individuals who possessed experience in the government agencies with which he would be dealing,[37] the Domestic Council under John Ehrlichman avoided appointees tainted by association with the bureaucracy. The result was a White House operation that presented all but insurmountable obstacles to senior executives who sought a mutually supportive relationship with the Office of the President. Though subsequent presidents have vowed not to repeat the Nixon mistakes, both Ford and Carter have followed his practice of using their staffs as a moat and making it wide and deep. Carter's "Georgians" have been regarded as no less effective in that role than Nixon's "Germans."

Occasionally, deteriorating relations between White House aides and departmental officials become humorous. Secretary of State Cyrus Vance reportedly had to employ extraordinary measures to bypass National Security Adviser Zbigniew Brzezinski. Desiring to deliver a speech draft to President Carter, Vance was said to have sent an assistant to the White House, where, by prearrangement, the chief usher of the White House living quarters came out to the South Lawn in his formal clothes to receive the draft and deliver it directly to the president.[38] Civil Service Commission Chairman Alan K. Campbell was the recipient of a written Carter directive to rewrite Chapter 410, Subchapter 8, of the Federal Personnel Manual to prohibit federal officials from participating in private conferences or meetings held in facilities which discriminate on the basis of sex, religion, or national origin, as well as race. Did this directive mean that officials could not address B'nai B'rith, the Knights of Columbus, or the Girl Scouts of America? Who, asked Office of Personnell Management officials, would know the intent of this surprise communique? At last published report, the source of the directive was apparently a young volunteer White House aide who was working on legal matters and who was no longer at the White House. Said Deputy White House Counsel Margaret McKenna, "I'm not quite sure we thought this all the way through."[39]

Departmental executives will find that they are also dealing more frequently with officials from OMB. OMB is naturally powerful by virtue of its control over the machinery of the executive budget extending down to the last detail of what gets printed in budget documents. OMB officials are the final arbiters of what is actually included in the budget, and the senior executive finds that making serious inroads in that secure power base requires preparation, time, and bureaucratic skill. Beyond that, OMB officials, working in concert with the White House staff, have enormous discretion in clearing legislation and in their various responsibilities with respect to departmental management.[40] In principle and for the most part in practice, departments and independent agencies must obtain approval from the OMB assistant director for congressional relations before submitting, endorsing, or approving the language of any statutes being considered by Congress.

The senior executive and his or her principal subordinates thus find themselves involved in continual skirmishes with partially concealed, mobile, and resourceful adversaries: the staffs who compose the Executive Office of the President. If the issue is important enough and the privilege has not been abused, the executive is officially allowed to go over the heads of these adversaries to the president. Such moves are not without cost; the executive is more often than not at a disadvantage in pleading his or her case. On other occasions, if the issue is unimportant, and again, the privilege has not been abused, the executive is able to bully the OMB or White House staff into submission. This, too, has a cost; ambitious presidential aides with grudges can work a good deal of mischief when it comes to approving appointments, clearing legislation, or arranging access to the president. In the vast majority of cases of conflict, neither option appears appropriate, and the departmental official is forced in frustration to acquiesce.

The presidential aides cannot act with complete impunity, however. The temptation is strong for the resourceful political executive to use conflict with the White House and OMB to advantage. William Ruckelshaus, appointed as the first administrator of the EPA by President Nixon, actually welcomed occasional conflict with the White House:

I felt that to a certain extent the desires of the White House and my feelings that we needed public support were antagonistic. From time to time to get whacked by the White House probably wasn't a bad thing—in order to gain more public support to do something about the issue. I didn't consciously go out and try to antagonize them into slamming at me. But when it did happen, as it did occasionally, I didn't feel that it had hurt the ability of the agency to move forward.[41]

Further confirmation of how senior executives can use conflict to advantage is provided by Leon N. Weiner, president of the National Housing Conference (a coalition of housing interest groups), who was quoted as saying of HUD Secretary Patricia Harris's role on one issue: "We have every indication that Secretary Harris did all she could, and we recognize that she was constrained by OMB."[42] During Carter's first term, it was often observed in the press that "even those who have been ineffective inside the administration have won friends outside it" by letting it be known that they fought the good fight with Carter's Georgians.

Whatever its advantages in terms of presidential control, subordination of political executives to the Executive Office staff takes its toll in executive morale and competence. "Confusion is created when men try to do too much at the top," wrote Robert Wood, who, as secretary of HUD, had experienced the institutional presidency under Joseph Califano.[43] "At the top minor problems squeeze out major ones, and individuals lower down the echelons who have the time for reflection and mischief-making take up issues of fundamental philosophical and political significance."[44] Upon leaving his post as under secretary of HEW in June 1979, Hale Champion said in a similar vein that his biggest disappointment was OMB, which he said was "too big, too complicated, and too inexperienced to run this government."[45] His boss, Califano, echoing this view, asserted that OMB is "simply not equipped to make decisions on the management of programs. They have no legal responsibility, no responsibility to the oversight committees of Congress. And they don't understand the details of the programs well enough."[46] Few competent, resourceful executives acquiesce to the rigors of such a working environment. If they are unable to circumvent its constraints, they are apt to leave.

The Renitent Bureaucracy

Despite contrary convictions on the part of the White House staff, a significant working distance is also apt to separate political executives from their career subordinates. A popular imagery has developed around the term "iron triangle," the informal coalitions of career program officials, interest group representatives, and legislators who often operate beyond the reach of political executives and are thus a constant challenge to those executives' ability to control their departments. By the efforts of these coalitions, government is segmented into relatively narrow, autonomous compartments resistant to penetration by appointed executives. "It is not a hidden government," observed Grant McConnell. "It is highly visible to anyone who spends time in Washington or who reads beyond the head-lines. It is obscure, certainly, but its obscurity is the result of dullness, routine, and the general acceptance of a largely unarticulated orthodoxy."[47]

Iron triangles sound, and are widely thought to be, unbreakable and unbendable. "Nothing can be more baffling to a fresh government execu-tive than the link between the congressional committees, special interest groups, and program bureaucracies," wrote Frederick V. Malek.[48] McGeorge Bundy, national security advisor to Presidents Kennedy and Johnson, observed following his government service:

My half-educated guess is that specialists in public administration might even say that the progress made by Presidents Kennedy and Johnson has been significant only where the network [of triangular alliances] was relatively weak, as in the conduct of diplomacy, or where there has been an administrator of truly excep-tional force and skill, as in the case of Secretary McNamara.[49]

A more sweeping judgment was that of John C. Whitaker, a member of Nixon's White House staff, then for several years under secretary of the interior, who insisted, "This 'iron triangle'—composed of the vested inter-est groups, select members of Congress, and the middle-level bureaucracy —*runs the federal government.*"[50] Bringing this view up to date, Suzanne H. Woolsey, an associate director of OMB in the Carter administration, com-mented that "the business of running large segments of federal domestic programs has been going on largely outside the power of any President or Cabinet secretary, much to the frustration of political officials who had been led to believe that they were in charge."[51]

Perhaps the most vivid example nourishing executive suspicions of the permanent government is the invasion of the Bay of Pigs early in the administration of President John F. Kennedy. A clear fiasco, the project, according to Kennedy aide Theodore Sorenson, "seemed to move inexora-bly toward execution without the President's being able either to obtain a firm grasp on it or to reverse it."[52] Historian Arthur M. Schlesinger, Jr., spoke of the "surrender of presidential government to the permanent government," of "barons" who wished to show "that the newcomers could not lightly reject whatever was bubbling up in the pipeline," of the "savage blow" dealt to the "elan of the newcomers."[53]

Most projects of the untamed bureaucracy are more benign. Career officials of the Job Corps, for example, were able to save the program from extinction at the hands of the Nixon administration by mobilizing its constituencies and thereby stiffening congressional resistance to the Nixon plan. Caught in the middle was Secretary of Labor George Schultz, who was pummeled in a congressional hearing by questioners who had conspired with officials from his own department. Said Schultz afterward: "No one should have to go through something like that."[54] His subordinates clearly had more power than he did.

These images, and the truth on which they are grounded, exert a profound effect on the behavior and performance of political executives. Notes Michael Maccoby and his colleagues following their study of federal management practices: "Reflecting the attitudes of the American public at large, political executives typically arrive in office expecting to deal with 'Washington bureaucrats,' not people." They go on:

... the political appointee usually is placed at the top of an unfamiliar organization. He expects to be there a brief period.... During that period, he is expected to leave a permanent monument, to make a name for himself. He is likely to push hard, sometimes at the expense of employee feelings. In fact, he may even take pride in pushing around the "bureaucrats." A new administration often arises fresh from a campaign against the bureaucracy, who promises to cut costs and red tape. The assumption is that the Civil Service is a recalcitrant mule that must be bribed and whipped, with carrots and sticks.[55]

Fearful of being coopted or outmaneuvered, political executives are tempted to go on the defensive immediately, issuing warnings that they will not be taken in and filtering or restricting their communications with bureaucrats. They surround themselves with special assistants, executive assistants, and other aides they can trust to serve as buffers, then place intense pressure on these loyal subordinates to override all obstacles in pushing policy downward and to build a wall of resistance to all proposals and ideas coming up from below. In his study of the relationships between appointed and career officials, Hugh Heclo concluded, "Communication among layers of political appointees readily substitutes for communication downward to the operating levels."[56]

The Nixon administration is now famous for its practice of instilling paranoia in its appointees by cautioning them against sabotage by career civil servants "because of their political persuasion and their loyalty to the majority party of Congress [the Democrats] rather than the executive that supervises them."[57] Nixon's managers were encouraged to insert their own appointees in new positions established between themselves and their disloyal subordinates. Stephen Hess quotes a former Nixon aide as recalling how a White House working group on education programs kept civil servants

in an adjoining room during the meetings, summoning them only when their expertise was required. Every time we invited one in, I could sense a certain coolness and reserve descend upon the room. After the presentation, the staffer would be thanked and invited to leave, whereupon the [Working] Group members loosened up and talked freely once again.

Concluded Hess: "Thus Nixon's proposals had few supporters when support was needed."[58]

The suspicion of bureaucracy nurtured during Nixon's presidency lingers. President Carter's Attorney General Griffin B. Bell let it be known to reporters that he had identified seven techniques or principles he believed bureaucrats used in their efforts to control him. They were "retaliation," "flooding," "burying," "leaking," "crying politics," "avoiding decision-making," and "expanding." Said Bell, "I think I've caught on to these simple techniques. They're no problem for me. If the bureaucracy is going to overcome me, they're going to have to get up something more sophisticated."[59] Said President Carter's Secretary of the Interior Cecil D. Andrus, "Bureaucrats have two ways of exerting control over you—get you to travel and deluge you with paperwork."[60] Of James Schlesinger it was said:

A retinue of assistants accompany him for his appearances before Congress, although Schlesinger can generally field any question tossed his way. The impression persists that he decides department policy pretty much by himself, and that only a few trusted assistants are allowed in his inner circle.[61]

A careful listener can hear a different theme in the tales of executives and their bureaucrats, however. Richard P. Nathan's observation, quoted above, noted attempts by career officials to explain, to warn, to supply facts. Career executives are not automatically hostile to an incoming administration or to a new political superior, nor are they typically reluctant to work hard in service to political executives. Business executives who served in government through the Executive Interchange Program said: "I found a surprising number of intelligent, hard-working, dedicated individuals at the managerial level of government" and "I was very impressed with their intellectual ability and with the hard-driving nature of many people in the supergrades."[62] During his tenure as HEW Secretary, Elliot Richardson wrote of his department's career officials: "They are typically people of strong principle and high competence who respect the role of the political appointee."[63] In other words, as political executives get involved with their work, they may well discover smart, energetic career officials knowledgeable about their department and perfectly willing to be of assistance.

A career subordinate's readiness to cooperate may prove all too fragile, however, and therein lies an important source of difficulties. A political executive who, out of insecurity, is too aggressive and authoritarian, or, alternatively, too timid or aloof, or who is careless in following through or following up, may discover that bureaucrats, inclined in the beginning to be cooperative, instead become everything they were reputed to be. Sensing this, one political executive said as he watched replacements enter Carter's cabinet:

If you, [a Cabinet member], come in and tell them, "Don't give me all that bureaucratic crap, just do it," you risk one of two results. Either the bureaucrats hunker down and prevent you from doing whatever it is you wanted. Or perhaps worse, they let you go ahead and do it. They don't warn you of the consequences and you end up with a bad press or the inspector general all over you.[64]

If a defensive or aloof attitude toward program subordinates infects the political executives' staffs, they are likely to be widely and regularly accused of arrogance by program people, who will resist rather than cooperate. Relations with subordinates seldom degenerate into open conflict. Often the problems are subtle. Notes Heclo:

Because most political appointees require considerable help in government, higher civil servants normally need do little by way of harmful actions in order to prevail. All that is usually necessary is for officials to fail to come forward with their services.[65]

He quotes one career bureaucrat as follows:

With [the former superior] we worked hard, but this guy is just here to further his career, not do a job. . . . We aren't trying to scuttle him, but what happens is you just perform your job at a merely acceptable level. . . . You don't find out things for him or volunteer information. No one's coming in early and staying late like before.[66]

Political executives' relationships with their subordinates thus are tenuous. With effort, these subordinates can often be won over. They are unlikely to abandon long-standing commitments to the programs, nor will they renounce their ties with interest groups and friendly legislators and legislative staffs. As is commonly noted, career officials will be there long after political executives have departed. On the other hand, they often will put their expertise and experience, and their functioning membership in iron triangles, in the service of political executives. If the political executive lacks the inclination or skill to enlist career subordinates in the overall management of the agency, however, these officials, too, will surely become antagonists in the political executive's struggle to manage.

Problems With Peers

Political executives soon become aware that many, perhaps most, policy issues of high importance involve other offices, agencies, or departments in the executive branch. National health insurance, for example, involves not only the Health and Human Services Department but also OMB, the Domestic Policy Staff (DPS), the Council of Economic Advisers, the Veterans Administration, and the Departments of Commerce, Labor, Defense, and Treasury. A wide variety of issues of lesser significance cut across departmental jurisdictions. Sugar policy involves, in addition to the Department of Agriculture, OMB, the DPS, the Council of Economic Advisers, the Council on Wage and Price Stability, the NSC, the Department of State, and the Treasury. Deregulation of the trucking industry involves the Interstate Commerce Commission, the Departments of Agriculture and Transportation, the Council of Economic Advisers, and the Council on Wage and Price Stability. International financial issues, such as the maintenance of buffer stocks for stabilizing community prices, almost always involve conflicts between the Treasury's economic orthodoxy and preference for free market economic doctrines and the State Department's preference for diplomacy and its sympathy for the views of other countries. The Carter administration's deliberations over urban policy became a fierce struggle among HUD, Commerce, and Treasury over the ends and means of economic development.

Departmental officials therefore come to realize that they are involved on many fronts in conflicts with the officials from other departments. Virtually all of President Carter's major initiatives—welfare reform, energy policy, tax reform, arms control, anti-inflation policy—involved more than one cabinet department. Indeed, in the first years of the Carter administration, the policymaking process was likened to "negotiating complicated multilateral treaties."[67] Yet a senior executive may hardly ever see or talk to these adversaries among his or her peers. There are few regularly used channels of communication with them. It may even seem unnatural to regard a peer as a working colleague, and conversations or meetings among cabinet and even subcabinet officials often become carefully staged events, with briefing books, talking points, whispered instructions, and elaborate protocol. For the most part, peers become known to each other through memoranda and secondhand and hearsay reports from aides and subordinates as well as through media accounts. It is entirely possible for conflict and rivalries to develop and be resolved without a face-to-face meeting among principals ever taking place. If chance encounters occur, say at a cabinet meeting, it is altogether likely that issues on which there is heated disagreement will not be mentioned by any of the parties in the absence of their seconds and handlers.

One may wonder why political executives engaged in bureaucratic conflicts do not simply pick up the phone and try to settle their differences. The explanation is to be found in the several factors that militate against the development of an interdepartmental or collegial state of mind among ostensible peers. Because of their mandates, departmental executives almost invariably become departmentally-minded. As Richard Fenno expresses it, "the psychology of departmentalism . . . militates against the establishment of what might be called mutual responsibility—a state of mind which stresses group concerns rather than separate and particular concerns. The subjective attitude hardest to come by among Cabinet members is this sense of corporate unity and common purpose."[68] Presidential assistants seldom try to overcome the department orientation of senior executives. The separatist instincts of these departmental executives are the basis for the power of central staffs. They are needed to coordinate the factions and ensure that a presidential perspective supersedes departmental perspectives. The rare examples of voluntary coordination among department and agency officials often arouse the suspicions of a White House or OMB official wary of having subordinates "cutting a deal" behind the president's back. The willingness, even eagerness, of Executive Office aides to superintend and referee interagency conflict reinforces the separatist tendencies of departmental officials, who are inclined to stand their ground in interagency disputes unless overruled by higher authority.

White House officials may, conversely, fail to recognize the interagency character or scope of an issue, and the departmental or agency executive may have to fight his or her way into the picture. The slight may be minor, such as when an aide to Lyndon Johnson, Joseph Califano invited Secretary of the Interior Stewart Udall to the signing ceremony for the Wilderness Act of 1964 but forgot to invite Secretary of Agriculture Orville Freeman because he overlooked the fact that wilderness areas could also be created out of national forests.[69] Former Secretary of Commerce Juanita M. Kreps was chagrined that she was excluded from Carter's top-level Economic Policy Group, whom she referred to as "the boys at the breakfast table."[70] A more serious slip is reported by former White House aide John Whitaker, who observed President Nixon at a cabinet meeting direct the attorney general to take charge of the drug abuse problem, evidently overlooking the important role in federal drug efforts played by HEW.[71]

Even if the president's assistants were to encourage them to resolve their differences, senior executives would be tempted, and would be encouraged by their subordinates, to follow separatist impulses because of another higher authority: Congress. A vivid case in point is the Carter administration's handling of welfare reform.[72]

At the outset of his administration, Carter asked Secretary of HEW Joseph Califano to create a comprehensive welfare reform proposal that could be announced by May 1, 1977. Though no formal communication to this effect was issued, Califano gathered from the president's occasional remarks in public and private that the proposal was to be developed in concert with Secretary of Labor Ray Marshall and perhaps with Secretary of Commerce Juanita Kreps and the DPS, but the charter was primarily his. Califano was wary of working with the White House staff, however. Remembers Frank Raines, a DPS member:

The Secretary of HEW established a rule that nobody from his department should deal with anybody from the White House without Califano Executive Assistant Ben Heineman's knowledge. That was Califano's notion of Cabinet government. And he was quoted as saying that he wasn't going to let the White House do to him what he did to Cabinet members when he was in the White House. As time moved on our role became more clear but they didn't make it easy for us early on, especially since Ben didn't know much about welfare initially. Califano, I felt, underestimated the view that the President had in favor of Cabinet government —even if we wanted to run HEW, the President wouldn't have let us.

The president apparently felt that welfare should be managed in the agencies. As another member of the DPS staff, Bert Carp, recalled: "The President didn't give us any specific guidance as to how he wanted the process handled. He viewed Califano and Marshall as the key people in putting this together."

In subsequent months, a sharp conflict developed between the two cabinet officers and their subordinates over the extent to which welfare recipients should be required to work as a condition for receiving benefits. HEW favored a sparing and selective use of work requirements. DOL wanted a large-scale public service jobs program to ensure work opportunities for welfare recipients, who would be given incentives to take a job. Though the disagreements were sharp and detailed, officials of the two departments were able to agree on one thing. A proposal initially favored by the president and some of his personal advisers, which involved separate programs for welfare recipients depending on their ability to work and on their prior attachment to the labor force, should be dropped from consideration as too expensive and administratively intricate.

The officials of neither department would budge from their fundamental position. As the president's deadline approached, the White House staff asked Charles Schultze, chairman of the Council of Economic Advisers, an excellent mediator and synthesizer, to assume an "honest broker" role between the two departments. In a four-hour session with subcabinet officials, Schultze was unsuccessful. He reported to the president: "I [was] trying to find an approach which would merge the best points of the HEW and Labor positions. I do not want to rule out the possibility that such an approach could be found. But at the moment the chances are less than 50-50." The basic, unresolvable difference was that Marshall and his associates believed that welfare payments should be as close as possible to a pure wage payment. In contrast, HEW officials believed that welfare payments should be based on family size and total family income and not simply on the work effort of one family member. Neither set of officials was inclined to compromise on this fundamental point.

The president missed his deadline for a proposal and instead announced a set of principles for welfare reform which, though general, still generated intense behind-the-scenes controversy. As the impasse dragged on, the DPS finally began to "crack heads a little bit" and an administration plan was finally lashed together.

Though given the charter to develop the proposal, Califano never attempted to overrule or subordinate Marshall. In an earlier book, Califano had written: "Cabinet officers will not take orders from one of their peers."[73] Throughout the entire episode, Califano and Marshall met on this issue only during briefings and well-attended meetings. Their conflict was fought by proxies—assistant secretaries, deputy assistant secretaries, and special assistants—who pursued their goals with single-minded abandon. In the end, the administration proposal was engineered by a forceful junior-level White House staff member, belatedly agreed to by departmental assistant secretaries, and reviewed in only a pro forma way by Secretaries

Marshall and Califano. The outside world was not to realize how the disagreements were resolved until years later. At the time, administration officials told the *National Journal* that the welfare benefit structure was engineered by Charles Schultze working directly with Califano and Marshall, and thus it constituted a "model" of efficient "Cabinet government."[74] The soundest argument against department-centered government, the one most often used to buttress the case for a strong and intrusive Executive Office of the President, is that virtually all important policy issues cut across departmental jurisdictions. No single party of interest is in a position to manage such issues; thus management must be supplied by the Executive Office. Political executives who must be routinely wary of superiors and subordinates, suspicious of how they will exercise what little discretion they have, must also be alert to their vulnerability to peers, whose noncooperative actions may give Executive Office staff members the excuse to take over responsibility for decision making.

The Measure Of Success

The terrain over which the senior executive must move is thus filled with hazards. As the author of one study of thousands of federal executives at various levels of responsibility concluded:

. . . for the executive functioning within the American political system, there is an [enemy] behind every tree. The executive cannot, however, in a fit of aggressive action go out and [destroy the enemy]. . . . To move aggressively, or even noisily, may invite undesirable or even disastrous attention from superordinates, opposite numbers, or the public at large. Power is so widely dispersed that the executives with the greatest prospects of surviving with their reputations intact are those who move within tight perimeters and avoid stepping on political landmines. Little is to be gained by fighting the White House staff, wrangling with Congressional Committees, and alienating the bureaucracy.[75]

To survive for a respectable length of time, the political executive has every incentive to choose a handful of savvy assistants, react to political and bureaucratic pressure with minimal competence, and chart a path of least resistance and danger through the perils of the job. Even if something goes wrong unexpectedly, quick wits and an instinct for public relations may be sufficient to deflect criticism and to maintain the executive's image of leadership and control.

The political executive who becomes merely dutiful and passive in exercising his or her responsibilities and avoids politically damaging controversy need not expect censure as a result. The same forces that militate against high achievement also protect against failure. Reliable anatomies of managerial incompetence are unlikely to be systematically produced in a partisan political process. Moreover, there are no agencies or institutions with a clear incentive to ferret out and publicize the truth about federal executive performance and to relate the executives' actions to their consequences. Ralph Nader's organizations may swoop down occasionally on an agency, as they did on the Federal Trade Commission or the Bureau of Reclamation. Investigations by the GAO, oversight committees of Congress, and academic institutions studying public management may likewise trace difficulties, occasionally even successes, in policy design and program administration to the actions of political executives. None does so systematically, however.

The major source of current information about executive performance is the daily press.[76] The primary sources are the occasional stories of agency affairs and officials in papers such as the *New York Times,* the *Washington Post,* the *Los Angeles Times,* and the *Wall Street Journal.* Columnist Jack Anderson routinely nips at bureaucrats and the executives who supervise them, as the following example illustrates.

The bureaucratic block in the gasohol project can be traced to the Agriculture Department, where Secretary Bob Bergland is dragging his feet on programs designed to extract ethanol from grain. Farmers and motorists throughout the country favor gasohol development, but Bergland and his Agriculture Department advisers are obstinately balking at any innovation that might cut into grain exports or drive up the prices of farm products.[77]

The *National Journal,* a weekly publication concentrating on executive branch policy making, may be, said *Newsweek,* "the nation's most respected nonpartisan source of information about how Washington's policy making machinery really works."[78]

Experienced government officials are frequently heard to remark, however, on how little reporters seem to know about how the government really works, about who is effective and who is ineffective. At a time when the *Washington Post* was describing Carter's OMB Director James McIntyre as "the little known McIntyre [who] was widely praised for his supervision of day-to-day activities" and saying he had "quiet competence," the reality, as viewed by the *National Journal,* was that few in OMB or other federal agencies respected his abilities. Said an OMB career staffer: "The only thing that distinguishes him from any other budget analyst in town is his former association with the President."[79] Even the respected *National Journal,* however, failed to penetrate the myth of cabinet government cultivated by the Carter administration in reporting its efforts at achieving welfare reform.

In writing about the complex affairs of government, reporters are hampered by their tendency to be intimidated by expertise and professionalism. "The cult of the professional is one of the journalist's most deeply seated attitudes, and one of his most profound problems," says James Fallows.[80] This shortcoming in the reporter's approach to government interacts with another. Fallows notes that writers "are so much a part of the world they are writing about that they can hardly step outside and analyze it. It would be like analyzing themselves."[81] Similarly, Douglas Cater, once a distinguished Washington correspondent, says, "The reporter is the recorder of government but he is also a participant. . . . He can choose from among the myriad events that seethe beneath the surface of government which to describe, which to ignore."[82] Sustained coverage of complicated policy and program issues by the press is as unrealistic to expect as sustained compassion from welfare workers.

Media sources occasionally attempt a dispassionate appraisal of government officials and their effectiveness. In October 1978, for example, *U.S. News and World Report* rated Carter's cabinet.[83] Interestingly enough, all four in what was termed the "bottom group" were gone before the end of Carter's third year in office. More often than not, however, coverage of political executives is most precise and searching when investigative reporters sense scandal. Not solely the result of the success of reporters such as Robert Bernstein, Seymour Hersh, William Shawcross, and Robert Woodward, the muckraking impulse is encouraged by institutions such as the Fund for Investigative Journalism, which channels foundation funds to journalists investigating potential scandals, and by the success of the TV program *60 Minutes.*[84] Writes Douglas Cater:

The Washington correspondent . . . clings to the image of the reporter as the supreme individual in the age of the organization man. . . . His prestige symbols encourage him in this notion. The Pulitzer Prizes, the Heywood Brown and Raymond Clapper Awards handed out each year go to the reporter who has beaten the system and gotten the "scoop"—to the one who has singlehandedly busted up the hidden enclave of intrigue and purified big government by the cleansing power of publicity.[85]

The weaknesses of the media in covering executive actions can be readily exploited by political executives with an instinct for public relations. Public affairs offices are often large, staffed with various communications specialists, and engaged in a wide range of activities from furnishing news releases to mounting media campaigns to preparing departmental officials for public appearances. Political executives often use their public information officers to take advantage of the publicity possibilities in mass circulation newspapers, magazines, radio, and television.

It is personal contact with journalists that counts most, however. Smart political executives often realize, as did former Under Secretary of Commerce Joseph W. Bartlett, that

the Secretary can delegate, and thereby ignore, the function of the chief press relations man for his department, but he does so at his [own] peril. If the Secretary eschews public relations and frequent interviews, experienced reporters will consult willing sources at lower levels who, by default, are awarded *de facto* power to frame the department's public image.[86]

Henry Kissinger, an acknowledged press relations expert, says:

I experienced the symbiotic relationship in Washington between the media and government. Much as the journalist may resent it, he performs a partly governmental function. . . . Officials seek him out to bring their pet projects to general attention, to settle scores, or to reverse a decision that went against them. . . . For the experienced Washington observer careful reading of the press or listening to the key commentators provides valuable intelligence concerning the cross-currents of bureaucracy, or the subterranean gathering of pent-up political forces.[87]

Clever executives learn how to flatter the reporters' sense of importance and status, to give in order to get, to deflect attention with a well-timed story, or systematically to build a reputation through interviews, social contacts, and friendship with sympathetic writers.

Because of the key role played by the press, many experienced senior officials suggest that appearances are far more important than reality in the formation of judgments about executive performance, even by those in a position to know better. As former Secretary of Commerce Peter Peterson observed: "In Washington, your ability to articulate your accomplishments in a way that is memorable and persuasive generally counts far more than the objective standards of efficiency and success as we know them in business."[88] Frederick Malek reports the contrasting impressions of Secretary of the Interior Rogers C. B. Morton and OMB Director Roy Ash. Morton, says Malek, "enjoys a public reputation as an effective and able leader, though it is difficult to pinpoint many major accomplishments."

Ash, who was instrumental in holding the executive branch together during Watergate and was a leader in major government reorganizations, "was often portrayed as a villain." Concludes Malek: "Ash's record of achievement easily eclipses that of Rogers Morton, yet the latter enjoys a public acclaim rooted in his sound sense of public relations."[89] Morton's sense of public relations was indeed well developed. A media consultant to Morton's Interior Department was once quoted as follows: "A part of greater use of television should be a continuing effort to get the secretary usually involved in newsworthy events which provide good picture materials for the print media, too. Secretary Morton is not only the most photogenic member of the Administration, but he's also able to participate physically in all kinds of outdoor situations and look natural."[90]

A public perception that one is effective is easier to come by than actual effectiveness. Indeed, the most sophisticated officials come to recognize that perceptions shape reality. If one is believed to be influential, one often acquires even greater influence. Bert Lance, for example, was reportedly all but uninterested in the details of his job as director of OMB; he left the preparation of the president's budget to others. Yet because of his intimate association with the president, he was celebrated in the national press as the man who was restoring OMB to its former position of power. A contrasting experience is that of Juanita Kreps, who, reflecting on her service as secretary of commerce, said:

I know that the glamor, the glory of this town centers on who's at the center of power. I am constantly plagued by this constant reference to the fact that I'm soft spoken and gentle and don't make waves. I keep threatening to change that image by coming in some morning and screaming and throwing things.

A low-key, substantive approach "does not pay off in Washington. Rather the fellow who can hold an audience, who can go with a minimum of information and a maximum of political savvy—that's the way to get ahead in Washington."[91]

It is not surprising that government executives are tempted to manage more for effect than for results and to present themselves to the public in ways that make their jobs appear more political than managerial. It is also not surprising that we do not really expect the senior executives in government to be managers. Observed *Fortune* in 1954, "The main job of the President and his top executives is not administrative but political."[92] A 1964 study by the Brookings Institution reported the striking finding, deemed "little short of astounding" by the Brookings researchers, that only 14 percent of the general public identify management work with government. College seniors, graduate students, and business executives—the very people whose skills the government most urgently needs and for whom such jobs would have the greatest appeal[93]—were about two and one-half times more likely to associate management work with business than with government. "The manager," writes Leonard Sayles, "is the most notable representative of the institution of business, as the politician is of the institution of government. . . ."[94] Indeed, the term "manager" is faintly pejorative when applied to political leaders. In his "national malaise" speech, President Carter faulted himself for being a manager of government rather than a political leader. Not long after replacing James Schlesinger as secretary of energy, Charles Duncan was said to have made no enemies, in part because "Duncan is a manager, not a policymaker, and has avoided ruffling feathers by doing little that is controversial."[95] Said Ed Rothschild, head of Energy Action, a Washington-based consumer group: "Duncan probably knows how to pay his gas bill. That's it for his energy knowledge. But he was not brought in as an energy thinker; he was brought in as a manager."[96]

Yet, we want the government to be well managed. Instead of relying on people to achieve it, however, we have preferred to rely on process, organization, and technique to coordinate the diffuse and disparate fragments of authority and resources scattered among the branches and levels of government. The efficacy of the systems approach to public management is explored in the next chapter.

CHAPTER 4

The System Is Not the Solution

RICHARD NIXON, perhaps more than any other president, authorized and supported measures to improve the management of the federal government. But, wrote Frederick Malek, the young business executive he relied on to bring about these improvements, "President Nixon wanted sound management but did not wish to devote his time to its attainment."[1] The improvement of governmental management without anyone having to spend too much time actually managing has been a persistent motivation for the major governmental reform movements in recent years. Said Raymond Jacobson, executive director of the Civil Service Commission during the 1977 debate on civil service reform, "a lot of people out there don't want to take the time to manage. There are ways to cut through the problems if you have a reasonable amount of management savvy."[2] Surely, recent reformers appear to believe, ways can be found to ensure that government employees perform to high standards without being cajoled and harassed by political leaders; surely modern management tools and methods should replace the clanking, hand-operated, antique, and unreliable machinery often still in operation and are capable of supplying government with automatic pilots, gyroscopes, infrared vision, and inertial navigation so that the crew will neither crash nor wear out. Surely, such reformers conclude, modern management systems and techniques are the solution to governmental incompetence.

The major reforms of recent years—PPBS, MBO, ZBB, policy analysis, program analysis, program evaluation, performance measurement, reorganization, productivity measurement, and sunrise and sunset laws—have had a family resemblance. Each has had the common goal of improving efficiency, accountability, and effectiveness through rational, goal-oriented, analytical management. At the core of each seems to be an economic calculus, a continuous comparison of measurable benefits and costs, and the creation of material incentives for behavior that will maximize the former and minimize the latter. With these systems in place, no program or individual would be automatically entitled to a secure or unchallenged existence. Being faced with the necessity of proving themselves or going out of business will, it is believed, instill in employees and their managers a determination to succeed that will insure competent performance. In this chapter we investigate this proposition.

Reform proposals recommend change in at least one of three areas: organizational processes, organizational structure, or organizational behavior.

Reforming Organizational Processes

All government organizations adopt standard routines and operating procedures by which they accomplish tasks and achieve internal coordination. Governmental performance can be viewed as a product of these routines.[3] Reformers seeking to change the performance of the government have often attempted to do so by changing these standard decision-making and operational routines. The most important routine is that of formulating the organization's budget, so budgetary reform has attracted the greatest attention. Early interest in budgetary reform, growing out of Progressive era concerns with increasing the integrity and efficiency of routine government activities, focused primarily on achieving fiduciary control over budget administration. With the growth of government in the 1930s, Congress, ordinarily reluctant to surrender its powers of the purse, cooperated with placing responsibility for the formulation of the budget in the newly created Executive Office of the President, with a dramatically upgraded staff capability. Following World War II, the first Hoover Commission popularized the concept of "performance budgeting." In 1950, President Truman submitted the first bona fide performance budget, and the Budget and Accounting Procedures Act of 1950 encouraged the extension of performance concepts throughout the federal government.[4] The seeds of the later reforms had been sown.

PLANNING-PROGRAMMING-BUDGETING SYSTEM

Enthusiasm for performance budgeting ebbed during the 1950s,[5] but as early as 1960 the budgetary process began to be transformed again. The budget came to be seen as a means of ensuring more coherent, forward-looking, and results-oriented performance,[6] and a formal planning function was introduced into the theory of the budgetary process. The bellwether of this transformation was the planning-programming-budgeting system (PPBS). On the strength of Secretary Robert McNamara's apparent success with PPBS in the Department of Defense in the early 1960s, President Johnson ordered the "new and revolutionary system" installed throughout the federal government in 1965.

In theory, PPBS required numerous structural changes in the budgetary process. Classifications within the budget were altered from objects of expenditure, such as personnel and maintenance, to activities with complementary objectives, which in turn were aggregated into programs and made the objects of systematic policy analysis. Finally, PPBS emphasized development of policy analysis and program evaluation as an ongoing means of adjusting and upgrading policy decisions.

Program budgeting represented a shift from using the budget as an instrument of expenditure control to using it for systematically analyzing policy choices and corresponding resource allocations. It required information in forms and in quantities not previously required in budget making and policy making. Beyond defining objective criteria for assessing policies, a controversial and technically difficult first step, analysts had to struggle with specifying costs and benefits in rigorous quantitative terms. The results, however, were often incomprehensible to political officials and program managers, who simply did not think about the issues before them in that way and who resented the intellectual abstraction and the implicit centralizing bias of systems approaches. Aaron Wildavsky has observed that "many defenders of PPBS . . . end up alleging, in effect, that the world is not good enough for it. The paradox is that the world PPBS is supposed to change must first undergo that change before it can accommodate PPBS."[7] For that reason, PPBS as a management system never really caught on, President Johnson's mandate notwithstanding. Even at the Defense Department its use faded after McNamara's departure.

The legacy of PPBS is the significant utilization of policy analysis and program evaluation in federal decision making. By insisting that it is better to have some idea of where you are going than to fly blind and that it is better to be orderly than haphazard about policy making, advocates of PPBS helped foster a new level of expectation concerning government administration and performance. Its institutional legacies are in departmental offices for planning and evaluation, and its intellectual legacies are in the emerging disciplines of policy analysis and in the growth of professional schools that teach it to people who are or will be making careers in government service.

MANAGEMENT BY OBJECTIVES

An oft-heard criticism of PPBS was that its routines failed to take into account the need to deal with policy and program issues that were not primarily budgetary in nature. Management by objectives, or MBO, chronologically the next major federal management reform, owes its lineage to both the performance and program budgeting movements in government and to management reforms that were fashionable in private business. Like PPBS, MBO initially emphasized the *process* of delivering goods and services, not the larger problem of determining policy objectives, and thus it was something of a retreat from the ambitions of PPBS. In the private sector, stimulated by Peter F. Drucker's *Practice of Management,* which first appeared in 1954, MBO was widely adopted as a management theme in practice and in teaching, thus enhancing its appeal to government administrators who viewed business management methods as models to emulate.

Contrary to popular impression, the advent of MBO in the public sector did not occur during the Nixon administration, though it acquired its status as a movement then. Prior to the 1970s, MBO was practiced in a number of government agencies—the Social Security Administration, the National Park Service, the Federal Aviation Administration, the Internal Revenue Service, and others—as a device for ensuring specificity in program objectives; for tracking, measuring, and evaluating results; and for redesigning programs and objectives.[8] In 1970, an MBO process was initiated in HEW with the larger ambition of "coping with a veritable explosion in the size and scope of its operations"[9] that had occurred during the 1960s. Under the direction of Frederick Malek, HEW's MBO process received widespread attention and was reported to be reasonably effective in coordinating flows of information and resources during a period of unruly growth.[10]

With the creation of OMB and Malek's appointment as its deputy director (under another Harvard Business School graduate, Roy Ash, former head of Litton Industries and chairman of Nixon's Committee on Reorganization), MBO was instituted throughout the federal government by the Nixon administration in an effort to tame what was perceived as a bulky and unresponsive executive structure.

As implemented by OMB, MBO consisted of six stages: (1) defining the overarching goals or mission of the agency; (2) conducting analyses of agency problems; (3) formulating objectives based on problems but tied to overarching goals; (4) developing an action plan for meeting objectives; (5) gathering information necessary for making program adjustments; and (6) evaluating performance in comparison to objectives. Within OMB, thirty new positions, termed "management associates," were created to oversee MBO in the agencies. Within the departments, overall responsibility for MBO was typically lodged in an office of administration and management headed by an assistant secretary. Unlike PPBS, MBO did not require the creation of extensive and specialized administrative structures and a redesign of budgeting and accounting systems.

In practice, MBO, like PPBS, impressed many critics as being politically naive. Frank Sherwood and William Page write that Rodney Brady, HEW's assistant secretary for administration, and Malek seemed to believe that management is "value-neutral, universalistic, applicable in all cases, and best functions when the situation is unambiguous and clearcut. If the situation is not that way, make it so."[11] The authors give as an example influences on the Federal Executive Institute "that technical knowledge be taught to the exclusion of discussion of executive values, moorings, and obligations."[12]

The most disindigenous feature of MBO in the federal government was its reliance on clarity of objectives to direct resource allocation, management performance, and evaluation. Objectives are seldom clear-cut, however, partly by design—political compromises are often founded on the obscuring of objectives and the conflicts among them—and partly because defining objectives in measurable terms is often inherently difficult. Ash and Malek initially attempted to finesse these problems by issuing broad, sparse directions: The objectives must be important to the president; the results must be observable; and the program must require no additional funding. In public statements, Ash further downplayed the formality of MBO design, calling MBO a matter of "style," not of process, and "management by common sense." Nonetheless, the submissions by the departments and agencies were carefully enforced and, under pressure from OMB, tight, ambitious deadlines were scheduled. Nominal compliance was almost complete, and the president was reported to have assembled 237 objectives in 1974 with only the Department of State abstaining.[13]

As might be expected, objectives varied considerably in scope, content, and rigor. Some, such as a 1975 State Department objective to formulate foreign policy on the basis of "a partnership between the government and people" requiring "a new consensus concerning our fundamental interests and evolving aims . . . a realistic view of our capabilities . . . and a positive and open public dialogue on issues,"[14] were comically amorphous. Others, such as a goal "to increase by four percent the proportion of total purchases by agencies at which SBA [the Small Business Administration] has procurement center objectives,"[15] were appropriate in a business sense but could hardly be classified as presidential concerns.

Most often, the problems faced by the departments in formulating objectives were overcome by stating objectives in process-oriented, rather than results-oriented, terms that were unambiguous, quantifiable, and usually controllable. Error rates, turnover, and other management indices were far more likely to be proposed as objectives than the substantive policy goals of the department. Where substantive goals were stated, their achievement was often beyond the control of the federal government. Richard Rose notes that "overall, 25 percent of 1974 objectives and 30 percent of 1975 objectives *cannot be accomplished by any organization,* public or private. They are the resultant of social and economic processes."[16]

Because of MBO's shortcomings and its dispensability, it was only a matter of time before it fell into disuse. OMB began canceling critical management review meetings shortly after MBO was implemented and personnel began to be diverted for fighting fires, most notably those caused by the energy crisis in 1973–74. In the end, interest in MBO was probably most seriously undermined by the politically sterile nature of the objectives generated by this process; 81 percent of the objectives in 1973 and 80 percent in 1974 were deemed apolitical in nature.[17] This result was not a fault of the participants but rather of the framework itself. Like its predecessor, MBO fell down because its routines suppressed substantive issues subject to political dispute and controversy. Executives, pressured by serious and immediate policy demands, did not have time for what they regarded as MBO's obscurity and triviality.

Beneath the surface, however, MBO made significant changes in the capabilities of the political executives who made imaginative attempts to use it. At HEW, for example, Elliot Richardson made effective use of MBO conferences with program managers to communicate in a personal way his sense of departmental priorities, regardless of whether they were captured by the formal objectives, and also to learn about obstacles to their implementation.[18] Secretary of Agriculture Earl Butz kept an "underground" list of objectives that were not divulged to OMB or even disseminated throughout the department. These objectives were far more controversial and speculative than the department's nominal objectives, and as a result they were treated with greater interest and expediency by the secretary and program managers. Butz, in fact, had meetings every two weeks to check on the progress of these confidential objectives.[19]

These unintentional and often covert possibilities inherent in the MBO process were its most intriguing, and for senior executives significant, characteristic. Richard Rose stresses the importance of this aspect:

> The chief clients for the MBO system are the political appointees in the departments, starting with the Secretary or the Under-Secretary responsible for overseeing the activities of the department. . . . The Secretary has more of a personal stake in the identification of his department's objectives than does any outsider. Similarly, a bureau chief is sensitive to the evaluation placed upon his programs within the department and may hope for tangible recognition of success in the annual departmental budget review.
> . . . In the hands of a Secretary or an Under-Secretary who is a good committee chairman, management conferences can be a forum for exchanging views about developments and shifts in emphasis within and between programs, and encouraging flexibility among both political appointees and program managers. The management conferences also ensure that those in attendance are fully briefed about a range of activities within the department, thus reducing the imperfections in the flow of information throughout the departmental hierarchy.[20]

After the presidential requests for objectives were issued in 1974, the formal pursuit of MBO in OMB and elsewhere dissipated in the general confusion that surrounded Watergate and rapid changes of administration. President Ford, for example, issued a "mega-management" directive in 1976 that buried executives in more than twenty simultaneous post-Watergate management reforms within a four- to twelve-week timetable.[21] MBO as a matter of style was overwhelmed by demands for information and adjustment during a turbulent period.

MBO did not introduce a new set of tools into the government, and it required relatively few structural changes. Its imprint on federal operations has been faint. Unlike the planning and evaluation officials, PPBS's contribution to the structure of government, the heads of administration and management offices have seldom achieved important roles within their departments. To a limited extent, MBO perpetuated the strengths and weaknesses of the program budgeting movement. To their credit, its supporters recognized the need to struggle with the intractable problems of shaping the department's mission with results in mind. Its flexibility allowed MBO to be remolded into more effective means of departmental communication when managers used the framework creatively. MBO's largest fault, however, was that it was "inaugurated without necessary understanding of motivation, authority, and power in public organizations."[22]

Zero Base Budgeting

President Carter assumed office promising to install, throughout the federal establishment, a zero base budgeting (ZBB) system which, in his words, "strips down the budget each year to zero and starts from scratch, requiring every [activity] that spends the taxpayer's money to rejustify itself annually." His February 14, 1977, memorandum to cabinet members and agency heads proposed that "by working together under a zero base budgeting system we can reduce . . . costs and make the federal government more efficient and effective."[23]

By taking this approach, Carter was not the first alumnus of state government to attempt ZBB in the federal government. In 1962 former Governor of Minnesota Orville Freemen introduced ZBB into the Department of Agriculture. The description issued by Freeman's Office of Budget and Finance was virtually indistinguishable from the modern version of ZBB.

A new concept has been adopted for the 1964 agency estimates; namely that of zero base budgeting. This means that all programs will be reviewed from the ground up and not merely in terms of changes proposed for the budget year. . . . The total work program of each agency must be subjected to an intensive review and evaluation. . . . Consideration must be given to the basic need for the work contemplated, the level at which the work should be carried out, the benefits to be received, and the costs to be incurred.[24]

Freeman's trial of ZBB, however, generated "entirely unsuccessful" management results and was dropped from budgetary procedures after one year. In their review of this experience, Aaron Wildavsky and Arthur Hammond found few positive consequences as a result of much effort.

> [This procedure] vastly overestimates man's limited ability to calculate and grossly underestimates the importance of political and technological constraints. The required calculations could not be made and would not have led to substantial changes. As a result, a great deal of effort went into zero base budgeting with few specific changes attributable to this method.[25]

Independently of Carter's forthcoming directives, ZBB was also tested in such agencies as the Consumer Product Safety Commission and the National Aeronautics and Space Administration. These applications of ZBB were initiated in 1977 to provide the House Appropriations Committee with information on the feasibility of this system. The results were discouraging. Essentially, the agencies defined minimum funding levels at current appropriation levels and refused to rank spending proposals in terms of priorities because they lacked criteria for making comparisons among programs.[26] In spite of these results and similarly discouraging experiences in the states, President Carter forged ahead with implementation of ZBB in the federal government.

In its purest form, ZBB simply requires development of the budget from scratch, without reference to the size, composition, or objectives of previous budgets.[27] This comprehensive approach to budgeting has long had advocates in the management literature. As early as 1924, E. Hilton Young, an English budget authority, advocated reassessing budget programs annually.[28] But it has only recently found its way into practice. The version of ZBB implemented by OMB required budget formulation via three steps: (1) identification of "decision units"; (2) translation of decision units into "decision packages"; and (3) ranking and consolidation within the budget. Decision units represent the smallest organizational entities—programs, functions, line items—for which there is an identifiable manager who can establish priorities and a budget within the unit. The manager is responsible for allocating decision units to decision packages that describe the program and analyze its likely effects at a minimum, a maintenance, and at an increased level of funding. For each decision package, an analysis of the costs and consequences of alternative levels of spending makes its way to department heads. Department heads must formulate a final and comprehensive ranking that includes decision packages down to the level of the formal budget request.[29] Decision packages are then forwarded to agency heads, who rank them with respect to their own priorities.

The comprehensive ranking procedures demanded by ZBB provoked the greatest protest from managers.[30] In the Department of Agriculture, for example, managers were faced with the unenviable task of ranking such diverse programs as food stamps, national forests, and meat inspection.[31] No accepted or politically acceptable criteria exist for such comparisons, and agencies realized that they would risk alienating constituents by ranking some programs below others in importance. In the Public Health Service (PHS), the ranking process generated considerable controversy. PHS made substantial changes in the rankings of its subordinate agencies with minimal opportunity for their rebuttal. Regina Herzlinger notes the predominant reason for these top-level changes:

> Most of the changes that PHS had made in the agencies' original rankings appeared to be for political not analytical reasons. For example, HSA [the Health Services Administration] had given a low ranking to the PHS hospitals established in the eighteenth century to aid impoverished merchant seamen, feeling they were no longer necessary. However, the PHS staff felt it was politically infeasible to suppress the hospitals and thus upgraded the ranking.[32]

The National Institutes of Health (NIH) submissions also created conflict. After refusing to submit rankings for minimum and maintenance budgets, NIH put together an alphabetical list and submitted it as a ranking.[33]

ZBB also suffered from problems similar to those of program budgeting and, to a lesser extent, MBO. ZBB required quantum increases in the quality and quantity of information required for decision making, but it made no provisions for the ways that this knowledge was to be generated.[34] If anything, ZBB exacerbated the information problem by requiring great amounts of data under severe time constraints. Moreover, if ZBB was practiced literally, its ahistorical nature would obscure the lessons and information of the past and permit the yearly invention of new relationships, program structures, and goals.[35] For agencies engaged in long-term undertakings, such as biomedical research and environmental protection, this "myopic bias" represents a large drawback.[36] Finally, the design of ZBB takes no account of expected political interference as decision packages are formulated, reranked, consolidated, and bumped up to successively higher levels of decision making. The resolution of these conflicts, as the PHS hospital example illustrates, has everything to do with the acceptability of ZBB outcomes.

In the best use of the ZBB process in the federal government, the EPA was able to improve flows of information within the agency and use the rankings to shift and optimize priorities which otherwise would have been unchanged. At the program level, the ZBB process brought together enforcement and research officials with program officials for the first time. Most important, ZBB at EPA demonstrated the power of a creative manager, Douglas Costle, to explore a given management technique for purposes other than the narrow ones for which it was intended. In this case, Costle utilized ZBB to educate the relatively green administrative corps he brought into the agency. As with Richardson's use of MBO, the primary benefit of ZBB to Costle lay in the improvement of intradepartmental communication. When it came time to consolidate rankings, ZBB brought together all six assistant administrators, none of whom had been at the agency for more than a few months. One of them, William Drayton, Jr., remarked that all six were "united by a common level of ignorance." James H. McDermott, head of the safe drinking water team that appeared before the top administrators, noted, "They were new to the business and they asked one hell of a lot of questions." In the end, the ZBB process facilitated a small shift in resources from noise control to safe drinking water, where it was felt that additional dollars would have the greatest impact. Even in EPA, ZBB was still not without its critics. One budget analyst remarked, "If we did the best job in the government, I'd hate to see what the rest of the government did."

Nonetheless, Costle's experience with ZBB suggests a lesson similar to McNamara's use of PPBS and Richardson's use of MBO. The particular management technique matters much less than the manager's willingness to exploit it for his or her own purpose. Under aggressive, interested leadership, PPBS, MBO, and ZBB had marked effects on flows of information and quality of decision making *in a few select cases.* The critical variable in these cases was the executive's willingness and capacity to prod for results, to take the time to manage.

As it was designed and implemented in most of the federal government, however, ZBB failed in its central purpose: to provide managers with the necessary incentives to perform the required analysis and indicate clear priorities for program choices. The framers of ZBB, seduced as were earlier reformers by the intuitive appeal of imposing an orderly, businesslike approach on federal management, ignored the imperatives of the political process and the necessity for adapting management practices to it.

Reforming Organizational Structure

"Reorganization has become almost a religion in Washington," wrote Harold Seidman during the early years of the Nixon administration.[37] Even so, the fervor then was mild in comparison to Jimmy Carter's early commitment to reorganizing the entire federal structure. The urge to reorganize is irresistible to political leaders. As Herbert Kaufman has put it, "the calculus of reorganization is essentially the calculus of politics itself" and thus is often a far more beguiling reform than altering internal management practices. He goes on:

> Reorganization of the executive branch is a commonly advocated weapon against inefficiency and complexity, but it is not the only one. Changes in public policy can also be effective. Improvements in administrative management, budgeting, personnel administration, standard operating procedures, methods of purchasing, incentive systems, and other techniques of handling the day-to-day business of the executive branch can increase efficiency and simplify operations. But compared to reorganization—the creation of new administrative organizations on a grand scale, the regrouping of old ones, the termination of outmoded units and the redistribution of their functions among others, changes in the degree of autonomy enjoined by existing bodies, and other such transformations of structure—they are often seen as superficial, trivial, and politically unrewarding.[38]

Carter had aggrandized his position as governor of Georgia by reorganizing state government, and he pledged to take advantage of his "outsider's" status to realign political power in Washington, D.C., as well.

The expressed goals of major reorganizations are usually to ensure maximum efficiency and economy, promote more effective planning and coordination, and reduce fragmentation, overlap, and unnecessary paperwork. But, as Kaufman noted, the real goals are almost always partly or wholly political. Reorganization may represent a challenge to entrenched interests, a hacksaw taken to iron triangles, as did Carter's reorganization in Georgia. Through reorganization, elected officials can gain greater control over the government bureaucracy by mandating change and then controlling the steps necessary to carry it out, thus altering existing patterns of advocacy. It may be a way to increase the visibility and political clout of a favored political goal or constituency, as was the case with the creation of the EPA and the Departments of Energy and Education. It is a way to weaken, eliminate, or take over rival organizations, as with the various efforts to reorganize the intelligence agencies or the breakup of the Atomic Energy Commission. It may signal a determination to do something about a problem when it is not clear what should be done, as with President Nixon's creation of a Special Action Office for Drug Abuse Prevention. "Periodic reorganizations," observes Seidman, "are prescribed if for no other reason than to purify the bureaucratic blood and prevent stagnation."[39]

The history of intradepartmental as opposed to interdepartmental reorganization is less well documented, but senior executives are invariably tempted to rearrange their organization charts to align internal responsibilities with the talents and interests of the people they want to appoint, to shake up a predecessor's arrangements in order to signal a change in approach or priorities, or to conform to specific ideas about how they want to manage their organizations. Departmental officials have been given substantial legal authority to engage in internal reorganizations, although the avalanche of substantive legislation in recent years has blocked many formerly open routes to internal change. Typical of internal shake-ups was the reorganization of the Social Security Administration by incoming Commissioner Stanford G. Ross in 1979. "One of my first tasks as Commissioner of Social Security was to evaluate our organizational posture," he said in a bulletin to all employees.

As I began my evaluation, I quickly sensed that SSA had not fully recovered from the organizational trauma of the 1975 reorganization and that there appeared to be a rather deep-seated fear of organizational change on the part of many of SSA's staff. . . . However, . . . [o]ur current organizational structure hampers effective and meaningful communications, inhibits the policy development and decision-making process, contains duplication, and isolates the field organization to the extent that field interests and concerns are not adequately represented at headquarters. The magnitude and diversity of these problems demand organizational change if SSA is to effectively perform its mission.[40]

Ross's boss, HEW Secretary Califano, was able to make a major department-wide reorganization—combining Medicaid and Medicare into a new Health Care Finance Administration, reassigning the Aid to Families with Dependent Children program to the Social Security Administration, assembling scattered social and human services agencies into the Office of Human Development, and abolishing the Social and Rehabilitation Service altogether. Indeed, the history of HEW from its creation to its demise was one of almost continuous internal reorganization.

Though organizational change has been a concomitant of the evolution of government since its creation, its salience as a political issue dates from the time of the New Deal, and virtually every president from Roosevelt on has dealt with it. (Moreover, 86 out of 109 reorganization plans since 1939 have been implemented.)[41] Franklin D. Roosevelt was a master craftsman in using reorganization to achieve his political and programmatic goals. Subsequent presidents fell under the influence of the two Hoover Commissions and their relentless pursuit of governmental efficiency. President Truman undertook significant structural changes in 1949, essentially following the blueprint established by the first Hoover Commission. These plans reinforced many of the Brownlow Committee recommendations and Roosevelt actions, increasing the authority and capabilities of department heads and enhancing the possibilities for presidential development of policy. President Eisenhower likewise followed the lead of the Hoover Commission and submitted fourteen reorganization plans. His Committee on Government Organization—including Nelson Rockefeller, Milton Eisenhower, and Arthur Flemming—developed several far-reaching proposals, though Eisenhower was reluctant to create undue political controversy, only going to bat for the creation of a Department of Health, Education and Welfare. He also accepted the advice of an advisory group that urged reorganization of the Department of Defense.

Unlike Roosevelt, President Kennedy showed no interest in or feel for organizational issues. The obligatory advisory group was established, but he largely ignored its recommendations. Kennedy's attempt to create a Department of Urban Affairs and Housing was soundly defeated, and by the end of his period in office, the president's reorganization authority had been allowed to lapse.

President Johnson overcame substantial legislative obstacles, successfully proposing creation of the Departments of Transportation and Housing and Urban Development. The pitfalls and consequences of consolidating federal departments, however, were lost on Johnson. Harold Seidman notes that Johnson's "reorganization program and decisions on organizational issues reflected little if any unity of purpose. His approach was episodic, pragmatic, and sometimes gave the appearance of being improvised on the spur of the moment."[42] A plan to combine Labor and Commerce, adopted at the last minute to spice up his 1967 State of the Union Address, represented a typically careless approach to organizational issues.

Working from the recommendations of the Ash Council, the Nixon administration proposed a major reorganization of federal activities in 1971. Appearing before Congress in his State of the Union Address, Nixon declared:

Based on a long, intensive study with the aid of the best obtainable advice, I have concluded that a sweeping reorganization of the Executive Branch is needed if the Government is to keep up with the times and the needs of the people.

To that end, Nixon proposed the compression of seven existing departments—Agriculture, Interior, Commerce, Transportation, Labor, Health, Education and Welfare, and Housing and Urban Development—into four "superdepartments": Human Resources, Community Development, Natural Resources, and Economic Affairs. He argued that the problem of government lay in the structure of its machinery, not its people or resources. The Nixon proposals, however, were short-lived, as they immediately faced a hostile Democratic Congress. The House Government Operations Committee, for example, concluded, "There are factors working against early enactment. This is the year of a national election, the President's party does not hold a majority in the Congress, and there is considerable skepticism about wholesale reform packages." John Ehrlichman attempted to accomplish the same result by persuading the president to designate four of his cabinet officers as "super secretaries" superintending the activities of their colleagues, but this scheme also was short-lived. Soon after, Watergate preempted the administration's organizational initiatives; reorganization authority expired, and the work of the Ash Council was quietly shelved.

While campaigning for the presidency, Jimmy Carter pledged to reduce the number of independent federal entities from 1,900 to 200. To carry out his pledge, he authorized creation of a Reorganization Project within OMB under a newly designated executive associate director for reorganization and management. On the advice of OMB Director Bert Lance and presidential assistant Hamilton Jordan, the reorganization effort was downgraded almost immediately, and Carter's most visible organization goals became the creation of two new cabinet departments: Energy and Education. Yet the reorganization staff continued its activities, and Carter appointed a veteran Florida legislator, Richard Pettigrew, to the post of assistant to the president for reorganization. Said Pettigrew:

We have specific goals to achieve greater economy and efficiency, to enhance employee productivity and government accountability, to improve the delivery of government services, and to reduce the private sector burden imposed by regulation and paperwork requirements, to improve the long-term capacity of the government to anticipate and confront problems that this country faces and to make policy effectively in the executive branch.[43]

At the end of this project, frustration reverberated throughout the government. More than 300 people worked on the project over a three-year period. The original OMB reorganization staff saw two years of work on economic development and natural resources reorganization plans dissipated in a matter of weeks by the DPS and the vice president's office, which feared the political costs of a major reorganization effort. One presidential assistant said he was waiting for the reorganization staff to convince him that the proposed major reorganizations would allow Carter to claim significant savings for the government. "I want as a criterion the ability to say we saved so many millions of dollars by doing this."[44] Indeed, said one White House aide, "You are going to see a lot more emphasis on waste and fraud in government, that sort of thing."[45] In Interior, morale in the Bureau of Land Management was undermined as professionals read reports in the papers telling how Agriculture's Forest Service would be brought over to improve its operation. Important reauthorizing legislation for the Economic Development Administration was put aside and later submitted late and deficient to Congress, while reorganization studies took precedence.

Along the way, the administration encountered the turbulence typical of this type of undertaking, but it was not able or willing to devote the requisite energy and competence to dealing with it. From city and county, by land and by sea, the critics attacked.

- Urban interests objected to the loss of a specifically urban-oriented department and feared their mission would be significantly diluted.
- Rural interests objected to the movement of such programs as the Farmers Home Administration (FHA) into a presumably urban-oriented Department of Development Assistance.
- Timber interests objected to reorganization because they feared a new department would emphasize environmental protection over timber production. The Sierra Club, on the other hand, did not support the move because it feared Secretary of the Interior Cecil Andrus's prospective timber policies.
- Ocean interests turned their objections to the transfer of the National Oceanographic and Atmospheric Administration (NOAA) into a call for a new cabinet-level Department for Oceans—composed of the Coast Guard, the Maritime Administration, and NOAA.

What about those reorganization efforts that succeeded? The travails of the Department of Energy and its first secretary became familiar because of their high visibility. President Carter claimed that the creation of this department would "bring immediate order" to national energy policy.[46] Eighteen months later, the president created by executive order an Energy Coordinating Committee, chaired by the secretary of energy but involving twenty-two other federal departments and agencies, "to provide for the coordination of Federal energy policies."[47]

Perhaps even more revealing of what reorganization entails is the tale of a reorganization that was barely noticed. Early in 1978 the secretary of the interior created the Heritage and Recreation Service (HRS) within the Department of the Interior in accordance with the provisions of section 2 of Reorganization Plan No. 3 of 1950 (64 Stat. 1262). The new organization consolidated the Historic Preservation Fund, formerly under the National Park Service, and the Bureau of Outdoor Recreation and its Land and Water Conservation Fund. The Historic Preservation Fund is now a principal source of financial support for the National Trust for Historic Preservation and its Historic American Buildings Survey (HABS) and Historic American Engineering Record (HAER). The Building Survey was born during the depths of the recession and a few months later, the Department of the Interior entered into a "tripartite agreement" with the American Institute of Architects and the Library of Congress to administer the survey. A similar cooperative effort was begun in 1958 with the American Society of Civil Engineers. The two surveys were part of the Park Service's Office of Archaeology and Historic Preservation.

In 1978, the newly appointed head of the HRS abolished the HABS and HAER advisory boards without first notifying them, prompting the professional associations and the Library of Congress to claim a violation of the tripartite agreement. Their ire was further exacerbated by the directors intent to merge the two surveys and decentralize their administration to seven regional offices. Would this be more or less efficient? Would the engineering survey lose out to the more popular architecture survey? Would rehabilitation and advocacy replace precise, scientific documentation as the primary goals? Would the quality of the effort be diluted? Could the morale of the historic preservation movement be restored and the professional associations be placated? Would the effort be worth it in the end? These were the questions facing the secretary of the interior as a result of a relatively simple internal reorganization.[48]

Experience with reorganization suggests that it can indeed have the political advantages claimed for it. No evidence has yet been produced, however, to suggest that reorganizing government leads to greater competence in the performance of its functions or to specific gains in efficiency or effectiveness. The contrary is probably the case. The instability associated with reorganization efforts often leads to reduced morale and productivity, confusion of assignments, caution in proceeding with important tasks, and defensive behavior in general. It may seem easier to place the officials of interrelated agencies in the same organization, so that they will be compelled by a common superior to cooperate, rather than having to make the effort to persuade them to work with each other. It seldom works out that way. As with other types of management reforms, reorganization may aid political executives who are disposed to become immersed in directing their organization's activities, but it is not a substitute for taking the time to manage.

Changing Employee Behavior

The most active area of recent management reform has been attempts to alter personnel performance through changes in the environment, incentives, and rewards of federal employees. These efforts have sought to alter the performance of government by changing the performance of its employees. Efforts to alter personnel performance seem to push and pull in often contradictory directions. A "soft path" to personnel improvement builds from the premise, associated with the human relations school of management, that long-lasting changes in performance require changes in the quality of the working environment and in the nature of the work itself. A second, and far more popular, route to performance improvement, the "hard path," relies on the conventional tools of hierarchy and competition to induce higher levels of performance.

Each path has well-developed traditions, and their cases have been vigorously argued. An admirer of hard path management approaches, Theodore Levitt, has observed:

Until very recently, inherited attitudes and ancient cognitive modes sought impotently for possible improvement in the skills and attitudes of the *performers* of service, rather than for possible redefinition or redesign of service itself. Manufacturing has outperformed service because it has for a long time thought technocratically and managerially about its functions. Service has lagged because it has thought humanistically.[49]

Michael Maccoby, speaking for the humanists, counters:

. . . greasing the system with rewards and punishments is inadequate since it is the managerial approach itself based on principles of standardization, specialization, compartmentalization and control, which undermines cooperation and effective performance.

Stated in psychological terms, the managerial system, based on hierarchical controls and standardization, reinforces motives of material rewards, power grandiosity, beating the system, and in some cases contributes to emotional and physical illness. On lower levels, it causes resentment, apathy and stress. It does not sufficiently reinforce the best in the Civil Service: the attitude of craftsmanship and the interest in bettering society.[50]

Recognition of the central problems of leadership in organizations accompanied the emergence of the human relations school of management, which was spawned by the Hawthorne studies and continues in revised form under the rubric of "organizational humanism."[51] In contrast to scientific management, which tended to view subordinate employees as passive instruments performing assigned tasks, human relations theorists viewed employees as social beings with beliefs, ideas, and feelings. The design and organization of work would have to take into account the social needs of employees through arrangements which permitted decentralized, participative management.

This view, developed in the period from the late 1930s to the early 1950s, drew sharp criticism for being manipulative, for violating the dignity of the individual, and for serving merely as a veneer to an authoritarian system, thereby subordinating the individual even further to the needs of the organization.[52] Critics of the human relations school began to draw the distinction between the leader and the administrator. William H. Whyte, Jr., and Eugene E. Jennings, for example, distinguish between

the administrator [as] one who fits into the organization and is commanded by it, and the leader [as] one who gives direction and character to that organization and represents a focal point of it.[53]

The basis for humanistic studies of organizational behavior began to shift toward the employees' psychological needs, and scholars began to suggest the incompatibilities between the needs of organizations for the maintenance of cohesiveness and the performance of tasks and the needs of individuals for self-actualization.[54] Such propositions have invited the rejoinder that the kinds of conflict and disagreement that attend the division of labor within a bureaucratic organization are not only inevitable but healthy and productive.

Out of this tradition most recently has come the field of organizational development (OD), which provides a representative challenge to rational, hard path approaches to personnel reform. In brief, OD is concerned with molding healthy environments (including administrative processes) that will foster supportive, collaborative relationships, commonality of purpose, democratic, nonhierarchical group decision making, and mutual adjustment to change. Although OD has been written about extensively, its applications, particularly in the public sector, are rare. The chief obstacle is simply the constant pressure within operating organizations for results. As Victor Thompson argues:

Somehow, the picture of a strongly identifying group of workers and their boss sitting around planning high group-production goals for latrine digging is ludicrous. Claims for success for organizational development often involve Research and Development or similar groups (often groups of salesmen). In any case, the stories are few, and we have no way of knowing whether organizational development was responsible.[55]

One of the few examples of OD in the federal government occurred in the Department of State during the Kennedy and Johnson administrations. Under the leadership of William Crockett—first as assistant secretary of state for administration, later as deputy under secretary for administration—a classical process of OD was developed with the help of five consulting groups. As a first step, an Action Program of Organizational Development (ACORD) dramatically reduced the number of operating layers in the department, effectively flattening the hierarchy. As Donald Warwick notes, "the axe was applied to 125 positions ranging from middle level to top management." At the same time, a new MBO system was installed to allow freedom of action and autonomy for each operating unit. State Department personnel were then invited to participate in off-site training sessions designed to provide "a conceptual understanding of their own roles and responsibilities and an experiential understanding of their own management styles." These sessions were headed by prominent behavioral scientists—Chris Argyris, Warren Bennis, Lee Bradford, and others—and were conducted at the National Training Laboratory. ACORD also emphasized "team-building" for groups working together, training of "internal change agents," development of evaluation capabilities, and dissemination of findings.

The experience of ACORD was short-lived, and for the period of time that it survived, its accomplishments were mixed. Among the participants, increases in communication, job motivation, and performance were reported. Among the clients, the responses were more ambivalent, and some reports of the experience were negative.

. . . The first year was far from organizational bliss. The reforms were hobbled from the outset by the initial suspicion and resistance of those most intimately involved. The hastiness of the changes, the narrow base of participation, and poor communication about its scope and intent also generated concern and resentment in other parts of the Department. . . . Acceptance . . . was further stymied by the long history of reorganizations in the department, leading to the feeling that "we've seen it all before"; by its glaring departures from managerial orthodoxy; by a string of other reforms undertaken at about the same time; and by perennial bad blood between [the Administrative Office of State] and the bureaus, between "substance" and administration. Some of these difficulties were surmounted during the first year; others persisted.[56]

Of significance is the fact that the upper echelons at State "were always too busy to be bothered with anything but exhortations about leadership."

Critics of the experiment pointed out that Crockett and his associates failed to understand the functional utility of foreign service officer behavior. Their real purpose, according to this line of argument, is to serve as a neutral and reliable channel of communication between the U.S. government and foreign governments. Prodding them into self-actualization would undermine their ability to perform in this role.

A second and more recent attempt to reform the working environment in the federal government was developed in the Commerce Department between 1977 and 1979. This effort, the Project to Improve Work and Management, was lodged in the Office of the Assistant Secretary for Administration and encompassed the twelve office directors under Assistant Secretary Elsa Porter. An additional part of the project focused on increasing the effectiveness and quality of human development in the Office of Publications and the Office of Audits.

Under Porter's direction, a Human Development Seminar produced a consensus statement of the organization's goal:

. . . to perform its assigned functions of facilitating the efficient and effective performance of the substantive program missions . . . in a manner that respects all employees, their rights and their sense of dignity and provides for their need for individual development.

In order to facilitate this goal, the seminar detailed four principles of conduct:

1. *Security in Performance of Responsibilities.* Directors will be secure in performing their duties with mutual trust and clear mutual expectations both to other directors and to the Assistant Secretary. Directors can expect the support of the Assistant Secretary and others in such performance. On the basis of mutual trust, directors will feel free to inform the Assistant Secretary of the complete facts of any situation; conversely the Assistant Secretary will be able to expect complete and accurate information regardless of its implications. The Assistant Secretary can be secure in the knowledge that problems or mistakes are not being withheld from her and that she is in full possession of the facts about all phases of her operation.

2. *Equity of Treatment.* Each director can expect to be treated fairly, on the basis both of his or her own office's situation and with respect to Administration. Equity

will not be achieved by flat uniformity, but by treatment which considers the needs of each director and office as an individual part of a larger operation and its goals.

3. *Individuation.* Each person is to be treated as a distinct individual distinguished by a unique set of characteristics. Individuation involves respect for the differences between individuals. This includes respect for different career goals and different needs for growth; it includes respect for the paramount importance of individual values and the creation of a work environment which promotes the highest human development.

4. *Participation.* Participation is both the opportunity and the responsibility to take part in decisions affecting the goals and operations of Administration as an entity, and as individual areas of responsibility. Participation includes responsibility for both the giving and receiving of judgments and information, with the Assistant Secretary and with the other directors. Implicit in participation is the need to develop skills required for participative problem solving: agreement on criteria, development of alternatives, and evaluation on the basis of the criteria. Participation includes re-examination and change according to principles. However, participation does not include a lessening of individual responsibilities, nor does it mean decisions by committees or by votes. It is a process by which all points of view are to be presented and seriously considered, and through which effective solutions can be found.

These principles amount to little more than guidelines for "I'm OK—You're OK" management relationships. In practice, emphasis on participative decision making held the potential to create havoc for the political executive juggling interests beyond the emotional well-being of his or her subordinates and facing severe time constraints for both individual decisions and tenure in office. The assistant secretary, for example, was charged with betraying her principles when she overruled a decision by the office directors concerning an organizational problem. The issue was eventually resolved, but the assistant secretary was committed by the principles of the agreement to "consultation, open discussion and justification of the reasons for her decision."[57]

The effectiveness of these approaches is limited by pressures of time and deeply embedded patterns of behavior in federal departments. Like the State Department, the top echelon of the Commerce Department was merely tolerant of the Project to Improve Work and Management:

Juanita Kreps was sympathetic, but not hopeful or supportive. When the new approach was presented to her, she said: "This seems to me very precious, and I mean that in both senses of the word," implying that the principled-participative approach was too delicate to survive in the bureaucratic soil of Commerce.[58]

Similarly, when it was suggested to OMB that budget cuts affecting the U.S. Travel Service be mediated through a cooperative, consultative venture, the budget analysts balked, bemused by the apparent naiveté in Commerce.

OD is little understood in the public sector, and there are few indications that it will be embraced by senior executives looking to trigger better organizational performance. The major handicap of this route is that it has shown little evidence of increasing the effectiveness or output of organizations given the kinds of deadlines against which managers must operate. Without this support from senior executives, it is unlikely that departments will adopt "T-groups," antihierarchical arrangements, or other characteristics of human relations in any systematic fashion.

A more fundamental objection is that approaches to reform of the work environment and employee motivation rooted in the human relations school overlook the extent to which bureaucratic rigidity serves an important protective function. In *The Bureaucratic Phenomenon,* for example, Michael Crozier argues that bureaucracy offers individuals both independence and security. A system of bureaucratic rules, he says, "provides the individual with the minimum of security necessary to him . . . in a world where the individual feels he is extremely vulnerable."[59] Further, and ironically, bureaucracy, he argues, "may be viewed as a very good way of maintaining some of the individualist values of a pre-industrial world" because it preserves for each participant a measure, albeit limited, of autonomy and discretion. The price to the individual thus partially cut off from reality and its incentives may be high, he points out, which "explains the paramount importance of human relations within the bureaucratic system." Thus, a more promising avenue for political executives than forced self-actualization may be accepting human relations as essentially a value promoting the simple and intuitively appealing notion that managers who are sensitive to the needs and concerns of their subordinates are likely to contribute more toward employee motivation and productivity than those who are insensitive, defensive, and aloof.

The most fundamental objection to employee-centered management reforms is that they violate the principle that government organizations exist to serve the public, not their employees. This view can easily be distorted into an oversimplification—high employee morale and service to the public are not necessarily antithetical—but it serves to express an attitude that inhibits widespread acceptance of these reforms by political executives.

Far more popular, for these reasons, is the hard path to changing employee behavior. In 1970, for example, the federal government inaugurated productivity measurement and improvement programs. The impetus for this effort was provided by a request by Senator William Proxmire (D-Wis.) to the GAO to study the feasibility of productivity measures for federal programs. The result was an interagency task force report concluding not only that federal productivity measurement was feasible but that a program to do it should be established. OMB was given overall responsibility for this program, and it in turn delegated data collection assignments to the Bureau of Labor Statistics; responsibility for personnel management aspects to the Civil Service Commission (now the Office of Personnel Management); and other technical assistance responsibilities to the GSA. The product of this effort, the Joint Financial Management Improvement Program (JFMIP), would provide analysis and conclusions concerning productivity improvement to the president and Congress.

Productivity in the federal government is measured as the ratio of goods or services (output) provided by an organizational unit to the resources consumed (input) for a given time period. The only input considered under this system is labor. Each year, this measure of the efficiency in providing goods or services is compared to that of previous years. Thus, each year's productivity measure provides a comparison with the output per employee year for previous years. Overall, this measure of federal productivity rose at an average rate of 1.2 percent from 1967 to 1976. Concealed within this aggregate, however, were variations from as much as an 8.2 percent increase for communications to a decline of 2.0 percent for printing and duplication.

Productivity measured in this way reveals nothing of the *quality* of work that is being done, however. The approach recalls Frederic Thayer's description of a National Bureau of Economic Research study in which the performance of surgeons was measured by a unit called the "hernia equivalent" (HE). A group of surgeons estimated that ten HEs was a reasonable workload per week. The work of the government manager could easily be recast in similar terms. The care and concern that should accompany decision making, program design, and evaluation are supplanted by a concern for how many transactions are performed. In the regulatory field, for example, this type of reasoning leads to shallow, diligent, and often arbitrary enforcement of rules despite their economic or social consequences.

The most recent initiative to improve federal management and employee productivity is civil service reform. In his January 19, 1978, State of the Union Message and in a subsequent nationally televised speech, President Carter made civil service reform the "centerpiece of government reorganization,"[60] the first time a president has placed such a high priority on reforming the civil service system.[61] The Civil Service Reform Act of 1978

97

split the Civil Service Commission into an Office of Personnel Management (OPM) and a Merit Systems Protection Board, a structural change first proposed by President Franklin Roosevelt in 1937.

The major innovation, however, was the creation of a Senior Executive Service (SES) of some 8,000 upper-level career civil servants. Adumbrated by the Brownlow Committee[62] and first proposed in 1955 by the second Hoover Commission, a senior executive corps would, according to President Carter, "restore the merit principle to a system which has grown into a bureaucratic maze. It will provide greater management flexibility and better rewards for better performance without compromising job security." Should an eligible candidate for the SES choose to join, he or she would be assigned to a designated SES position at a new, higher pay scale and become eligible for promotions and for financial bonuses of up to 20 percent of salary for high performance, which close to half of SES participants might receive, awards of $10,000 for "meritorious" performance, to be given to 5 percent of the executives, and a top award of $20,000 for "distinguished" service, for up to 1 percent of the executives. Other incentives include paid sabbaticals once a decade and accumulation and redemption of retirement or annual leave time. (A special system of incentive pay based on performance also applies to middle managers in grades GS13–GS15.) Holders of SES positions could also be reassigned to other SES positions and to other geographical locations within the agency or, if they agree, to positions in different agencies. If their performance was unsatisfactory, they could have their pay reduced, be demoted, or be dropped from the service and returned to their former civil service rank and tenure. In theory, the existence of an SES makes it easier for political appointees to choose their own teams from among the top career civil servants, thus making them more politically responsive, and for top career managers to gain broad experience.

Decisions on promotions, reassignments, or demotions are based on an annual performance appraisal. In fiscal year 1977, prior to reform, noted Alan K. Campbell, then chairman of the Civil Service Commission, who became the first director of the Office of Personnel Management, 500,-000 federal employees received grade increases, while only 700 were denied them. Moreover, "last year," President Carter said, "out of about 2 million [federal] employees, only 226 people lost their jobs for incompetence or inefficiency. That's about one-hundredth of 1 percent." (Critics pointed out, however, that annual turnover in the federal work force actually exceeds 20 percent, much of it a result of unsatisfactory performance.)[63] In other words, existing performance appraisals were simply not being used to motivate employees to do a better job. The new system would utilize methods, according to President Carter, "that are used widely and effectively in private industry."[64] Under it, prior to the beginning of a fiscal year, each SES participant must draft a statement of personal goals for the coming year. The statement is discussed with the participant's supervisor, then reviewed, and, if the employee and the supervisor disagree on what it should contain, arbitrated by the next highest supervisor. The statement is again reviewed at the end of the fiscal year by the supervisor, and the participant's performance is graded as unsatisfactory, minimally satisfactory, or fully satisfactory. These grades are assessed by a five-member performance review board, and all recommendations are passed along to the presiding executive, who makes the final determination.

The premise on which this reform is based is that the prospect of monetary rewards is a significant and effective motivational device. Though the prospect of increased income will often induce people to work harder and more effectively, it is far from established that this is always or even usually the case, especially with executives whose incomes already greatly exceed the level needed for basic comforts. In his study of pay as a motivator, E. E. Lawler questions its efficacy when the level of trust between superior and subordinates is low, when individual performance is difficult to measure, and therefore must be assessed at least in part subjectively, and when the pay rewards are limited[65]—circumstances characteristic of the civil service environment.

The efficacy of performance appraisal has also been questioned. Years earlier, Douglas McGregor warned of the problems associated with performance appraisal based on twenty years of experience with it in private industry. The chief problem, according to McGregor, was that supervisors did not like the judicial role they were forced to play, and they resisted it.[66] The approach of the Civil Service Reform Act incorporates the corrective McGregor recommended: Place responsibility for establishing and assessing performance goals as much as possible on the subordinate. Nevertheless, the willingness of supervisors, especially political appointees, to fulfill their role in performance appraisal is problematic. Former Executive Director of the Civil Service Commission Bernard Rosen, a thirty-year civil servant, remembered complaints by both Kennedy and Nixon administration officials that careerists were resisting new directions.

In each case, Rosen told the concerned officials that the senior career executives were ready and willing to carry out policy directives, but that since no clear signals had emanated from the new cabinet officers, in the interim the programs and laws had to be administered according to existing policies.[67]

"I work in the federal government," one civil servant was quoted,

and am deeply concerned about the attitude most people have toward us who are employed by it. The word is bureaucrat, but I cannot bring myself to say it. I know that the people hate the government, and that the people who work for it hate it even. And I think the reason is that there is such poor supervision everywhere—absolutely everywhere.

She feared the civil service reform, however, saying, "things can only get worse, because it gives the supervisor power to fire at will, but doesn't require the supervisor to *supervise*."[68]

The likelihood is, however, that the level of supervision will be higher under the 1978 act. Said Rosen:

. . . no longer is it acceptable for political executives in the agencies to detach themselves from their fundamental responsibilities for managing. Characterizing poor performance by the bureaucracies they lead as "their" failures instead of "ours" will quickly identify at least one reason for the failures.[69]

Indeed, his observation suggests the possibility that performance appraisal might just as well have the ironic effect of making political appointees more responsive to the bureaucracy in that, as supervisors, they have a stake in having successful subordinates and therefore in negotiating achievable performance goals with them, ones that will make them both look good. Because responsibilities at senior management levels are more diverse, less routine, and therefore less susceptible to precise identification and measurement, accountability is a more amorphous and negotiable concept, and senior executives, anxious to avoid pressure from OMB and OPM and inquiries from congressional committees, will no doubt discover that performance appraisal can be manipulated to good advantage.

The new system has also fostered fears of political manipulation and subversion of the higher civil service. Employees who receive bonuses, for example, may be more susceptible to pressure from superiors and become sycophantic lest they lose them. Adverse judgments can be appealed, but the burden of proof is on the employee to prove that he or she was wrongly appraised. In defense of this philosophy, Campbell said, "A manager must have the right to be arbitrary to be effective."[70] Some critics feel this will inevitably exacerbate tendencies toward authoritarianism, management by inducing fear in vulnerable subordinates.[71] Some see an open invitation to increased unionization of middle and higher grades. Still others fear that proposed amendments in the Hatch Act which would permit greater political participation by federal employees would further increase their vulnerability to political manipulation.

There are limits to the possibilities for abuse, however. The Merit Systems Protection Board submits its budget directly to Congress and thus enjoys considerable independence from the Executive Office of the President. SES participants are prohibited from being placed in positions for which they are unqualified and thus may not be transferred to another agency involuntarily. Indeed, lateral mobility may not be much easier or much greater than it was before the act was passed.

Though these reforms have been highly touted, their history has a peculiar quality. Many are launched with great fanfare, often with ardent presidential support. Yet their half-lives have been remarkably short and appear to be getting shorter. Serious students and practitioners of government do not take these reform movements all that seriously, and few mourn their usually unpublicized demise. Before Jimmy Carter's many reforms had even got off the ground, for example, the Brookings Institution, under the heading "No Miracle Cures," was warning that "those . . . who cling to the belief that any combination of means will instantaneously transform the character, image, or performance of the executive branch are doomed to disappointment."[72]

Perhaps a better sense of the recurring search for a systemic solution lies in historical and political contexts of their adoption. The reform of governmental administration is a permanent theme in American politics at the federal, state, and local levels. The rhythms of electoral politics guarantee that the latest ideas for making government work better will be advocated and tried, imparting a trendy cast to the reform enterprise. Indeed, the urge to reform government is so strong that little forethought or preparation goes into the reform enterprise. Any technique that might work, especially if it has been "proven" in business, has its advocates. Thus it is not surprising that "the history of management improvement in the federal government is a story of inflated rhetoric, shifting emphasis from one fashionable managerial skill to another, and a relatively low level of managerial achievement."[73]

These reform movements have unquestionably brought constructive changes to public management: the executive budget, job classification, professional accounting practices, policy analysis, and systematic approaches to planning and decision making such as the one discussed in chapter 7. As government has grown more complex, however, comprehensive management reforms are more and more being proposed as cures for ailments that are in reality caused by the centrifugal forces of partisan politics and as solutions to the dilemmas of achieving accountability in completing the countless transactions that constitute the daily work of government. Unfortunately, they can do no such thing.

A recurring theme of these reforms in the processes, organization, and performance incentives of government has been the idea that government should and can be more businesslike. Policy analysis, program budgeting, productivity measurement, performance appraisal, and program evaluation conducted within properly structured organizations can simulate the bottom-line orientation of business organizations with similar results. Government can be as effective as the best-run and most profitable corporations. The enduring strength of this idea of businesslike government—despite evidence to the contrary—suggests the value of examining it more closely, which is the purpose of the following chapter.

CHAPTER 5

The Nature of the Public's Business

THE IDEA that the management of a business enterprise is a valuable source of ideas for governmental management—that the problems of public and business administration are the same—has been popular since virtually the beginning of the Republic. The idea was initially simple: The people and methods that could direct and coordinate the efforts of others so as to accomplish tasks of production, distribution, and service provision could surely be useful in accomplishing the tasks of government. Recent formulations stress the similarities among complex organizations of all types and, in particular, the similarities between large corporations and government agencies. In this view, though the environments and missions of corporations and government departments differ, the general management function is the same in both. Senior executives must motivate subordinates, provide leadership and a sense of direction, and maintain relations with the organization's constituencies.

This is a pivotal issue. If the public's business is like private business—if government transactions are or can be made analogous to private transactions—then the relatively well-developed body of ideas and practices from corporate management can be applied to government, and the pool of potential managers for government will be much larger because business leaders can be regarded as natural candidates for top-level appointments. The failures of PPBS, MBO, and ZBB can, if business and government are indeed analogous, be interpreted as failures of execution, not failures of concept, and a well-conceived business management system for government, the design of which reflects lessons from previous failures, should again be attempted. If government and business are in crucial aspects dissimilar, however, then applying business management concepts may be futile or even counterproductive, necessitating a distinctive field of public management to assist the high-level government executive and to aid in identifying as well as training potentially capable executives.

Arguments concerning the similarity or dissimilarity of government and business organizations are based on three distinct types of intellectual support. The first is historical and analogical and, in some measure, normative; managing the government is similar to managing business, the argument usually goes, but to the extent it is not, it should be made so. The second is derived from various theories of social processes, especially those concerned with the role and function of bureaucratic organizations, and, like the first, stresses similarities. The third is in part impressionistic and based on systematic observations of the behavior of top officials of complex organizations on the job. It is this type of evidence that most convincingly refutes the notion that we can think about public management in the same way that we think about private management.

The Business Analogy

Because the former colonists were administratively ill-prepared for self-government, political leaders of the new Republic turned to businessmen for help. "The country possessed a substantial body of men experienced in business management, some of whom dealt in large affairs," Leonard D. White wrote. "As a class it was they who carried the wisdom and lore of the management art; it was their methods which provided the foundation for the business operations of government."[1] Yet this source of assistance was limited; there were few large business undertakings at the time, and most business success reflected individual effort in small undertakings. The typical businessman of the time was a merchant.

For most of the nineteenth century, the business-government analogy was in eclipse. Government was viewed as fundamentally political, deriving its distinctive character from partisan politics and Jacksonian concepts of democratic government. The analogy revived, however, and reached its zenith in the business-dominated years from the latter decades of the nineteenth century to the mid-1930s, owing to the conjunction of the transformations occurring in business organization and the Progressive era's reformist spirit.

From the time of the Civil War until 1896, business was affected by several interrelated developments. Technological advance was causing a shift of emphasis in industry from the processing of agricultural and forest products to manufacturing based on machinery, chemical processes, metallurgy, and other advances in science and technology. In new industries, with their high capital requirements, large size had significant economic advantages in lower unit costs and the possibility of large-scale marketing and advertising. Thus large firms began appearing in these industries through mergers and takeovers. The capital requirements and complexity of large-scale enterprises increased the popularity of corporate organization, which separated ownership from control, limited the liability of owners, facilitated decentralized management, and made possible working partnerships between individuals with capital but little managerial ability and individuals with managerial ability and relatively little capital (between, for example, J. P. Morgan and the man he selected to run U.S. Steel, Elbert Gary).[2]

The declining prices and serious depressions of this era, which stimulated ruinous price competition, further promoted the concentration of economic power in large manufacturing firms which could survive falling prices and periodic depressions and in the investment banks which provided their capital needs. Economic revival after 1896 coincided with the height of the merger movement and of the formation of large trusts. Following this period, growth in the scale and concentration of industrial enterprise in the first decades of the twentieth century was to occur via vertical integration rather than via further concentration of production in a few large firms. "By the 1920s," according to business historian Alfred D. Chandler, Jr.,

the first stage of growth of the large enterprise in the United States was essentially complete. The large firm had come primarily in the newer and most technologically complex industries where size had real economic advantages, and where the necessity of assured supplies had encouraged vertical integration.[3]

As the size and diversification of business organizations grew, business leaders began to recognize the need for appropriate organizational forms and for internal management techniques to substitute for the personal contacts and incentives that had been effective in the days of smaller, owner-administered business units. The creation by merger of large, vertically integrated companies such as Standard Oil, Du Pont, General Electric, and United States Rubber created the need for a centralized top management structure to direct and coordinate subsidiary operations. The new managers of these companies tended to be full-time salaried professionals rather than individuals qualified by an ownership interest, which further widened the separation between ownership and control. Functions such as marketing, finance, and production were organized into departments operated from corporate headquarters.

The creation of centralized, functionally specialized management structures went hand-in-hand with the professionalization of business practice. Prior to the 1920s, the professionalization of business administration occurred mainly in the specialized and departmentally organized fields of accounting, finance, marketing, and production. But the function of general management was becoming recognized as of central importance, and in 1919 the founding of the Administrative Management Association created a forum for the discussion of general management problems.[4] In 1925, the American Management Association was formed and "quickly became the leading professional organization for top and middle management in American business corporations."[5]

During the 1920s and early 1930s, and to a degree even up to the 1960s, a reasonable case can be made that public and private management of large organizations were more alike than different. Both types of organizations were or appeared to be growing more or less vertically integrated, functionally organized, professionally staffed, and centrally administered. The notion that government might be made more businesslike, and that both might draw on a core doctrine of management, was not farfetched.

It is also possible to reach the same conclusion from the opposite perspective. Business could be said to be growing more and more like government. Business was becoming more bureaucratic and thus the distinctions between public and private managers were becoming blurred; both needed political and bureaucratic skills.[6]

After 1920, for example, the growth of business organizations occurred mainly via diversification: industrial firms adding new product lines or altogether new lines of business. At the same time, the control and owner-ship functions, despite stock option and bonus plans, were becoming even more widely separated. These changes provided the context for a major innovation in business management: the decentralized administrative structure. Pioneered by General Motors's Alfred P. Sloan, this structure comprised administratively autonomous operating divisions superin-tended by a functionally organized general office. Adoption of this struc-ture by other successful industrial firms was not only a response to the diversification of the firm; it tended to institutionalize it.

The modern diversified enterprise represents a calculated, rational response of technically trained professional managers to the needs and opportunities of chang-ing technologies and markets . . . strategies of diversification were rarely if ever carried out by individual financiers or owner executives. They were undertaken by professional managers, anonymous bureaucrats. . . . These men were executives who, because of their educational background and their experience in the manage-ment of the large, vertically integrated enterprises, had developed the necessary technological and administrative skills to initiate and execute a new and complex strategy of expansion.[7]

As diversification and decentralization increased, the functions of general management became more significant and more specialized. The numbers and specialized duties of vice presidents, assistant vice presidents, assistant secretaries, assistant treasurers, assistants to the president and vice presi-dents, staff officers, and specialists proliferated. Similar structures were created in the subordinate divisions, each of which had its own central management.

In short, the large industrial firm was becoming a bureaucracy, with significant implications for the management of the enterprise. The notion that profit was the proximate motive for *all* business behavior was being undermined. As Peter Drucker observed in his classic study of General Motors, "The individual department or unit in one of the many big divi-sions is too far away from the market for its performance to be related to market success . . . it is subject to the yardstick of cost accounting."[8] In diversified and decentralized corporations, then, market and market price cannot perform their "social role" of supplying "objective performance tests for managerial ability."[9] A second implication noted by Drucker is that this type of organization fails to discover and develop leaders. "In the big divisions, because of their centralized organization, men are likely to remain specialists with purely departmental knowledge right up to the very end of their careers."[10] Leaders were more likely to be found in the smaller divisions, where individual performance in command was more likely to be tested.

The history of business and governmental enterprises through the 1930s suggests that the management problems of large private organizations selling products to their customers and large public organizations providing services directly to the public might not be all that dissimilar. Testing the proposition required a motive, one that was furnished by the reform politics of the decades around the turn of the century.

With the emergence of large-scale business enterprise and a laissez-faire ideology that bred distrust and skepticism of government, the ideal of political government "was challenged and gradually subdued to the ideal of a 'businesslike' government."[11] The appeal of this idea was powerful, especially when linked to the goals of the political reformers active at the time. In his 1887 article on the study of public administration, Woodrow Wilson stated, "The field of administration is a field of business. It is removed from the hurry and strife of politics." In proposing the Keep Commission, President Theodore Roosevelt said, "There is every reason why our executive governmental machinery should be at least as well planned, economical, and efficient as the best machinery of the great business organizations."[12] In his 1916 book *Federal Executive,* John Philip Hill wrote of "the business that the great governmental corporation conducts."[13] In his first report to the president as director of the Bureau of the Budget, Charles G. Dawes declared in 1921 that heretofore all of the defects in the routine business administration of the government resulted directly from the fact that "the president of the corporation gave practically no attention to its ordinary routine business. He avoided his responsibility for the proper conduct of the business of the corporation, and neither assumed nor delegated active control over it."[14] In his 1924 book *With Congress and Cabinet,* William C. Redfield, secretary of commerce during most of the Wilson administration, wrote:

Do you ask just what government departments are? I reply that in general they are great business establishments running factories, buying goods, distributing products, employing workmen of many kinds, engaged in building, navigating, traveling, research, publication, farming, instruction, and in almost every kind of production activity.[15]

In the 1920s the phrases "business operations of the government," "application of uniform business principles and methods to the expenditure of public funds," and "the public's business" were in common usage.

Perhaps the greatest success in the application of the business analogy to government was at the municipal level. In 1910, Richard S. Childs, general manager of the Bon Ami Company and an ardent political reformer in the Wilsonian tradition, began advocating a plan for municipal government whereby an elected commission would make public policy but an official appointed by the commission and accountable to it would exercise all administrative functions.[16] Such a plan, he said, would ensure that city management resembled that of "the private business corporation, with its well-demonstrated capacity for efficiency," thus ending domination of municipal administration by political machines. When Dayton, Ohio, adopted the manager system on January 1, 1914, following a campaign pressed by an alliance of the chamber of commerce and the Dayton Bureau of Municipal Research, the idea caught on, and by 1920, 140 cities had adopted the system.[17] Support for the new arrangement united reformers in the Wilsonian tradition, who saw efficiency as the goal, with businessmen who, according to Martin J. Schiesl, sought, in addition to efficiency,

the replacement of the ward system of public affairs with a centralized administration that would organize municipal services according to the business view of what was good for the community [thus reducing] the influence of lower-class groups in city government. . . .[18]

The goal of efficiency in municipal government accomplished through an organizational framework similar to that employed by the business corporation, generally regarded as the most effective of American institutions, united enough reformers behind the city management plan to create what can be judged in retrospect to be the most successful movement in the history of public administration.[19]

The popularity of the business-government analogy has never again reached the level it enjoyed in the first half of this century, but the idea has far from disappeared. The following statement is typical of post-World War II expressions from the business community:

To a greater extent than is generally appreciated, the best-managed corporations develop their managers chiefly by assigning them real job responsibility, rotating their jobs, evaluating their performance resolutely against rigorous standards, and eliminating poor performers. I simply wish to emphasize that these measures— rather than manpower charts and other forms of paper work—do the development job. These measures that are proper in private enterprise should be more widely used in government.[20]

Richard Nixon's notion of management in 1969, reports Richard P. Nathan, "seemed to be that it was a profession or science, that expert managers from the business world could neatly improve the performance and efficiency of the government."[21] In *Why Not the Best?* Jimmy Carter wrote, "The vast bureaucracy of government often fails to deliver needed social services to our people. High ideals and good intentions are not matched with rational, businesslike administration."[22] In a position paper distributed during his campaign for office, Carter said that to improve government efficiency, "tight businesslike management and planning techniques must be instituted and maintained utilizing the full authority and personal involvement of the President himself."[23] Nixon and Carter offered nothing new in presenting their views, however. They were presumably based on the old notion that, as America's most successful organizations, corporations can serve as models for government.

The notion that large-scale, complex organizations—whether business or government—are similar has been reinforced by academic studies of social process and organization. The systematic study of organizations and their management in America is customarily said to have begun with Frederick W. Taylor, as interpreted and applied by writers of the scientific management school. To his influence was added that of Henri Fayol, whose universalist ideas on management processes were made fashionable by Luther Gulick in the 1930s. Taylor and Fayol were engineers, and their concern was with the articulation of routines for organizing and managing the performance of repetitive tasks.[24] Their engineering view of management was substantially enlarged in the late 1930s by the reports of the Hawthorne experiments, which shifted attention from work to the worker and his or her motivation, and by the publication in 1938 of Chester I. Barnard's *The Functions of the Executive.*[25] Motivated by the "universals of organization," Barnard stressed the indispensable role of the executive as maintaining the organization by providing a system of communication, promoting the output of essential efforts, and formulating and defining purposes. He also stressed the importance of the activity of decision making and, following the Hawthorne results, of informal relationships among people in organizations.

The most powerful and enduring early contribution, however, is Max Weber's classical theory of bureaucracy and the intellectual tradition to which it gave rise. Weber developed the concept of an archetypal bureaucracy, a continuing organization, arranged hierarchically, having an administrative staff performing official functions within specified spheres of competence, and bound by rules. Its administrators do not own the means of production. They are pursuing careers, are subject to discipline from superiors, and their official rights and responsibilities are kept strictly separate from their private spheres. All administrative acts, decisions, and rules are formulated and recorded in writing.[26] This model, Weber believed, "may be applied in profit-making business or in charitable organizations, or in any number of other types of private enterprises serving ideal or material ends. It is equally applicable to political and to religious organizations."[27]

Many students of social and economic change have found these works to offer powerful analytic tools for explaining the emergence, power, and functioning of large-scale organizations. Their authors have been consciously searching for universal formulations and principles and hence have downplayed or ignored differences among formal organizational types. The popularity of this universalist approach has endured, moreover, because "its focus on authority and managerial control appeals to upper management, as does its emphasis on formality and economic incentive, variables over which managers have some control."[28]

During this so-called classical period of organizational studies, James Burnham developed a formulation with similar implications. He observed the emergence of managers:

. . . those who already for the most part in contemporary society are actually managing, on its technical side, the actual process of production, no matter what the legal and financial form—individual, corporate, governmental—of the process.[29]

Burnham argued that any distinctions between government and private managers are disappearing. "The active heads of the bureaus are the managers-in-government, the same, or nearly the same, in training, functions, skills, habits of thought as the managers-in-industry."[30] Unlike classical theorists, who tended to see the emergence of a managerial class as a natural concomitant of economic and social development, Burnham saw it as a threat to democratic processes.

In the past few decades, studies of organizations and of the role of organizations in social and economic change have mushroomed, with virtually every academic discipline contributing. Some researchers have tried to bring a sense of unity to the study of organizations, while others have pursued specialized paths of inquiry. Though they differ in important respects, for the most part these approaches assume that complex organizations are similar, and references to distinguishing characteristics of government bureaucracies are infrequent and casual. Indeed, for most social scientists studying organizations, investigating the distinctiveness of public bureaucracies would only distract them from the primary task of formulating theories applicable to all types of organizations.

In contrast to sociologists, economists and political scientists are students of management, especially those associated with business schools and actively involved in management consulting, whose views are based primarily on systematically ordered observations of the behavior of managers and who rely more on psychology and anthropology. Their intellectual roots are in the Hawthorne experiments and in the work of Fritz Roethlisberger, George Homans, Kurt Lewin, Douglas McGregor, William F. Whyte, Chris Argyris, and others composing the human relations or organizational behavior school. Their questions are: What do managers do? How are successful managers different from unsuccessful ones?

These observers take an essentially skeptical view of managers and management competence. "One is continually surprised," writes Leonard R. Sayles, "by the number of obvious mistakes made by otherwise sophisticated organizations."[31] Writes Kenneth R. Andrews, "a clear majority of businesses, in even the most sophisticated economy in the world, are mismanaged in some obvious and preventable ways."[32] "There is . . . evidence of widespread managerial weakness," writes Robert B. Buchele.[33] Says David Finn:

. . . corporate top management does not deserve its reputation for marvelous efficiency and decisiveness. It gets the job done more often by mastering the "science of muddling through," as one observer has put it, than by directing an orderly system of administration.[34]

The basic reason for poor management, in this view, is that it is exceedingly hard to manage a complex organization. The following observations are typical:

Clearly, the managerial job, at least in the upper ranks, is getting harder and harder. . . . the causes of trouble are so varied that they seem to yield only the lesson that management is a many-sided process in which there are various ways of going wrong. . . .[35]

The organizational setting within which managers must manage is more recalcitrant than one first imagines. . . . these institutions impose extraordinary constraints on managerial effectiveness.[36]

Managerial work is enormously complex, far more so than a reading of traditional literature would suggest.[37]

The Nature of the Public's Business

Most observations of this nature are based primarily on the experiences of large corporations, but their authors generally believe that both their diagnosis and their prescriptions apply to virtually all complex organizations. Perhaps the most expansive statement of this character is that of Peter Drucker:

Certainly there is a worldwide generic function which we call management and which serves the same purpose in any and all developed societies.[38]

Henry Mintzberg is more specific:

Managers' jobs are remarkably alike. The work of foremen, presidents, government administrators, and other managers can be described in terms of . . . basic roles and . . . working characteristics.[39]

Leonard Sayles reduces his depiction of the manager's role to two basic elements: contingency responses and uncertainty reduction. The specific formulations of these authors are less important than the general idea that managers in all types of organizations must do the same kinds of work—assume the same roles, accomplish the same tasks, engage in the same kinds of activities. To the extent that the government manager is seen as different, it is primarily in that some goals are politically mandated and managers must develop political sensitivities.[40]

Businessmen who have served in government are another source of evidence for determining the similarities and contrasts between business and government. Though most evidence of this type supports the view that public management is different, a point to which we shall turn next, a 1958 study of businessmen in government by the Harvard Business School Club of Washington, D.C., reported that "it seems evident that the functions performed in government are about the same as in business or at most constitute an obstacle in only a small part of the [businessman in government's] job."[41] Differences tended to be collectively characterized as the "red tape" associated with government, a term encompassing size, complexity, absence of a profit motive, rigidity, and outside pressures. Such differences were regarded as a matter of degree rather than kind, however.

Government Is Different

Yet the notion that government is fundamentally different has also been argued on many of the same intellectual bases as those underlying the propositions positing similarities. But there is one important additional source of evidence and insights that on balance favors this side of the debate: the testimony of people who have held high-level positions in both business and government.

Peter Drucker has argued that business management and nonbusiness management cannot be equated; indeed, he seems to say, management means business management:

Management is the specific organ of the business enterprise. . . . Management must always, in every decision and action, put economic performance first. It can only justify its existence and its authority by the economic results it produces. [Thus] the skills, the competence, the experience of management cannot, as such, be transferred and applied to the organization and running of other institutions. In particular *a man's success in management carries by itself no promise—let alone a guarantee— of his being successful in government. . . . What to the manager must be the main focus is to the politician, of necessity, only one factor among many.* [42]

This proposition has been stated with equal force by Paul H. Appleby, whose primary orientation was to government, not business:

. . . the dissimilarity between government and all other forms of social action is greater than any dissimilarity among those other forms themselves. . . . In broad terms the governmental function and attitude have at least three complementary aspects that go to differentiate government from all other institutions and activities: breadth of scope, impact, and consideration; public accountability; political character. . . . Government administration differs from all other administrative work to a degree not even faintly realized outside, by virtue of its public nature, the way in which it is subject to public scrutiny and public outcry. [43]

With Drucker, he argued that "even possessed of patriotism and zeal, the most capable business executive in the country might be a most dismal failure in government. Indeed, in actual fact many such persons do fail in government." [44]

Both authors propose that there is an enormous existential difference between public and private management, especially at the top of the organization. Whatever the similarities of task, activity, or even social setting, private management is oriented toward economic performance as determined in markets, whereas public management is oriented toward the public interest as determined in political forums. It is a difference in degree so great as to constitute a difference in kind.

The most fundamental rationale that has been offered for this difference is constitutional in the broadest sense. Prof. Emmett S. Redford has drawn attention to the basic difference between administrative law—what Eugene V. Rostow has termed the "public law of American capitalism"— within which corporate authority is exercised. The former is directive— increasingly so, as chapter 1 indicated—whereas the latter is enabling and restrictive. Thus, in the case of public executives, there are more things they must do, and fewer that they may do, than is true of their private counterparts.

An alternative explanation is historical. In 1934, in a later edition of his famous 1926 text *Introduction to the Study of Public Administration,* Leonard D. White observed:

> The antecedents of American public administration are profoundly different from those of American business. For over a half century the spoils system held undisputed sway in government affairs, and for a century its influence has been great. The gigantic struggle to loosen the grip of the politician has inevitably left its marks upon the body of the civil service. Many of the conditions which seem to lessen the efficiency of government offices are the product of the legal protection [which] evolved to guarantee even a moderate level of efficiency and integrity. . . . Business has not been scarred by a similar struggle to free itself from incompetence. . . .[45]

He went on to note that "profits also furnished business an intelligible test of success, but they are of no help whatever in assessing the achievements of government";[46] "government is constrained to a rigid observance of the principle of consistency, which may be ignored by business";[47] and finally, government affairs are subject "to a degree of accountability which is far more minute and pervasive than business."[48] White quotes former Secretary of Commerce Redfield in a passage as relevant today as it was then: "Congress sits outside on its hill eager to detect any departure from the precise rules it has laid down. The only possible course a subordinate may take with safety is to follow laws in their strict literal meaning."[49]

The essence of the difference between business and government was summed up by Marver Bernstein as follows:

> In contrast to the business executive, the political executive tends to work with a less homogeneous group of executives, administers programs that are generally larger in scope and public significance, lacks privacy in his unofficial as well as

official life, and periodically undergoes trial by public debate. He must devote more time to a defense of his programs and policies even though his tenure on the job is relatively brief. Unlike the business executive, he directs activities that often lack a clearly defined purpose and that normally are matters of some concern to other political and career executives, congressional leaders and staffs, interest groups, and the general public. Except in rare cases, previous experience in private life has not prepared him adequately to deal effectively with Congress.[50]

A set of familiar propositions has been offered concerning the differences between business and government.[51] Few have been rigorously derived from conceptual models, and even fewer have been subjected to empirical tests. Many represent assertions founded on normative biases such as those stemming from a desire to justify the separate study of public administration or, in the contrary view, from a commitment to the values propounded by economic theories of competitive efficiency. Others are offered on the basis of casual and unsystematic observations on how government agencies operate. The most degenerate form of such distinctions is the familiar comparison between efficient, innovative business firms and sluggish, procedure-bound government bureaucracies.

A collage of these views is as follows. Government agencies are not exposed to competitive markets and to tests of profitability and efficiency. Indeed, government activities are subject to political influences and to public scrutiny and accountability. Because of the civil service system and the political process, government executives have far less control over the internal activities of their organizations than private executives, and subordinates are resistant to political leadership. Government programs have vague, multiple, and often conflicting goals—or no goals at all—and thus the measurement of both costs and overall performance is virtually precluded. The technology appropriate for achieving program goals is often unknown or indeterminate. How should an agency prevent drug addiction, rehabilitate a criminal offender, or revitalize a neighborhood?

Few theoretical or conceptual studies have attempted to explain systematically the differences between government and business organizations. Those that analyze government organizations implicitly regard them as distinctive but seldom bother to argue the case beyond superficial references to the exigencies of politics and "publicness."[52]

There are two significant exceptions. In *Bureaucratic Behavior in the Executive Branch,* [53] Louis C. Gawthrop creates an analytic framework from a synthesis of several traditions in the study of organizations and uses it to assess how executive departments and large, complex, private industrial and other business organizations respond to demands for change arising in their environments. He offers the generalization that the executive bureaucracy of our federal government reveals a much greater tendency to follow the consolidating-satisfying-bargaining patterns of organizational development than do the large, complex bureaucracies of private industrial and business corporations. To a great extent, the administrative hierarchies of this latter group reveal a strong commitment to the innovation-optimizing-objective analysis pattern of organizational development.[54]

He cites four major causes of this difference: (1) government executives lack control over internal resources; (2) effectiveness in government is more a matter of earning favorable political judgment than of achieving measurable performance results; (3) goals or standards in government are lacking or unclear; (4) government executives are under greater pressure to achieve immediate results.

Peter M. Blau and W. Richard Scott have developed a typology of formal organizations based on the principle, who benefits? Thus they distinguish among "mutual-benefit associations," where the membership is the prime beneficiary; "business concerns," where the owners derive the benefits; "service organizations," such as social work agencies and mental health clinics, where the client group benefits; and "commonweal organizations," such as police and fire departments, where the public at large is the prime beneficiary.[55] They argue, based on their empirical studies, that special problems are associated with the administration of each type of organization. For example, whereas the business firm must be concerned with operating efficiency in a competitive situation, service organizations must worry about conflicts between administrative procedures and service to clients.

Finally, a rich body of evidence that government is different from business can be derived from the attributes and experiences of people who have served in government. There are three types of studies of this character.

One group of studies compares the types of people who serve in managerial positions in business and government. W. Lloyd Warner and his colleagues, for example, studied the careers of nearly 13,000 civilian and military executives of the federal government in 1959 through a variety of statistical and interview procedures and compared the results with a similar study of business executives.[56] Though they concluded that business and government executives are more alike than unalike, they cited notable differences: "The business leaders take longer to reach high position, and they are correspondingly older than the federal executives. . . . The government men are significantly more often college graduates and holders of higher degrees."[57] Another study, a recent Korn/Ferry/international survey of 3,600 senior-level executives working at several hundred of the largest U.S. corporations, found that the average senior vice president has worked for the same company for nearly twenty years. The composite executive emerging from the survey is a fifty-three-year-old white male, educated at a large public university, a registered Republican, Protestant, father of three, whose wife does not work outside the home, with a background in accounting or finance, and a belief that hard work rather than exceptional intelligence or activity is the key to success.[58] Thus there may be a significant cultural difference between top businessmen and their counterparts in government, especially among subcabinet or second-rank officials. This in itself is less interesting than the implication that self-selection accounts for many of these differences. A third study based on research conducted on graduate students in management showed that individuals planning to join or rejoin nonprofit (mainly government) organizations differed significantly in personality, values, and behavior from those planning careers in the profit sector.[59] Individuals oriented toward the public sector demonstrated on tests and in their behavior at school that (1) their personalities tended more toward dominance, status, and flexibility, (2) they were more skillful at and interested in being change agents, and (3) they were less interested in wealth than those preferring the private sector. Test data suggested the possibility that they were also better at personal relations, higher in self-acceptance, social presence, and responsibility, more concerned with power, and less concerned with security. The authors conclude:

Given these significant differences in personality characteristics, personal values, motives, and occupational values, management schools and schools of business administration [particularly those which allege that management is a generic subject which can be applied to either public or private organizational settings] will need to reassess their current programs and teaching methods. . . .[60]

Another kind of evidence is derived from studies of the attitudes and behavior of people in business and government. Exemplary is a 1974 study of the organizational experiences, job satisfaction, and organizational commitment of 279 managers in three industrial and five government organizations.[61] The business managers were significantly more involved in their work, more loyal to their organizations, and more strongly identified with the aims of their agencies than government executives. Most other studies in this vein have produced similar results: "Business executives typically report more positive attitudes toward their organizations than comparable government executives,"[62] though some evidence suggests that satisfaction increases with rank.[63] There are several possible explanations for these findings that bear on the distinctive character of public management. For example, the connection between the manager's efforts and the achievement of specific organizational goals is weaker in government because goals are vaguer and more diffuse. Policies and purposes change more frequently in government. Thus managerial commitment tends to be more tentative, expectations less certain, and loyalty to specific objectives less intense. Management teams in government are likely to be less homogeneous socially, to feel less pressure for cooperative effort, and to respond to a more diverse set of incentives than management teams in business. Thus senior government executives face a much greater problem in defining and achieving organizational goals through reliance on the energies and commitment of subordinate managers.

Corroborating evidence was provided by a study of the images of public service held by both private citizens and federal government employees. "In every federal and nonfederal group interviewed," the authors report, "the government is placed below the large business corporation as a route to outstanding success."[64] Yet the federal groups rated the government as equal to or better than the corporation in the chance to get to the top of the organization. "Apparently," the authors conclude, "the *nature* of the top jobs in government, rather than the *opportunities for getting to the top,* compare less favorably with what the business world has to offer."[65]

In some respects, the most compelling evidence concerning the difference between business and government is the observations of people who have served at high levels in both business and government. The number of such individuals did not become large until after World War II, which drew large numbers of business executives into such agencies as the War Production Board, the Office of Price Administration, the Office of Defense Transportation, and the like.[66] A great many subsequently expressed frustration with public service, with the red tape associated with personnel, financial, and legislative processes, with politics, with poor working conditions, and with the constant public and congressional criticism to which they were subject.[67] Secretary of Defense James V. Forrestal once said that

the difficulty of government work is that it not only has to be well done, but the public has to be convinced that it is being well done. In other words, there is a necessity both for competence and exposition, and I hold it is extremely difficult to combine the two in the same person.[68]

Critical attitudes toward public service created what many termed a "crisis" in staffing the Eisenhower administration with able executives.

Though many corporate executives nevertheless joined the government, John J. Corson, the first executive director of the social security system and later a high official of the United Nations Relief and Rehabilitation Administration, who advised the Eisenhower administration on top-level staffing, reported in 1954:

A majority of business executives are uncomfortable and unsuccessful in the federal government's top-most political, policy-making posts as department heads and assistant secretaries. They are unaccustomed to and sometimes resentful of the interest of the legislative branch in administrative affairs. They are unfamiliar with the necessity for clearance and coordination with numerous other departments. They are irritated by public scrutiny of their actions and by the rigid controls exercised over recruitment of personnel, budgeting of funds, and procurement of supplies and equipment.[69]

Four years later, Marver Bernstein reported on Eisenhower appointees who had served in business. One participant in the Bernstein study summarized the views of these appointees as follows:

In a business enterprise, the executive is always told in advance exactly what the aims and purposes are of the organization he is joining, and he is sold on those aims from the beginning. But in government, we have to find out for ourselves what the aims of our departments are and what our role is supposed to be as secretary.[70]

These officials were quite surprised and even shocked to realize how extensive their responsibilities would be and how much they were expected to know about a wide range of matters that somehow concerned their departments. Bernstein further observed, "The insecurity of the political climate often makes executives more cautious. Since authority is rarely commensurate with legal responsibility, the executive must establish his own alliances and temporary coalitions within the executive branch."[71]

In a section of his book entitled "Government Is Different," Bernstein quotes several experienced executives who had high government posts. George M. Humphrey, who served as chairman of the board of the M.A. Hanna Company before becoming President Eisenhower's secretary of the treasury, said, for example:

When I came to Washington in January [1953], I did not realize so clearly as I do now how different government is from business, and how much more difficult it is to get things done. The job of making changes looked a lot easier from the outside.[72]

. . . in government the executive management must operate under a system of divided authority. . . . [W]hen a government executive decides on a course of action not already established under law, he must first check with other agencies to make certain his proposal does not conflict with or duplicate something being done by somebody else. It is common in government, much too common, for several agencies to be working on different facets of the same activity. The avoidance of overlapping or conflict calls for numerous conferences, for painstaking study of laws and directives, for working out plans in tedious detail so that what one Cabinet officer does will not bump into what another is doing—or run counter to our interests and activities abroad. . . .

Before coming to Washington, I had not understood why there were so many conferences in government, and so much delay. Now I do. Everything is more complex. . . .[73]

Bernstein quotes another executive with extensive experience in both government and private business:

This operation in a goldfish bowl does seem to make the tensions of the public service much greater than does those I see in business. In business you can delegate to a greater degree and hold people down the line responsible. In government the focus of responsibility on the top executive is much greater than in the corporations I have worked with.[74]

Still another said:

The man who makes a mistake in the shoe manufacturing business by picking the wrong styles can measure his judgment in terms of the volume of sales. He may be able to recover his financial losses next year. In any case, after all, it is his money, and you can't take that with you. But the fellow in a bureau of the Atomic Energy Commission deals with the survival of the country and even the fate of mankind. His job accomplishments cannot be calculated neatly and objectively. He feels a kind of wearing responsibility that few business executives feel. The consequences of error are so catastrophic and irreparable that sober and serious fellows would feel worse in administering that responsibility than they would in making financial decisions.[75]

And another said by way of indicating the relatively favorable aspects of government service:

Compromise is something I didn't know before I came here, at least in the same degree. I learned that compromise is vitally important in government and society. This is a lesson that more Americans need to learn. Many of us come into government with a fixed and simple picture of government operations only to learn, if we stay for more than a few months, that things can't be done here as they are handled in a single company by a president and his board of directors.[76]

Frederick Malek believes that successful management of any organization makes the same demands on its leaders: setting goals, selecting people, allocating resources, motivating people, and evaluating results.[77] Yet he notes "enormous differences" between business and government. Indeed, the qualities that assure success in business may assure failure in government. The three most important differences he cites are that the government executive (1) lives in a fishbowl in the glare of publicity; (2) must influence and gain the confidence of Congress; and (3) must contend with partisanship at every turn; proposals cannot be judged on their own merits.[78] He quotes James Hodgson, a former businessman and, at the time, secretary of labor, as follows:

The most general of the reasons for the failure of successful businessmen in government is a lack of breadth—an inability to conceptualize rather than merely achieve, an inability to understand and be effective in the *relations* elements of a governmental role, and an inability to deal with problems indirectly rather than through authoritarian line control.[79]

Another former businessman (president, Bell and Howell) and cabinet officer (secretary of commerce) is quoted as follows:

In business, a man's ability to communicate, while important, is hardly the dominant consideration. If confronted with the choice between someone with a great track record or great ability to articulate, the businessman would take the track record. But in government, the choice might be different.[80]

Another chief executive officer (American Motors) and cabinet officer (Housing and Urban Development) observed to Malek that "success in government depends on the attitude of the people you deal with—the bureaucracy, the Congress, the media, the public. To shape this attitude there is a much greater need for the ability to communicate than exists in any business I can think of, including advertising."[81]

Among businessmen who have most recently served in government, W. Michael Blumenthal has provided a lengthy assessment of the contrasts between business and government.[82] They can be outlined as follows:

BUSINESS	GOVERNMENT

Measure of Success

• Bottom line: Either you are making profits or you aren't.	• No bottom line: Success is often measured by intangibles: how often you meet with the president; whether you are viewed favorably by the press; whether or not you are believed to be affecting policy.

Decision Making

• It is clearly defined as to who is involved; there is much more autocratic control over personnel, information, and so on.	• Everyone gets involved: interest groups, congressional committees, OMB, different departments, the press. Decision making is "a floating crap game." *"To move within the process and still come out with the right decision is the essential difference* between what you do as a senior executive in government and what you do in business."

Management

• How well you managed the place is worth something on the bottom line.	• Concern is not with management but with whether the policies you are responsible for are judged successful or not.
• You can easily make administrative and personnel changes throughout the organization.	• It is extremely difficult to make administrative changes except for your top people.
• There are several ways to motivate staff: move someone around and up quickly, increase pay, give extra responsibility, bonuses, and so on.	• It is difficult to motivate staff because of bureaucratic obstacles.

Relationship with the Press

• You can change your mind and make changes in your internal policy without having to defend your moves publicly.	• If you change your mind, you are being inconsistent.
	• You must learn to be evasive or to express yourself very carefully and build defenses against being misquoted.
	• If you appear to the press to be influencing policy, your actual influence on policy is strengthened.

Government and Business: A Comparison[83]

How does one assess this conflicting evidence? Unfortunately, public and private management cannot be compared on strictly objective grounds. There are both similarities and differences in the tasks, activities, contexts, personal demands, and rewards of public and private executive jobs. Individuals are likely to weigh the relative importance of similarities and contrasts in sharply different ways depending on their personalities, values, cognitive styles, and expectations. For example, executives who aspire to a visible role in major public events and who enjoy bargaining and compromise with adversaries may welcome the political challenge of a cabinet office. Those who crave the exercise of authority and opportunity for individual entrepreneurship may regard a politicized environment as distracting and inhibiting. Individuals who give subordinates a loose rein and who react to their ideas rather than initiate policies and activities themselves may find government and corporate environments quite similar and congenial. Individuals who like to lead others, deploy resources, and see results attributable to their actions may be stifled in a government department and find it hard to manage one. Thus comparisons between government and business almost invariably contain significant elements of subjectivity, and for this reason, they are difficult to interpret.

One is left with the need to sort out and make sense of the mixed accumulation of ideas and evidence just presented. This is best done by organizing the discussion under four topics or themes recurrent in this type of analysis: the organization's ownership and purpose; the relationships of the organization with the environment; the scope and content of executive decisions; and the structure of organizational authority.

ORGANIZATIONAL OWNERSHIP AND PURPOSE

It would be a mistake to resurrect the myth that corporations maximize or maintain profits to the exclusion of other goals. More than forty years ago, Chester I. Barnard conceived of the corporation as a complex organization the continued existence of which depends on cooperation among individuals in the achievement of a commonly understood purpose. "It appears utterly contrary to the nature of men," he observed, "to be sufficiently induced by material or monetary considerations to contribute enough effort to a cooperative system to enable it to be productively efficient to the degree necessary for persistence over an extended period."[84]

In their pathbreaking book *A Behavioral Theory of the Firm,* Richard M. Cyert and James G. March introduced the concept of "satisficing" to the theory of corporate behavior. Drawing on organizational theory, they viewed corporate decision making as the selection of the first alternative that is satisfactory in terms of the organization's goals, which in turn are a product of internal bargaining among participants with disparate interests. Corporate management invariably has many goals, some of which may even be antithetical to profitability. Corporations have constituencies other than their owners: the Securities and Exchange Commission, the U.S. Attorney General, the Federal Trade Commission, unions, state regulatory agencies, local interest groups, the managers themselves. Further, to a growing though hardly compelling extent, corporations are faced with pressures to be socially accountable and to cater to public opinion and organized interests. The campaign against Nestlé's marketing of infant formula in Third World countries is illustrative.

It would be equally mistaken, however, to create the opposing myth that earning profits is merely one, and not necessarily the most important, goal of business decision making, that business is as bureaucratic as government. A fundamental objective of corporate management is to provide an economic return to its owners, to reward their investment. While it may take the form of maximizing profits or sales (either in the short or long term), maintaining a steady—or a steadily increasing—profit, stream of revenues or market share, or even maximizing the growth of the firm in terms of size, diversification, and market power, the achievement of economic results, the maintenance of a healthy bottom line, is a powerful unifying force in corporate organizations. The company must make money, and the more profitable it is, the more successful it is judged to be. Indeed, some students of business argue that profitability is a more conscious concern of management than it was in the business-dominated early decades of this century because it is now a more complex achievement.[85]

It has become a commonplace that ownership is separate from control in the modern corporation. The firm's managers, who control its actions, seldom have a substantial ownership interest. This might seem to attenuate the influence of the owners' economic interests in management decisions, but the corporation's owners, with their narrow concern for profitability, have powerful allies to pressure management to be mindful of profits. Insufficiently recognized, for example, is the role of investment bankers and securities analysts in appraising corporate management. Concerning a 1972 decline in the price of its stock that was to have profound effects on corporate management, the president of General Foods, C. W. "Tex" Cook, complained that Wall Street analysts were "all rushing to the same side of the boat."[86] In 1979, business publications reported that General Electric stock was not selling at a premium because analysts judged General Electric's management to be too cautious. The chairman and president of United Technologies Corporation, Harry Gray, was reported to be annoyed in 1979 that the company's stock was selling at only six times earnings, below the industry composite, because securities analysts found the company too complicated to study.

Another ally of owners is the powerful business press, which analyzes corporate management and, by publicizing aggressive, profit-seeking general managers and criticizing questionable management actions, affects the reputations of senior executives in building and leading profitable enterprises. *Fortune* magazine's "business triumphs of the seventies" celebrated the bold, the profitable, the successful: the Boeing 747, McDonald's, ABC's rise to the top of the network ratings, Philip Morris's prosperity in spite of the U.S. surgeon general, and the executives who produced such triumphs. Widespread publicity that a company's management is weak may make it the target of a takeover attempt by a more aggressive firm.

Moreover, corporations can fail and can be perceived as approaching failure. Even if there is no simple market test or profit motive, there is a conclusive economic test of management competence. Dun and Bradstreet publishes regular reports on the causes of business failures, including neglect, lack of managerial experience, and, the largest category, incompetence. The general managers of a corporation are expected to manage their organization. If the organization falters or fails, its management is held responsible by the financial community on which it depends.

There is nothing remotely approaching an ownership interest, a bottom line, or a Dun and Bradstreet analysis of organizational failure in government departments.[87] Governmental purposes, and the means of achieving them, must be authorized by or created in accordance with law, and the purposes and behavior of lawmakers in no way approximate those of stockholders or their allies. Indeed, the purpose of much, if not most, government activity is to do what the private sector will not do or will not do in the same way as government. A goal of numerous public programs is precisely to "incur losses,"[88] to provide services that private firms could not provide at a profit, or to subsidize their provision by those firms. Further, there is no analogue to failure, no competitors waiting to move in, no independent group of auditors or analysts whose profession is to assess management performance.

Government executives must be directly and immediately concerned with a range of effects on society vastly wider than that confronting private executives. Secretary of the Interior Cecil Andrus, for example, found himself facing the choice between a proposal by the International Whaling Commission that the United States endorse a moratorium on all killing of the endangered bowhead whale and an opposing view by the Eskimo, Indian, and Aleut communities of Alaska, which hunt the whale according to age-old customs for dietary subsistence and for the income garnered from carvings and other handicrafts made from their catch. Andrus decided, against the wishes of the Departments of State and Commerce, to oppose the moratorium while working with native groups to develop a self-regulating program for reducing the take.[89] Choosing between the survival of a species and that of an entire way of life is a problem that does not confront the corporate executive.

Most issues faced by government executives are less dramatic but no less socially consequential. In an interview early in his term as secretary of transportation, for example, Brock Adams was expected to address the following questions: "What are your views on subways?" "Is this country ever going to get people out of their own private automobiles and into something bigger?" "Are you really confident that the auto industry can meet the 1981–85 gasoline standards?" His authoritative views were sought on the actions and future prospects of whole industries—automobiles, mass transit, airlines, trucking—and on such matters as safety, financing, construction, technology, and regulatory approaches.[90] In a similar interview, HEW Secretary Califano was asked about health insurance, health care cost control, health maintenance organizations, the supply of practicing physicians, social security financing, and the financial capacities of state and local governments. Andrus was asked, "What is the answer to the nation's water problems?" and about the effectiveness of strip mine controls in the West, outer continental shelf leasing, the costs of environmental protection, the management of Indian affairs, and the efforts on behalf of endangered species. The priorities facing the first secretary of education, Shirly Hufstedler, were generally considered to be school desegregation, the distribution of federal funds to schools, student loans, the persistence of functional illiteracy, and shoring up financially troubled colleges and universities.

Not only that, as the discussion in chapter 2 emphasized, senior government executives are placed in the position of having to resolve or reconcile conflicts among the goals of public policy as well as conflicts between policy goals and the means by which they are to be pursued. Lawmakers with widely diverse views concerning organizational purposes influence the language of statutes. Moreover, the enactment of a statute does not necessarily mean that consensus or agreement has been reached; often it means only temporary agreement to proceed to the next step or to turn the problem over to the executive branch. Thus the writing of a law does not settle the question of purpose. In the face of conflict, purpose may be left deliberately vague. The statute may incorporate conflicting statements or be subject to conflicting interpretations or expectations. Thus not only does the public executive have the problem of deciding which formulation of purpose is appropriate, he or she confronts the possibility of continuing conflict with lawmakers and their constituencies over what ought to be done, how, and why. The official is subject to Murphy's Law of Politics: No matter what you do, you should have done something else.

RELATIONSHIPS WITH THE ENVIRONMENT

A corporation is a creature of the state. However, most business corporations are created to carry out any purposes their incorporators want to give them, provided the purposes are consistent with state corporation laws. The owners of rights in private property are not free of obligations to society, and corporations are subject to a variety of legal requirements. In general, however, the owner of private property enjoys certain fundamental protections. Public access to information on and public control of the activities of corporations and their executives are limited. The definition of corporate purpose, if lawful, is not subject, in general, to external dictates or manipulation.

The amount of privacy enjoyed by private managers is admittedly eroding. "Executive insulation is a luxury of the past," declares one study.[91]

No longer can the company chairman or president . . . remain obscured behind a one-way mirror, seeing and manipulating his subjects while remaining hidden from view. . . . Chief executives must now spend more time dealing with outside groups.

Peter Drucker has observed that "managers are not private, in the sense that what they do does not matter. They are public. They are visible. They represent. . . . Managers have a public function."[92] Harry Levinson goes even further: "Since he serves by consent, the executive is in many ways an elected leader. As time goes by, judgments of *all* those who are affected by his power will be heard more frequently in his selection."[93] In their pursuit of purpose, corporate managers can no longer ignore the effects of the corporation's activities on local employment, on air and water quality, on the consumer's safety and health, or even on the consumer price index. Multinational companies cannot ignore the effects on U.S. domestic or foreign policy interests of their operations abroad. Argues John Quarles, former deputy administrator of EPA, corporate decision making on capital investments may well be in the process of being transferred from the private to the public aegis.[94]

Thus corporate managers are drawn increasingly into public forums and into defenses of their decisions before groups with no ownership stake whatever. As the former chairman of AT&T, John D. deButts, put it: "Today more and more of the time that used to be spent in running the business must now be devoted to representing it to the many constituencies on which its future depends."[95] When problems mounted with respect to the steel-belted radial tires of the Firestone Tire and Rubber Company, its officials had to contend with media inquiries, critical attacks by governmental bodies—the National Highway Traffic and Safety Administration and an investigating subcommittee of the House Interstate and Foreign Commerce Committee—and lawsuits. This is far from the first time in our history that business has been on the defensive or that the public interest has intruded in corporate policy making. It is not even clear that these intrusions threaten the perceived prerogatives of private management to nearly the same extent as the antitrust or union movements once did. Without question, however, corporate managers are faced with a broad variety of formal regulatory and informal political constraints on their freedom of action.

What is a constraint for the private manager, however—a restriction on the pursuit of corporate purpose—is a mandate for the public manager—the very definition of purpose. The corporate executive is a public person in addition to being an organizational and a private person. There is a substantial question about the extent to which the public executive is anything but a public person.

Government organizations are much more than creatures of the state. The public has a right of access to them at almost every point. Through elected officials, the press, and the courts, the public can interrogate public executives about their actions. Indeed, most of these officials cannot even take office without a public hearing on their qualifications and the approval of the U.S. Senate. Whereas the burden of proof is on those who would require disclosure of or access to corporate executives in the public interest, the burden of proof is, for the most part, on the public executive who would restrict access to the public's business. One should not be misled by the fact that government agencies often seem as impenetrable as corporations. The public executive has nothing like the security from external authority that corporate officials enjoy.

That government executives can be expected or required to explain or justify their actions with little or no notice is one of the primary factors shaping public management. The ease and frequency with which this is and can be done is an enduring obstacle to genuine delegation of authority in government departments. Often the cabinet officer or agency head is called to testify before a congressional committee, even when the committee realizes that a subordinate knows more, because the executive attracts more media attention and boosts the status of the committee. Alan K. Campbell, director of the Office of Personnel Management, notes "the fishbowl character of what you do and therefore the need to really be careful that you are not signing off on something which could be on the front page of the *Post* or the *Times* the next morning."[96] Recalled Secretary of Education Shirley Hufstedler, "I wrote a letter to Senator [Clairborne] Pell [D-R.I.] about the Higher Education Reauthorization Bill, which was unacceptable to the Administration. I didn't know that any time a Cabinet member writes a letter, it's on every desk on Capitol Hill the next morning, plus in the *Higher Education Daily.*"[97] By inadvertently slighting features of the bill sought by House Subcommittee on Postsecondary Education Chairman William Ford, she drew a caustic letter from him and immediately had to set about repairing the damage.

The extent and frequency of public scrutiny are also an obstacle to orderly planning or even an orderly allocation of executive time. The executive's agenda—what he or she must consider important, when, and why—is largely formed by the sudden actions of others: the president or one of his aides, a congressional committee, or a state or local official. Said Patricia Wald of her job as assistant attorney general for legislative affairs:

It is not possible to set your own schedule. You can try, but you have to be ready to junk your whole schedule and go to whatever the crisis is. I literally come in in the morning with a list of things to do and the whole day goes in a different direction.[98]

It is not unlike a top corporate executive having to cope with the demands created by a new takeover bid or an unanticipated strike every week.

SCOPE AND CONTENT OF DECISIONS

The typical decisions made by senior corporate executives include those concerning new product development and market strategies; acquisitions and spin-offs; principal financial management decisions such as those concerning the financing of expansion; major personnel actions; plant expansions, additions, and location decisions; and the major features of relationships with employees. The actual decisions made by senior executives vary with the nature of the organization. For example, senior executives in a less diversified firm make more of the substantive decisions concerning products and markets than those in a conglomerate.

It is difficult to generalize concerning the intellectual demands of these types of decisions and the qualifications needed for successful performance of senior responsibilities. Kenneth Andrews states that

to be a leader in the activities of searching out and analyzing strategic alternatives and finally making or ratifying decisions among competing choices, the general manager must be an analyst. His need for intellectual ability equal to this requirement is fundamental; it becomes more compelling as alternatives become more difficult to evaluate and choices become harder to make. The rough-and-ready opportunist is not our preferred prototype, valuable as are his energy and ingenuity.[99]

Chris Argyris notes that "most chief executives have three characteristics in common—they are articulate, competitive, and persuasive. They compete vigorously for 'air time,' excel in one-upmanship, and stimulate win-lose competition."[100] He further notes, however, that "most of the executives in my sample are highly intelligent [and] are especially adept at conceptualizing problems and issues."[101] According to Leonard Sayles:

highly effective managers can solve apparently insoluble contradictions by creative synthesis, a higher level of cognitive development. . . . managers with the sophisticated view of reality don't simply respond to pressures; they seek to change what pressures there will be in the system, so they're not repeatedly coping with the same problems. . . .[102]

In short, among his or her other attributes, the effective business executive must be intelligent, conceptual, and creative in order to cope with the demands and pressures emanating from the environment, the organization, and the nature of the task at hand.

Aiding the corporate executive in such tasks are important characteristics of profit-making enterprises: the prevalence of economic measures of performance; a high degree of reciprocity between getting and spending money, so that corporate management decisions can be closely tied to performance measures; and a structure of authority which permits direction from the top. These characteristics produce tendencies toward conceptual coherence, a restricted scope of activity, and opportunities for creative synthesis.

These characteristics are much less dominant in government departments. The getting and spending of money are distinct and only loosely related processes. The definition and pursuit of purpose are dominated by Congress and thus by centrifugal forces. The possibilities for authoritative direction from the top are greatly restricted. Former HEW Secretary Elliot Richardson could complain of his department: "The structure was so complex, accountability so much subdivided, and the number of separate funding decisions so vast that only the specialist could hope to be adequately informed about the ways in which the money was parceled out."[103]

The executive skill most vital to success under such circumstances is creative, incisive, and analytical intelligence, the ability both to establish communications with program specialists and to transcend the compartmentalized thinking prevalent in government bureaucracies. To an extent seldom approached in business organizations, the successful public executive must, as chapter 2 suggested, master the basic substance of a wide variety of complex issues, perceive relationships among them, and devise policy ideas that are both politically attractive and programmatically sensible. Indeed, one of the most effective ways to motivate subordinates in a government department is to earn the intellectual and empathetic respect of the program specialists and bureau professionals. For example, in dealing with Social Security Commissioner Robert Ball, one of the federal government's most astute program officials, Elliot Richardson said, "If you were smart enough to ask the right questions, he would give you honest answers."[104]

A typical program decision may have several distinct dimensions: purpose and desired outcome, a much more complicated notion than contributions to profitability; target group, a concept somewhat analogous to the concept of projected market but usually more precise and often quite confusing; plan implementation, usually vastly more complicated in government than the kinds of routine delegations of authority that are possible in manufacturing corporations; roles for different levels of government, with no private analogue; program design, which, as the discussion in chapter 2 suggests, also has no private analogue; and availability of resources, a uniquely political process in government. The executive who wishes to work the problem must understand not only each of these aspects but their interrelationships as well. Moreover, he or she is usually working several problems simultaneously. These simultaneous demands on executive attention can constitute a formidable intellectual challenge.

STRUCTURE OF AUTHORITY

Large, complex business organizations are bureaucracies. There is specialization of function, sharing of power, insulation from external influences, inertia, and problems of internal communication and control. One
observer has stated the circumstances pungently:

> The company president . . . is not a baronial lord. He is a servant, like other servants
> of the corporation. His position at the top of the hierarchy does not enable or entitle
> him to have a markedly greater influence on the behavior of the corporation than
> other members of top management . . . or, even more significantly, than the
> engineer in the product development department.[105]

The heads of good-sized, publicly owned companies may not see themselves as having great power. They seldom believe that they can do anything they want in the industrial world. Indeed, a powerful reason for the
emergence of the human relations school of government was the recognition that the human beings in a corporate bureaucracy were not physiological adjuncts to the machine but were individuals with psychological and
emotional needs who would not respond to just any kind of direction.
Thus we read of the difficulties faced by the head of a General Electric
manufacturing division in persuading his subordinates to reduce their load
growth forecasts for electrical generating equipment in line with changed
energy markets. We read that the executives and employees of acquired
companies refuse to regard themselves as members of the new parent firm.
Chris Argyris has supplied a fascinating account of a newspaper pub-
lisher's inability to resolve a bureaucratic deadlock between the editorial
department and the news department over establishment of an op-ed
page.[106] Donald N. Frey, chairman and chief executive officer of the Bell
and Howell Company, said of his joining the company in 1971: "When
you first join a company you don't know who to believe. It's the simple
truth. Who's good and who isn't? Coming up with an answer is probably
the most time-dependent process of all for a chief executive."[107]

The bureaucratic nature of corporations and its implications for top
management are probably underemphasized; subordinate divisions are
often as parochial as government bureaus. "The local operating companies
[of AT&T] are like states, with their own state governments," asserts the
New York Times. "AT&T, like the Federal Government, acts to bind them
all together into some sort of sanity."[108] Said one observer of the company,
"It's a kind of anarchy. It's so big it's really not run by anybody. It just
goes on." Said a former corporate planner of the International Paper Company: "There's no atmosphere of objective analysis and planning. No one

feels that if they do a good and correct analysis, anyone would listen to him. It's so incredibly political that it just destroys any sort of rational objective management."[109] One of the most celebrated successes in television news broadcasting was the product of a simple bureaucratic compromise. Advocates for Chet Huntley and those for David Brinkley finally agreed to create a Huntley-Brinkley team as a way to keep the NBC news department together.[110]

Yet the business executive—the top management team—nonetheless has substantial internal control. A recent article in a national business magazine described how a company had systematically acquired control of weak and failing manufacturing enterprises and made them profitable in a short time by cutting the number of products in half, consolidating management operations, reducing staff by one-third, replacing weak managers, and introducing improved cost accounting down to the level of pencils and paperclips. "More than half of the businesses of the Bell and Howell Company, circa 1971, are no longer there," reported the *New York Times*.[111] Chairman and chief executive officer Donald N. Frey's strategy called for narrowing the company's horizons and investing in its strengths, an approach which led to the sale of the "profit-draining" consumer photo division, the business on which the seventy-three-year-old company was built. Another top executive was described in a flattering *Fortune* article as propelling himself upward by "deftly replacing [subordinates] who don't measure up" and "turning languid businesses around."[112]

Business executives have substantial authority over corporate strategy, personnel, resource allocation, and technology. John deButts, as chairman of AT&T, could say, "The purpose of the other managers in this company is to advise me. That's it. There can be only one person in an organization who makes policy decisions. In our case, that's me."[113] Though the effective exercise of this authority is difficult, there is nonetheless substantial scope for effective leadership. Authority—to acquire and divest, to hire, fire, and relocate, to spend or not spend, to accelerate or slow down—is there to be used.

No public executive wields nearly so much authority. No political executive would dream of saying, "I am the one who in the final analysis makes the decisions." As Prof. Joseph L. Bower has put it, "the United States has very nearly denied the public executive the tools of management. It is almost true that the business executive's enabling resources—structure and people—are the public executive's *constraints*."[114]

The public executive can seldom act except pursuant to statutory authority, as continuously interpreted by the courts. Former HEW Secretary Joseph Califano tells of being ordered by a federal judge to request OMB to approve an additional 1,800 people to staff the Office for Civil Rights. Not only that,

> the court demanded to review the memorandum I had sent to the Director of the Office of Management and Budget asking for the additional staff. . . . During oral argument on one of the various contempt motions to which I was potentially subject, the judge even asked counsel to describe the vigor with which I presented the argument to the Director of the Office of Management and Budget during a meeting.[115]

Imagine the situation if a corporate executive could not reorganize his or her company or commit its resources unless specifically authorized to do so by the legislature of the state of incorporation. In dealing with personnel, the public executive must conform to the requirements and standards of the civil service system, as administered by the Office of Personnel Management, and thus he or she has only limited control over personnel appointments, movement, compensation, working conditions, dispute resolution, and work rules. Indeed, Harold Seidman has observed that "probably more executive branch officials have been fired or reassigned as a result of pressure from the Congress than by the President."[116] Imagine the situation if a corporate executive had to negotiate with a management union to which all managers except the members of the front office management teams and their assistants belonged. In making policy decisions —in attempting to shape organizational purpose—the public executive must clear his or her actions with numbers of people who have, or believe they have, a stake in them. Imagine the situation if the members of a company's board of directors were appointed by the governor, included representatives of its unions, its consumers, its competitors, and the legislature, and were in continuous session.

In short, public executives are not accorded the kind of authority exercised by private managers. The framers of the Constitution did not want an unchecked executive. The author of *The Federalist*, No. 51, made this principle explicit:

> . . . the great security against a gradual concentration of . . . powers in the same [branch], consists in giving to those who administer each [branch] the necessary constitutional means and personal motives to resist encroachment of the others. . . . Ambition must be made to counteract ambition.[117]

Over the long run, Congress has been unwilling to have executive authority slip beyond its reach and control. Congressional ambitions counteract the ambitions of the executive. Even in those instances in which discretion is granted to a public executive, his or her actual use of it almost invariably invites subsequent legislative or judicial restraints or directives, and the initial grant of discretion is whittled away.

The Bottom Line

The senior executives of virtually all types of complex organizations have common preoccupations—with goals, people, organization resources, and constituencies. They spend much of their time meeting with people with whom they must compromise to achieve their goals; they must choose a leadership style that motivates rather than inhibits subordinates; they must deal with substantive and organizational complexities. But as Wallace S. Sayre once observed, "business and government administration are alike in all unimportant respects."[118] Though each of the differences just discussed could plausibly be viewed as a matter of degree, when added up they constitute a difference in kind. This difference is suggested by a comment of Grant G. Simmons, chairman of the Simmons Company: "The professional manager is apt to be running against a short term: He has perhaps only ten years to make his mark. He's less relaxed. He may run a vessel with too much sail up for rough and stormy seas, figuring, 'I'm not going to be at the helm when it's struck!' "[119] Ten years with too much sail! The typical public executive may rationally plan on spending three years in a trireme with mutinous oarsmen in weather that is far worse. It is an environment virtually without charts and horizons. Theodore Levitt confirms this view:

. . . [It] is now unanimously acknowleged . . . that, after the Arab oil embargo in November 1973, it took only one week of intensive around-the-clock work by the managers of the oil industry to rearrange completely the entire sourcing, shipping, pipelining, and delivery of the world's oil and petroleum products to get things back on a new, functioning track. I have been told personally by extremely high placed officials in Europe, the United States, and Japan that they viewed this as an almost miraculous achievement that none of the governments themselves could have conceivably accomplished.[120]

Indeed, it would not be farfetched to argue that business administration and public administration are less alike now than they were when large, complex business and government organizations were in their formative period. At that time, a great many of the functions of government were routine direct service operations, and the analogy to the management of production in business was not strained.

In the years since World War II, the fastest-growing firms have been to an increasing extent conglomerate and multinational companies, that is, combinations of apparently unrelated or loosely related businesses with extensive overseas operations. Though fundamentally new forms of organization, such as those pioneered by General Electric and General Motors, have not appeared recently, the functions of the top management of these firms have changed. The conglomerate manager is less likely to be involved in product and market strategy decisions and more likely to be involved with overall financial performance and with long-term resource allocation among businesses. An understanding of product markets, production, and labor relations is less important than an understanding of capital markets and of the behavior of foreign bureaucracies. Because of their psychological distance from the businesses they are in, conglomerate managers are apt to be more motivated by financial incentives and profitability than by maintaining or enhancing the company in other ways.

Government has changed as well, as chapter 1 recounted. Few of the current activities of government, or at least few of the current activities of senior executives in government, are concerned with direct service provision. Their concerns encompass virtually the entire range of social problems. In a real sense, their goal as managers is to influence the behavior not only or even primarily of their own employees but of other social institutions: state and local governments, private industry, and the family, for example. This transformation in the role of government is far greater than any that has occurred in business in the last fifty years. Indeed, it is no wonder that the public executive is subject to so much scrutiny and constraint. In a governmental system that requires its executives to be accountable to elected officials, it could not be otherwise.

The case for regarding public management as unique and uniquely difficult seems strong. Concepts of public management founded on hierarchical, profit-oriented enterprises are unlikely, therefore, to provide perspectives for executive public management. If managing a government department or agency is not like managing a corporation, and if we cannot depend on analogies to business for insights into public management, are there any other models or frameworks that are operationally useful to political executives? This question is taken up in the next chapter.

CHAPTER 6

Public Management: Levels of the Game

IN November 1973, HEW Secretary Caspar W. Weinberger proposed in testimony before Senator Edward M. Kennedy's Subcommittee on Health of the U.S. Senate Committee on Labor and Public Welfare to publish regulations that would "limit drug reimbursements under programs administered by his Department to the lowest cost at which the drug was generally available unless there is a demonstrated difference in therapeutic effect."[1] This proposal conformed well with the interests of the subcommittee, the chairman of which had proclaimed his determination to control drug cost inflation by curtailing the practice of prescribing relatively expensive brand-name drugs and encouraging instead the substitution of less expensive generic drugs. The proposal was also popular within HEW, which was contending with rapidly rising costs in the Medicare and Medicaid programs, and it satisfied the conservatively inclined Weinberger, who saw a limitation on federal cost reimbursement as far preferable to the compulsory licensing of drugs by their manufacturers and to the restriction of drug cost reimbursement to drugs on a list approved by HEW. The secretary's proposal seemed to represent an idea whose time had come.

It is more accurate to say that the time had almost come for a somewhat different idea. The final regulations were issued in August 1976, nearly three years later. Moreover, Weinberger's straightforward-sounding proposals for controlling drug cost reimbursements had become a complex bureaucratic solution.[2] The proposed regulations created (1) a Pharmaceutical Reimbursement Board (PRB), with five members from within the department, to identify which drugs should be subject to maximum allowable costs (MACs), to gather and analyze price information on them, and to recommend MACs; and (2) a Pharmaceutical Reimbursement Advisory Committee (PRAC) to review PRB recommendations and advise the secretary on their appropriateness, as well as to provide more general policy advice. Following PRAC review, the PRB's MAC recommendation would be published in the *Federal Register,* and thirty days would be allowed for written comments and requests for a public hearing. Each state was required to set reasonable dispensing fees for pharmacists based on periodic surveys of the regional costs of dispensing drugs. For multisource drugs (drugs available from more than one manufacturer), reimbursement, including dispensing fee, would be limited to the lesser of either the maximum allowable cost or the estimated acquisition cost plus, if the drug was provided on an outpatient basis, 25 percent of the amount by which the MAC exceeded the actual acquisition cost (AAC).

What happened in the meantime can be attributed in part to the tyranny of the task. In the course of working the problem, complications steadily multiplied as Weinberger and his associates sought to make the effects of the new policy precise and accountable to the diverse interests at stake. The outcome was also shaped, however, by the pressures generated in the course of working with these interests and responding to their criticisms and concerns. Handling these kinds of pressures while working out a complex policy problem is the essence of public management. The question we address here is whether or not it is possible to create a model or framework of the political and substantive pressures associated with problem solving in government that we can use to develop criteria or yardsticks by which the performance of political executives can be judged. To be effective, how should political executives relate to their environment?

Groups and Elites

The term "pluralism" has come to be a standard way of characterizing American democratic processes.[3] Pluralism "is the conception that power, or the ability to make decisions, in American society is diffuse and that decisions are reached through bargaining."[4] A pluralist approach focuses on *behavior* in the making of *decisions* on *issues* over which there is an observable *conflict* of (subjective) *interests,* seen as express policy preferences, revealed by political participation."[5] For the most part, bargaining occurs among groups organized to achieve a particular purpose or set of purposes. Groups "operate with varying mixtures of ideology and self-interest and seek to effect changes through: (1) strong internal organization which can concentrate power, and (2) the exercise of predominating influence when they encounter other groups."[6]

In the pluralist model, the role of governmental institutions is to adjust and continually readjust conflicting group interests so as to achieve a never-ending succession of temporary equilibriums. Though group influence impinges on all branches of government and on officials at all levels, the main focus of pluralist decision making and the process of change from one temporary equilibrium to the next is the legislature. "The legislature referees the group struggle, ratifies the victories of the successful coalitions, and records the terms of the surrenders, compromises, and conquests in the form of statutes."[7] The function of political executives is to work with Congress to adjust antagonistic interests, to negotiate compromises, and to arrange settlements.

This model has enormous intuitive and ideological appeal. It conveys a sense of checks and balances, of a kind of self-regulating adjustment to competing interests with virtues akin to those we ascribe to the "invisible hand" of the free market. Pluralism seems to explain most of American political life. Individuals organize themselves into a cohesive force and make claims on politicians, who balance these claims against others and respond in an appropriate way. Sometimes the focus of group effort is intense and highly concentrated on specific issues. At other times, it is more general and programmatic.

The working out of the MAC regulations can be viewed as typical of pluralist decision making and of the role of political executives in the process. Several groups were involved:

- The U.S. Senate Subcommittee on Antitrust and Monopoly—headed by Senator Edward Kennedy—which consistently sought to lessen the differential between drug manufacturers' costs and the prices charged to consumers.

- Officials of the U.S. Department of HEW, charged with administering Medicare and Medicaid, as well as testing and regulating the marketing of prescription drugs, including its Task Force on Prescription Drugs, made up of top federal health officials.
- The Pharmaceutical Manufacturers' Association (PMA), the trade association of the large, research-based pharmaceutical manufacturers, the profits of which come primarily from patented, brand-name products.
- The American Medical Association (AMA), the leading organization of the medical profession, whose journal depends for a substantial portion of its revenues on drug advertising.
- The American Pharmaceutical Association (APhA), the professional organization of pharmacists, which tends to represent independent pharmacists, who favored a fee system by which a flat rate was charged for professional services.
- The National Association of Retail Druggists (NARD), which favored a system for collecting fees from the dispensing of prescription drugs by which a percentage of the retail cost of each prescription was added to the total cost.[8]

Weinberger's initial proposal to the Kennedy subcommittee triggered a protracted discussion among these groups. The PMA announced its opposition, though not all its member companies were equally upset. The AMA, after equivocating, questioned the proposal, listing six different factors to be considered in assessing the equivalence of prescription drugs: therapeutic equivalence, chemical equivalence, quality control, bioavailability, stability (the rate at which drugs deteriorate on the shelf), and "patient acceptability." The APhA, though split internally, strongly supported the proposal; the NARD, in contrast, strongly opposed it. As the debate developed, the issues became more complex and esoteric. Could the Food and Drug Administration (FDA) actually determine the equivalence of drugs? Did the pricing of drugs and prescriptions include excessive profits? Should the implementing regulations be simple, permitting considerable discretion in individual determinations, or detailed? Should the regulations cover all multisource drugs or only the most frequently prescribed ones?

The final result was a compromise among the contending groups. Though the APhA, which endorsed recognition of a separate fee for the professional services of pharmacists, had supported the use of the AAC in determining the MAC, the final regulations yielded to drug industry criticism and substituted "estimated acquisition cost" for ACC to eliminate the necessity for detailed auditing of pharmacies. Weinberger supervised the process of identifying the issues, determining both the substantive and political merits of various proposals, and arranging the compromises.

The term "pluralism" conjures up a vision of political processes that is relatively benign, as it appeared to be in this case, at least on the surface.

A far less democratic vision is offered by those who hold that "every society can be divided into those who rule and those who are ruled."[9] Social policy reflects the values, commitments, and interests of ruling elites,[10] and changes in social policy occur as the structure and composition of these ruling elites change. By and large, these elites are immune from public influence or mass political movements; political parties and popular elections are largely decorative. Only policy alternatives which fall within the elite consensus are given serious attention.

Many elite perspectives are rooted in some form of economic determinism. Elites are those groups which through various means gain control of the economic surplus generated by a capitalist economy. In short, wealth confers political power. However, C. Wright Mills's "power elite" is not a Marxian "ruling class." Membership is based not on ownership of property but on the control of the "great organizations." "No one . . . can be truly powerful unless he has access to the command of major institutions."[11] This elite is united by a shared social and educational background and by common values and interests.

From a radical perspective, elites rule for their own benefit.[12] They exploit the masses of powerless people for their own gain. The proper political goal of those so exploited is not only the elimination of the rulers but the abolition of the ruling class. In contrast, the conservative perspective stresses the responsibility of the ruling classes for the moral and material well-being of society. "For their willingness to assume such responsibilities, they are entitled to the powers and advantages of office."[13] Ruling elites are necessary for the stability, cohesiveness, and productivity of social arrangements. Within this conservative perspective, however, there are substantial differences between democratic theorists who stress the accountability of ruling elites to an informed citizenry and those who stress the obligations of ruling elites to serve an essentially incompetent citizenry.

From the elitist perspective, the creation of MAC regulations takes on a different significance. The result can be interpreted, for example, as a compromise worked out between the bureaucratic and industrial members of a ruling elite whose goal is the protection of the existing distribution of economic power. In this interpretation, Weinberger's objective as a member of this elite was less the protection of prescription drug users against inflation than the restraint of the growth of government expenditures and regulations. To the extent that the original proposal threatened the profits and market position of both the large pharmaceutical manufacturers and drug wholesalers and retailers (inadvertently, we must assume), compromises were made. Even if Weinberger could be supposed to have been acting out of a sense of stewardship for the well-being of Medicaid and Medicare recipients (a tenuous proposition, since their drug bills were to be paid by third parties no matter what approach was taken), the debate occurred within the framework of minimal government interference in private markets dominated by the large drug companies. The MAC case, in this view, confirms the elitist model.

What are the implications of these two models for the political executive? Pluralist approaches contribute the notion that power is dispersed, that interests and ideologies are enormously diverse, that political organization matters, and that there is democratic access to political influences and policy making. Elitist approaches contribute the notion that some associations or groups are more powerful than others and that their power often is based on their ability to control the distribution and use of material resources: income and wealth, access to jobs, professions, or markets, and the allocation of public expenditures. Elites can and do bring well-financed pressure to bear on political executives whose actions affect their vital interests.

Even after one accounts for such factors in the shaping of political activity, however, governing in practice still is not fully explained. The set of vital forces bearing on and shaping executive behavior has somehow eluded these relatively abstract and unintegrated perspectives. Effective performance involves more than identifying groups, their interests, and their relative power and reconciling where possible the differences among them.

Levels of the Game

For government policy or programs to be conceived and put into operation, several distinctive types of questions must be answered by participants in the policy-making process:

- Is there a need for government action at all? If so, what would be the purposes or fundamental directions of such action?
- To move in a general direction or to accomplish broad purposes, what means or instruments should government employ? Which agencies or branches or levels of government should be authorized to act? How should financial, personnel, and other necessary resources be allocated among them?

· Precisely how shall the means or instruments of government action be designed
and used? How shall programs be organized and administered? What procedures, rules, and routines shall be adopted?

Before specialized services can be made available to a handicapped child,
regulations imposed on auto makers concerning the fuel efficiency of automobiles or on federally chartered banks concerning their financial hold-
ings, charges assessed against users of inland waterways or national parks,
or prices established for prescription drugs financed by Medicaid and
Medicare—that is, before government can engage in specific transactions
that have effects on people or organizations—these kinds of questions *must*
be answered, implicitly if not explicitly, in action if not in conscious
thought.

An examination of numerous cases of policy determination and program
design suggests that a distinctive kind of political process is associated with
resolving each type of question. Dominant participants, the modes and
language of communication they use, the forums in which actual resolution of specific issues occurs, and the bases for these resolutions differ
depending on the type of question being addressed. The politics associated
with each type of question may be viewed as a different *game,* where
"game" is employed as a metaphor for ongoing, sequential activity governed by both formal and informal rules, involving a high degree of interactive decision making, and with winning as an objective.[14] This is not
a customary way of thinking about the practical problems of public management. Political executives are often tempted or pressured by circumstances into organizing their thinking and their activities around specific
events or routines, such as an appearance before a congressional committee
or the promulgation of regulations. They may see the world in terms of
simple, intuitively appealing images such as "bureaucrats," "politicians,"
and "iron triangles." Some officials react to problems by searching for the
right answer.[15] Others see the challenge as survival in a contest with
omnipresent enemies. Still others see the challenge as one of successful
persuasion or salesmanship. More sophisticated executives may set about
finding the inevitable compromise, creating an imaginative solution, or
applying a known body of professional principles. Each approach, or combination of them, can be associated with a managerial style: autocratic or
rigid behavior, "jungle fighting," dominance and manipulation, or con-
ciliation and negotiation.

What these approaches fail to do is help political executives recognize
and react constructively to the essential characteristics of the political and
bureaucratic reality with which they must cope: the time-consuming, se-

quential nature of policy making; the fluid, interactive, polycentric character of political relationships; and the necessity to recognize and balance
competing considerations of process with those of task or substance, efficiency with equity, what is accomplished with how it is accomplished.
Public management, political leadership, is neither all substance nor all
process; it is a complex blend worked out over time in concert with others
with whom one shares power and interests. It is, says Richard E. Neustadt,
"a great game, much like collective bargaining, in which each seeks to
profit from the other's needs and fears. It is a game played catch-as-catch-
can, case by case. And everybody knows the game, observers and participants alike."[16]

Thus the game metaphor can have immense practical value to executives
attempting to orient themselves to new issues and circumstances involving
uncertainty, ambiguity, and conflict. Successful public management can be
viewed as effective gamesmanship.

A public management game begins when an individual or group advocates a change in the status quo and is able to persuade those with power
to influence change to consider doing so. Sometimes an individual—the
president, an influential legislator, a respected cabinet officer—is sufficiently influential to initiate a game merely by stating a desire or intention
to do so. In the case of the MAC regulations, the game that led to the
regulations was initiated when Senator Kennedy declared that he would
hold hearings to discover how HEW planned to deal with the problem of
drug cost inflation. Usually, however, mere advocacy or sponsorship of
change is not enough. A critical mass of influential people must be per-
suaded to become actively engaged in discussing the matter seriously, thus
making it an issue and placing it on the agenda of political debate. The
game of drug cost control might not have gained momentum had Weinberger chosen not to put forward a substantive proposal. Thus a game is
being played when a question is being discussed or debated and government action (or the termination of government action) is being urged by
at least some influential participants in policy making.

A game ends when a matter actively under discussion ceases to be an
issue. The end of a game may indicate that a question has been answered
or an issue resolved through the formation of a consensus favoring or
opposing change. An act may pass or be defeated, funds appropriated, final
regulations promulgated. A game may end, however, because participants
lose interest, are diverted to other issues, or conclude that nothing is to be
gained by continued discussion and efforts to win. The end, in other words,
may be conclusive or inconclusive.

A careful analysis of governmental activity suggests, however, that there is not just one game but games on many levels. Students of government have often conceived of government in terms of levels of activity or of the functioning of "subsystems." In *American Government and the Economy,* for example, Emmette S. Redford distinguishes micropolitics, subsystems (or intermediary) politics, and macropolitics.[17] Charles E. Summer distinguishes the level at which the formulation of what he calls "broad strategic alignments" occurs; the administrative level, which is concerned with "the elaboration of broad strategies into more specific details," and the "operating or work" level, where the performance of the actual operations and work necessary to carry out the alignment occurs.[18] In *The Power Elite,* C. Wright Mills refers to "the top, the middle, and the bottom levels of power."[19] Reacting to such ideas, Daniel A. Dreyfus, a longtime legislative aide, divided congressional decisions into "little decisions," called "legislative oversight and policy adjustments," and "major policymaking."[20] Both scholars and participants have seen and felt the existence of levels or layers in political life.

Following this kind of thinking, three different policy games can be said to characterize governmental activity. The "high game" involves deciding on whether or not there is a role for government, the first type of question mentioned above. The "middle game" involves deciding more concretely what that role will be. The "low game" involves the precise design of that role, that is, the choice of the details of its execution.

THE HIGH GAME

Should the government restrict the sale and possession of firearms? Does government support for abortions violate a human being's right to life, or does the failure of government to subsidize abortion services restrict a woman's freedom of choice with respect to her body and her well-being? Should public elementary and secondary educational opportunities be available without regard to the income and wealth of parents, school districts, or states? What are the obligations of the government in providing equal opportunity for handicapped children and adults? Should government spending be permanently restricted to a specific fraction of the gross national product?

These are the kinds of questions characteristic of the high game. The explicit issue is, does society have a problem that requires governmental action? What is the nature of that problem? Do we need more—or less—government? Why?

The nature of the questions that are at the center of the high game, in turn, determines the character and content of high game politics. Debate focuses on the right thing to do, on philosophies of government and the fundamental responsibilities of our institutions, on what kind of nation and society we should be, on social justice and our basic principles. Intense controversy is likely, often fueled by the activities of single-issue constituencies or powerful elites. Participants almost invariably include the president (personally), the leaders of both political parties, and the Supreme Court. Indeed, these officials can hardly avoid being drawn into questions of such importance.[21]

Political executives whose departments are affected by the answers to such questions become participants in the high game, too, though, depending on whether the White House maintains firm control, they may be either major or minor players. It is a dangerous game for them, however, because social values are explicitly at issue; no matter what position they take, their own political and social values will be questioned. The credibility and influence of senior executives may depend on how skillfully and sensitively they handle such issues.

Playing in the high game is a matter of gaining and effectively using access to and influence with the president, the national media, legislative leaders, and powerful private interests. The language and content of the game are predominantly philosophies, values, and ideologies, and the participant must be effective and persuasive in these terms. Success requires an understanding of the broad currents of public opinion, of the larger strategic issues of national politics, and of the influence of large power blocs. For the most part, the high game is played in the open rather than behind the scenes and entails a willing involvement in controversy and the power to persuade and to dramatize.

THE MIDDLE GAME

Should the states or the federal government administer public assistance programs? Should a federal development loan bank be established to aid cities in distress and, if so, what department should administer it? What emissions standards should be applied to new sources of air pollution? Should previous emissions standards be revised in the light of new information and changed values concerning the maintenance of clean air? Should oil and natural gas producers pay taxes at the wellhead? Should drug costs to consumers be controlled by compulsory licensing or by ceilings on reimbursements? Should food stamp recipients be required to purchase their stamps, or should the stamps be given to those eligible to receive them?

These are the kinds of questions characteristic of the middle game. Government must act, and the question now is, what type of action should be taken? How should responsibility be assigned among government agencies and the levels of government? How much should be spent and on what, that is, how should budgetary resources be allocated? Answers will reflect the incidence of benefits and costs and the political power of those who will benefit and those who must pay. The middle game was accurately described by C. Wright Mills twenty-five years ago. "American policies," he said, "as discussed and voted and campaigned for, have largely to do with these middle levels [of power] and often only with them. Most 'political' news is news and gossip about middle-level issues and conflicts."[22]

Primary participants in the middle game include the senior officials of executive departments, senior aides to the chief executive, chairmen of legislative committees and legislators with a special stake or interest in the issue, and organized interest groups, especially those with concrete professional or economic stakes. Debate is about results—that is, the effectiveness and efficiency of governmental actions—about the fairness, appropriateness, and consequences of distributional effects, about administrative competence, and about costs. Debate is likely to be fueled by organized groups acting, at least in significant part, out of self-interest.[23] Controversies and disagreements are probable but, though sharp, they are likely to be less intense. They are more political in the traditional sense, and reasoned compromises are easier to strike.

This is the predominant game for political executives, as well as the bread-and-butter game for legislators. Senior executives are involved in several of them all the time. It is a game, moreover, that they are in a good position to play, though the middle game, too, has its dangers. It is in the middle game, which requires continuous political interaction with other participants, that the problem of divided loyalties arises. In contrast to the high game, playing in the middle game is a matter of establishing effective working relationships with committee and subcommittee chairmen, program officials, and the executive staff of interest groups with high stakes in specific outcomes. It requires familiarity with the basic substantive and political issues associated with programs, budgets, and legislation. It requires a sense of timing and maneuver, opportunism, and an instinct for identifying trade-offs and fashioning attractive compromises.

THE LOW GAME

What accountable period should be used in measuring income for purposes of determining welfare eligibility? How should construction dates for the various features of a water reclamation project be established? How should ambient air quality be measured for purposes of determining compliance with the Clean Air Act? How should cosmetic surgery be distinguished from medically necessary surgery for purposes of determining eligibility for health insurance benefits? What information should be included in the annual program plan required of each state under the Education for All Handicapped Children Act?

These are the kinds of questions associated with the low game. The government must act, and the type of action has largely been determined. The question in this game is, precisely how should the government act? How should eligibility, or standards, or exceptions and exclusions be defined? How should compliance be determined, monitored, and enforced? How should vendors be chosen and payments made? To a much greater extent than in high and middle games, the answers will reflect the judgments of specialists, professionals, and technicians concerning such criteria as administrability, legal sufficiency, costs, personnel availability, controllability, and the like. Low games involve the fine resolution, small-motor processes of government. They tend to reflect the concerns of those with operating responsibilities, whether the concerns be functional—budgeting, enforcement, auditing—or programmatic—administration, staffing, efficacy.

Primary participants in the low game are subcabinet officials, the senior specialists in executive agencies, experts on legislative staffs, and experts associated with interest groups and professional associations. Protracted litigation over the applicability of the law to particular cases may also be part of the low game. Debate and associated controversies are usually highly technical and often inscrutable to nonspecialists.[24] Playing in the low game is a matter of learning how to communicate with experts and technicians and earn their respect and loyalty, of acquiring a feel for the strengths and limitations of expert knowledge and perspectives. If the middle game requires quick political reflexes, the low game requires quick intellectual reflexes and a mastery of, or at least surefootedness with, substance. It also requires a sense of how specialists work, how long it takes them to produce answers to questions, the incentives which motivate them, and the limitations on their perspectives.

The distinctions among these levels of the game are not clear-cut and unambiguous. An issue, for example, may be characterized as a middle game in Washington, D.C., from a federal perspective but as a high game from a state or regional perspective. The Carter administration's attempts to cancel or scale back federal water projects were a middle game to the federal agencies involved in Washington but a high game in the states of the arid West. The question of how much of Alaska's lands should be protected from economic development was also a middle game everywhere but in Alaska, where it was the quintessential high game.

Though the questions central to high, middle, and low games imply both a logical and a chronological order, in reality they need not be played sequentially. Indeed, games of different levels often are played concurrently. While EPA Administrator William Ruckelshaus was playing a middle game on the question of whether the Clean Air Act required a policy of nondegradation, for example, (see chapter 2) specialists from his agency, environmental groups, state agencies, and legislative staffs were simultaneously debating issues concerning the detailed design of approaches to nondegradation. It is possible to argue that debates over governmental policy toward the handicapped were occurring at all three levels simultaneously.

At times, a middle or even a low game may appear to have begun without a high game ever having occurred, though reflection on the historical background of the policy may reveal that the high game was completed years earlier. The Age Discrimination Act of 1975 is a good example of the latter phenomenon. The act ostensibly extended the protection of the Civil Rights Act to older Americans. At one point, the secretary of HEW warned sponsors of the act in the House that it "would leave to the Executive Branch . . . momentous policy decisions in wholly uncharted areas without benefit of any specific legislative guidance."[25] Yet there was no high game associated with passage of the act, though administration witnesses appeared to be indicating that they wanted to play at that level. The president never became involved, nor was much national debate sparked. Instead, the game was played at the middle level. Even at this level, it was brief. The idea was first broached at a congressional hearing early in 1975, and the act was signed by the president in November of that year. "During the entire legislative journey of the ADA, only one legislator, Senator Thomas F. Eagleton (D-Mo.), had bothered to raise important questions about its meaning." In effect, a high game, centered on the question of the governmental role with respect to the problems of older Americans had already been played, largely during the previous ten years, when acts creating Medicare, indexing social security benefits against inflation, creating the Supplemental Security Income program, mandating pension reform, and prohibiting age discrimination in employment had passed and a White House Conference on Aging had occurred.

Nor do issues relating to social values occur only in the high game. Value-laden issues arise at all three levels, but at lower levels they are apt to be unstated, suppressed, or obscured by technical issues. When their significance or implications are realized, however, the game may well escalate to higher levels. At one time, the question of Medicaid coverage for abortions appeared as a relatively technical question, but realization of its implications by groups opposed to abortion rapidly led to the initiation of a high game.

The Political Executive as Gamesman

The political executive must be a game player. Game playing is the nature of the job. Moreover, political executives may have little choice concerning which games they play, with what objectives, or even with what intensity. When he became secretary of the interior, Cecil Andrus had no choice but to play in the game over federal water policies. He was no doubt chosen for the job in part because the president believed that as a westerner (from Idaho), Andrus would be an effective player in that game, in which the president had already made clear his objectives. When he became HEW secretary, Joseph Califano was immediately rushed onto the field in two games: welfare reform, where the president's goal was not clear, and the creation of a federal Department of Education, where it was crystal clear. Whether he relished the prospect or not, EPA Administrator Douglas Costle became involved in rethinking U.S. policies for the maintenance and enhancement of air quality, and Treasury Secretary Michael Blumenthal became involved in federal income tax reform, games which neither might have played had they been free to choose. The president and Congress, acting in response both to internal or institutional interests and to external events such as energy shortages, pressure from governors, or crises abroad, initiate and establish the content and pace of the games senior executives play. "People ask what we're going to do first," observed Neil E. Goldschmidt shortly after becoming secretary of transportation in 1979, "and the answer is, we don't have any choice but to take it all on."[26]

Even when faced with the inevitable, however, political executives usually retain substantial discretion in deciding how to play. HEW Secretary Califano was virtually unmolested in deciding how to tackle welfare reform. His only constraint was a deadline by which a proposal had to be presented to the president, and even that turned out to be quite elastic. How executives use or interpret their discretion in playing the games initiated by the chief executive or the legislature can have a crucial bearing on their success or even tenure in office. Califano's main problem as secretary of HEW, for example, was the irritation of presidential aides with his apparent choice of tactics in such middle games as those associated with obtaining congressional approval of the Department of Education, which Califano personally did not favor, or of creating momentum on behalf of the mental health proposals of a presidential commission sponsored by Rosalyn Carter, where again the secretary exhibited a lack of zeal.

The issue of toxic substances control, that is, the regulation of disease-causing chemicals, offers another example of executive discretion in policy games. Here, the high game issue is largely resolved. In a series of statutes extending from the Food and Drug Act through more recent legislation concerning air and water pollution, carcinogens in drinking water, solid waste disposal, ocean dumping, and occupational health, Congress has declared that government will take action to protect us from disease-causing chemical agents. But how? A middle game began with developments leading to passage in 1977 of the Toxic Substances Control Act, which directed the EPA administrator to formulate a comprehensive approach to the problem. Such an approach would have to involve not only controlling substances such as lead, mercury, benzene, and asbestos, which are known to be hazardous, but detecting potential hazards among thousands of candidate substances so that health hazards can be prevented. The Toxic Substances Control Act left it up to the EPA administrator to determine whether premarket testing for carcinogenicity or other toxic effects should be carried out for new products containing potentially hazardous substances. In May 1980, under court order to expedite the implementation of the act, the EPA published draft regulations covering 500 substances that ran to 2,000 pages. Environmental groups immediately protested that most dangerous chemicals were not covered and that exemptions were too liberal. EPA officials defended them as striking a proper balance between protecting the public and cutting out unnecessary paperwork. A hard-fought middle game was in progress, with the play under the direction of the EPA administration.

Though senior executives must play in certain games, they retain substantial discretion as to whether or not to initiate or participate in many others. Taking advantage of an opening created by Senator Kennedy, for example, Caspar Weinberger chose to play a middle game on the drug cost control issue. He might have attempted to sidestep the issue altogether or to play it another way, such as by insisting that drug cost control be taken up in the larger context of regulatory reform or national health insurance. Instead, he saw an opportunity to achieve a concrete policy objective which he, as a manager, believed would mean tangible budgetary savings for his department, and he played accordingly.

The case of gentian violet[27] illustrates a situation in which political officials were able to keep a game being played at the low level from escalating to a higher level. For twenty-five years, the FDA has questioned the use of the substance gentian violet in products to control infectious diseases in poultry and the growth of mold in animal feed. The high game issue—should the government regulate the marketing of food and drug products?—had, of course, been settled in 1906 with the passage of the Pure Food and Drug Act. A variety of middle game issues had also been resolved. New products that may enter the human food chain cannot be marketed unless first subject to premarket testing, and according to the so-called Delaney Agreement to the Food and Drug Act passed in 1958, no substance may be added to food if it causes cancer in humans or animals. The issue regarding gentian violet is whether products containing it are new products, and thus marketable only if subject to premarket testing for safety and efficacy when ingested by poultry over long periods of time. The FDA decided that products containing gentian violet were indeed new products, and the agency has been repeatedly upheld in the courts. These rulings are ardently opposed not only by the manufacturers of such products but also by the poultry industry, which regards these products as of major importance to its economic well-being.

The FDA rulings, and their affirmation by federal courts, are decisions being made in the low game. Poultry industry spokesmen argue that other mold inhibitors are two or three times more expensive and less effective. The principal FDA officials involved—the director of the Bureau of Veterinary Medicine and officials in the Office of Compliance—are making technical judgments that, though viewed by them as merely enforcing the law, clearly affect the economics of an industry and the viability of several firms within it. However, though a handful of legislators and even the FDA commissioner have worried about whether this is an example of FDA overregulation, thus raising large issues, the game has remained at the low level.

Decisions concerning initiation and participation in middle games are typically less problematic for political executives than two other types of decisions.

The first concerns low game participation. An increasing number of consequential decisions are made in the low game. Such decisions have profound effects on the costs and effectiveness of governmental activity, and no political executive who purports to be concerned about government performance can afford to remain aloof from low games. Further, mistakes in the low game—failures of execution or poor choices—can shift an issue up to the middle level in a way that is distinctly disadvantageous to the political executive. Observed Francis E. Rourke, "The sustained attention which bureaucrats can devote to specific problems gives them a decided advantage in framing policy decisions over political officials who deal with a wide variety of problems and confront each issue of public policy only at sporadic intervals."[28]

Controlling the costs of government and the administrative burdens they impose on others, for example—high game concerns expressed in terms of a Proposition 13 or an amendment to the Constitution requiring a balanced budget—demands involvement in the tediously complex games at the low level. Consider the issues that arose in connection with preparing regulations for implementing the Education for All Handicapped Children Act. To what extent should federal program administration reinforce and protect existing professions and professional practice: changing the term "recreation therapist" to "therapeutic recreation specialist," drawing careful distinctions between the "hard of hearing" and the "deaf," and requiring certification or licensing of all personnel? How much red tape should be required of states and educational agencies? These are issues in a low game, but they are most assuredly policy issues of significance to the performance of government.

Another example of the significance of the low game is the issue of whether clinical psychologists and other psychotherapists should be eligible, as psychiatrists are now, for direct federal reimbursement of services they provide to Medicare recipients. A favorable decision would set an important precedent; if psychologists gain this status, nurses, social workers, and other nonmedically trained professionals who provide care to recipients are sure to follow. Recognizing the implications of allowing direct reimbursement for clinical psychologists' services, Jay Constantine, veteran staff member of the Senate Finance Committee, proposed in October 1979 that different therapies be tested for efficacy over a five-year period just as drugs are tested before being released to the market.[29] Psychologists and other mental health professionals vigorously opposed the proposal, suspecting a plot by psychiatrists, aided and abetted by Dr.

Gerald Klerman, head of the Alcohol, Drug Abuse and Mental Health Administration, to ensure a medical component in any program of psychotherapy. The medical director of the American Psychiatric Association said that physicians support the concept of clinical trials. This is a low game with far-reaching implications for the helping professionals as well as for the recipients of their services.

Most of the policy issues discussed in this book—welfare reform, Clean Air Act implementation, the education of handicapped children, for example—and, in fact, most policy issues of any consequence have important low games associated with their formulation and implementation. These are the games being played by the specialists, by the program administrators, scientists, researchers, and interest group staffs according to the distinctive rules characteristic of games at that level. They are games of enormous significance for governmental competence because, more than the games at other levels, they define the precise terms according to which governmental transactions are conducted.

Political executives must be players in the low games, which is another way of saying that they must become immersed in the substantive problems they confront. But playing at this level poses problems. To play at the low level requires taking the time to understand the work of the specialists and to earn their respect and cooperation. Not all political executives have the ability to play at this level; not all of them have an interest in doing so. Influencing such games, at least on the handful of issues of greatest importance to the executive's program, is a virtual necessity if the executive's management responsibilities are to be properly fulfilled.

The second troublesome choice facing political executives concerns the level at which to play in order to accomplish desired results. Choosing the wrong level can be costly. The long-standing disagreement among welfare reform advocates over whether change should be incremental or comprehensive is basically a disagreement over whether welfare reform should be played as a high game or as a middle game. Repeated attempts to play a high game used up several public officials, whereas reforms achievable at the middle level have been more successful politically. Health care cost containment is a good example of where a public official, in this case President Carter, attempted to play the game at the high level by arousing widespread public concern and a sense of crisis but could not do better than stimulate a middle game in which his cabinet officer was the executive branch's principal protagonist.

The fundamental problem of public management, using the game metaphor, is to recognize which games are being played and which style of play is most appropriate for each. The public manager, then, needs to know how to answer several questions. How can one tell which game is being played? How does a game begin? When is a game over? What are the formal and informal rules of play? Are there winning strategies? Is participation mandatory? If not, when is it advisable or inadvisable to become involved?

Though they are by no means excluded from high or low games, political executives are most often engaged in—or drawn or forced into—middle games; they are naturally found at the middle levels of power. They tend to be most effective and to have the greatest control over outcomes at this, their natural or customary level. Political executives are usually at a distinct disadvantage in playing in games at levels above or below them. The executive content merely to survive will not stray beyond his or her natural level and, for this reason, may not even notice that the other levels exist. The successful executive must play at all levels, however, especially at the low level, where the policy decisions governing day-to-day relationships between government agencies and those whom they intend to affect are made. To do so, political executives must adopt tactics appropriate to the level of the play. They must be good at the kinds of communications outlined above for each game.

Another implication for public management of the game metaphor as it has been presented here is that policy is not merely the province of high-level political officials. Policy making is not a special activity separate from administration or implementation. Policy is being made continuously, at all levels within a governmental organization, at all levels of government, and by all branches of government. "Policies," wrote Carl Freiderich, "are decisions about what to do or not to do in given situations. . . . administrative officials participate continuously and significantly in this process of evolving policy."[30] As Herbert Kaufman put it, "if policy is defined as what is actually done rather than what is said or intended, policy and administration cannot be separated in practice."[31]

Thus, in this view, a congressional authorization committee makes policy when it establishes a program. An appropriation committee makes policy when it decides how much may be spent on the program. The author of regulations that prescribe the qualifications of the personnel who are to be involved in the program is a policy maker, as are those people or groups whose comments on proposed regulations lead to revisions. So are the state officials who design and approve applications for federal grants financed by the authorized and appropriated funds and who thus determine where and to whom program services are to be delivered. So is the judge who decides how congressional intent should be interpreted or what the Constitution requires in a disputed class of cases arising in connection with the use of grant funds. All of these actions are necessary for government to have a particular effect through the transactions it conducts.

Policy making, in other words, when conceived of as the determination of precisely what actions will be taken, is a ubiquitous activity of government. Policy significance impregnates decisions and actions taken at all levels: high, middle, and low. Political executives who would be concerned with policy making must be concerned with activities taking place above, beside, and below them, with games at all levels. Policy making is virtually indistinguishable from public management.

Acceptance of this proposition provides a powerful motive for rethinking the proper relationships among participants at different levels of the executive branch. Decisions taken at different levels should somehow be interrelated. Competence in government is a matter of establishing patterns of communication and mutual influence from high to low levels of the game. Improving governmental competence requires, among other things, improving these patterns of communication and mutual influence. This is the subject of the concluding chapter.

CHAPTER 7

Improving Governmental Competence

POLITICAL EXECUTIVES are central to the performance of government. Their formal authority is the basis for many of its most important actions, and their competence and judgment shape the content and ultimate effect of those actions. Neither the president and his assistants, nor the staffs and committees of Congress, nor federal judges are as well positioned as are these executives to take the time to direct and manage the activities of government so as to accomplish public purposes.

The demands on these executives continue to grow. Congress continues to load additional responsibilities of all kinds on them with little regard for order, coherence, or consistency. Further, the specific responsibilities increase in substantive, technical, and administrative complexity. Whether the task is to create a new industry, solve a newly discovered social problem, fix a broken-down program, or make existing governmental machinery work better, the political executives in charge have to contend with the pressures of being, in effect, the architects of accountability.

Though they are given formal responsibility for countless tasks of real consequence, these executives at the same time face continual frustration in their attempts to assemble the power and resources to accomplish them.

Because of the centrifugal forces that diffuse their authority to act, political executives' performance continues to be judged by diverse and conflicting criteria. For this reason, they may experience considerable confusion in deciding how to judge their own performance—in choosing, in other words, which games to play and how to play them.

Conflicting Expectations

The more popular view of the standards that ought to guide the behavior of political executives is that executives are first and foremost *presidential aides.* From this perspective, the central question facing each one is, "How can I most effectively serve and support the president?"

In laying the foundation for the institutional reforms that are the framework of the modern presidency, the Brownlow Committee asserted:

> . . . the President is the Chief Executive and administrator within the Federal system and service. In many types of government these duties are divided or only in part combined, but in the United States they have always been united in one and the same person whose duty it is to perform all of these tasks.[1]

Enabling the president to be commander in chief of all of the activities of government was the theme of subsequent committees and commissions formed to study the presidency, from the first Hoover Commission to President Johnson's Task Force on Government Organization and President Nixon's Advisory Council on Executive Organization.

In questioning the command perspective of the presidency, Richard E. Neustadt has argued that the sharing of power among the separate institutions of government places inherent limits on the president's ability to command the departments and agencies. Presidential power, he argues, is in reality the power to persuade, the power to bargain with others in the game, including subordinate officials in the executive branch. As far as these officials are concerned,

> operating agencies owe their existence least of all to one another—and only in some part to [the President]. Each has a separate statutory base; each has its statutes to administer; each deals with a different set of subcommittees at the Capitol. . . . The more an officeholder's status and his "powers" stem from sources independent of the President, the stronger will be his potential pressure *on* the President. Depart-

ment heads in general have more bargaining power than do most members of the White House staff; but bureau chiefs may have still more, and specialists at upper levels of established career services may have almost unlimited reserves of enormous power which consists of sitting still.[2]

Thus the president cannot command them to see things his way. He must persuade them, using the various means at his disposal, to view their own interests as closely allied to his.

But persuasion is time-consuming, and presidents and their immediate staffs become impatient with it. They want to assume the prerogative to command. Much of the thinking concerning the president as general manager of the government has been devoted to identifying techniques and instruments of central direction and coordination, that is, to widening presidential influence and strengthening presidential control over the executive departments and agencies. The results are reflected in the dramatic growth in the size, complexity, and ambitions of the Executive Office of the President since Franklin Roosevelt's time. They are also reflected in the propensity of presidents to adopt sweeping administrative reforms—PPBS, MBO, and ZBB were all supported by the full weight of the presidency —which would enhance their control over subordinate officials and agencies.

Thus, though the Brownlow Committee insisted that the expanded White House staff they were recommending—six new assistants—"would not be interposed between the President and the heads of his departments,"[3] the Executive Office has assumed a size and an institutional presence that appear to place departmental officials in a subordinate role to dozens of his plenipotentiary assistants, all seeking to augment the president's ability to command. President Carter, for example, announced three days after he was inaugurated that "the major decisions will be made ultimately by me as President, which is my constitutional prerogative."

Why not minimize the need to cajole and persuade subordinates by appointing people who are imbued with loyalty to the president from the outset? Why not make the Executive Office of the President the focal point of executive branch loyalty and leadership? McGeorge Bundy has made this argument most explicitly:

. . . what is wrong is that the Cabinet office is still not understood at all levels, and by all hands, as truly presidential in its character and power. . . . In its relation to the White House it must be at once highly autonomous and deeply responsive. It is political, but only in the President's interest. It is managerial, but only on the President's terms . . . a Secretary should never choose his departmental interest as against the wider interest of the Presidency. At a test—unless he means to resign

—the Secretary should always be the President's agent in dealing with the bureau-cracy, not the other way around.[4]

Bundy's view is fully consistent with what presidents want. Presidents have a political and psychological need for loyalty. The president as chief executive wants to establish a chain of command from the White House through the cabinet secretaries to the subordinate career officials.[5] The aim is to achieve political responsibility and, as the Brownlow Committee put it, coordination through hierarchy. According to this view, a president should not have to persuade the members of the cabinet to do anything; loyalty to the presidential office should be taken for granted.

A second and altogether different perspective on political executives is that they should be viewed primarily as *heads of their organizations*. In this view, the central question facing each is, "How should I manage my organization to achieve effective performance?"

Viewed in their role as organizational managers, political executives should act both as leaders and as administrators, that is, they should both articulate purpose and see to its execution. The latitude to do either is limited, however, because these executives typically assume responsibility from positions outside of the organization and do not stay long in their government jobs.[6] Thus the incoming executive who wants to achieve the power to direct department activities—who wants, in other words, to have followers—must actively court and cultivate his or her subordinates in an effort to gain influence both with them and, through them, with their network of contacts in and out of government.

There are relatively few well-developed ideas about how the political executive can fulfill the role of organizational manager in a sense other than executing presidential commands. Two are particularly worth noting in light of the complexity of political executives' responsibilities. Based on a decade of high-level public service in foreign affairs, Harlan Cleveland in *The Future Executive* offers this view:

> The organizations that get things done will no longer be hierarchical pyramids with most of the real control at the top. They will be *systems*—interlaced webs of tension in which control is loose, power diffused, and centers of tension plural. "Decision-making" will become an increasingly intricate process of multilateral brokerage both inside and outside the organization which thinks it has the respon-sibility for making, or at least announcing, the decision. Because organizations will be more horizontal, the way they are governed is likely to be more collegial, consensual, and consultative.[7]

Michael Maccoby and his colleagues offer a complementary notion of an ideal leadership style for government based on their study of management and work behavior in the Department of Commerce. The ideal leader shows concern

for service to society and the professional and personal development of those who work with him. In areas where he maintains authority such a leader explains the reasons for decisions. When he invites participation, he attempts to develop consensus by rational argument and systematic study based on principles of human development—security, equity, participation, and individuation, pragmatically applied. . . . Given the realities of power in the government, which is by law vested in certain positions, such a leader can at best combine structured consultation with participative study of problems and design of control systems.[8]

When developed in the context of business organizations, views of this general character have come to be associated with the term "contingency theory." The idea is that prescriptions for organizational effectiveness are contingent upon the organization's environment and context, that is, the system of interrelationships in which the organization is enmeshed. Paul R. Lawrence and Jay W. Lorsch, whose ideas are based on a study of how large, complex business organizations adapt to changing technology and markets, argue that "the essential organizational requirements for effective performance of one task under one set of economic and technical conditions may not be the same as those for other tasks with different circumstances."[9] They see private corporations afflicted to an increasing extent by rapid changes in technology and markets and therefore becoming more complex.

All the evidence of this and other research points to the need for multiple leadership in these complex organizations. As they cope with heterogeneous and dynamic environments, the issues and knowledge involved become too complicated for only a few leaders to understand.[10]

The problem of leaders in these complex organizations is "to create and use multiple centers and multiple styles of leadership"[11] within a general framework of purpose that guides the separate parts.

A useful translation of this idea to the public management context is that political executives must know the state of play at each level of policy making and be purposeful albeit selective participants at all levels. This is the practical meaning of the term "multiple styles of leadership."

A third perspective on criteria for executive performance, and the most recent to emerge, views political executives in relation to *the issues they must face and the decisions they must make.* The key question from this perspective is, "How can I be an effective policy maker?"

This perspective is the chief legacy of the management reform movements of the 1960s and 1970s, which made planning, policy analysis, and program evaluation central activities in departmental management. Most incoming executives inherit a policy, planning, or program evaluation staff, perhaps headed by an assistant secretary.[12] The executive is expected to rely on this staff in leading the department's policy-making activities. In contrast to the executive who is frightened by any form of intellectual discussion, who is briefed on the run, and who reads only highly condensed digests of available information if he or she reads anything at all, the policy maker is a thoughtful, rational actor who becomes immersed in the substance of important issues. Because most of these issues are at once technically complex and politically prickly, they must be carefully, rationally, and dispassionately studied before judgments that are sound both politically and technically can be made.

It is often claimed that the rational actor, that is, the intellectual executive who seeks to identify the best policy through systematic thought and analysis, then implement it, is largely an academic fiction. Yet Robert McNamara was conceded to be such an executive, as were James Schlesinger and Elliot Richardson. Of Richardson it has been said:

He is by nature analytical . . . a man who wants to approach problems objectively [and] who is perfectly willing to put aside for a time the obvious and sometimes overwhelming political forces that may be pushing him in certain directions in order to think carefully through what the problem is and determine whether or not or how he wants to operate, what proposals he wants to make, how he wants to rationalize the positions he wants to take.[13]

Less publicized but equally adept at rational policy making infused with good political judgment have been political executives such as William Ruckelshaus, Caspar Weinberger, and Douglas Costle. Indeed, President Jimmy Carter has often been regarded as a prototypical rational actor. In July 1976, following his nomination, he gave the following account of the process he intended to follow in making policy decisions.

Exact procedure is derived to some degree from my scientific or engineering background—I like to study first all the efforts that have been made historically toward the same goal, to bring together advice or ideas from as wide or divergent points of view as possible, to assimilate them personally or with a small staff, to assess the quality of the points of view and identify the source of those proposals and, if I think the source is worthy, then to include that person or entity into a group I then call in to help me personally to discuss the matter in some depth. Then I make a general decision about what should be done involving time schedules, necessity for legislation, executive acts, publicity to be focused on the issue. Then I like to assign task forces to work on different aspects of the problem, and I like to be personally involved so that I can know the thought processes that go into the final decisions and also so that I can be a spokesman, without prompting, when I take my case to the people, the legislature or Congress.[14]

From this perspective, the political executive's primary responsibility is to understand the substance of issues and to make the right decisions and recommendations. Though such a view might sound bureaucratically and politically naive, it is viewed by its proponents as having considerable practical value. Depending on an analytically based decision-making process, Charles Schultze argued, "improves the capability of the agency head to shape the program of his agency, and increases his power relative to his operating subordinates."[15] In other words, "policy" or "program," rather than "president" or "organization," is the senior executive's proper preoccupation.

Political executives who adopt any one of these roles to the exclusion of the others soon discover that the different perspectives are essentially in conflict. A cabinet officer who, acting as a loyal presidential aide, resolutely seeks in a determined way to translate presidential wishes into departmental action, no matter what the objections that subordinates may offer, is driven to an authoritarian style of leadership that is counterproductive to being an effective organizational leader. Feeling that they are neither heard nor respected, subordinates passively or actively resist directives that are forced on them without discussion. However, a senior executive who is sensitive to his or her subordinates' views and who takes the time to achieve agreement through persuasion and compromise is apt to be regarded as "going native" by the president and his staff and therefore lose their support. Such an organizationally minded executive may also be regarded as too political by his or her policy advisers and thus may see high-quality advice drying up as analysts and planners go elsewhere or seek other clients for their work. A senior executive dedicated to optimal policy and to making the right program decisions is likely to be seen as politically naive or too technocratic, and thus faces deteriorating relationships all around.

Conscientious political executives feel pressures to strike a balance among all these roles. They realize that they must serve as aides and advisers to the president and as members of a partisan administration accountable to those who elected it. At the same time, they realize, in a way that executive office staff assistants do not, that they must supervise and bear a significant measure of responsibility for the productive functioning of their organizations. Further, they learn that they must direct or participate in the substantive aspects of the tasks assigned them by the president, by Congress, and by the courts. It is these multiple and conflicting imperatives, and the personal and practical tensions they create, that make the political executive's job unique and uniquely difficult.

Choosing to shape and judge their performance by criteria derived from this balanced perspective confronts political executives with a dilemma, however. No one else judges them in the same balanced terms. To the president and his staff, competence in other roles is valued only to the extent that the executive's loyalty to presidential concerns, as defined in the executive office, is not fundamentally compromised. The political executive's subordinates, in contrast, will ask whether he or she is there to "do a job," that is, to understand and cooperate with them in carrying out their programmatic responsibilities or merely to transmit directives from above. The committees of Congress present no consistent incentives for performance, and the political executive is judged on the Hill now by one standard, now by another.

Faced with confusing and conflicting signals, their authority disintegrating under centrifugal forces, and nearly overwhelmed by the pressures of the job, it is no wonder that political executives are tempted or driven into paths of least resistance, investing their energies in hobbies such as sexy new initiatives and favored programs, in traveling and speech making, and in passive reliance on advice that comes their way from sources they trust or fear. Small wonder, too, that government executives as a group enjoy little prestige as managers and that the public has little confidence in government.

Perhaps the ingredients for effective management of governmental organizations cannot be assembled or the centrifugal political forces overcome. The Constitution did not provide for strong general management in the executive branch, and neither presidents nor congressional committees perceive it to be in their interest to enhance the power of departmental and agency executives. Yet persistence in the creation of impossible jobs is likely in the decades ahead to produce the same results as in the past: desultory executive performance, irresistible urges to try technical and procedural fixes that preclude continuity and stability of administration, and deepening disillusionment with governmental competence that corrodes the capacities to lead in all public officials. The question seems urgent: Can anything be done about it?

Presidential Prerogatives versus
Governmental Performance

During the crisis created by the Iranian taking of American hostages, following his decision to expel Iranian students from the United States, President Jimmy Carter gave an order that no demonstrations by Iranian students were to be permitted on federal property. Yet demonstrations did occur, despite his order, and the president found himself on the phone with a number of worried officials discussing these incidents. "I've never chewed ass over mistakes—we all make mistakes," Carter was reported to have said to his staff with heat. "But when I give an order, I don't want to have to spend 12 hours on it the rest of the day."[16] To his cabinet he said on another occasion, "Once a decision is made, I will not tolerate opposition or unenthusiastic support from people involved in that decision."[17] "Poor Jimmy," Harry Truman would have said. "He will give an order and then have to spend the next 12 hours or the next 12 months saying that he really meant it."

On another occasion, Carter vetoed a military procurement authorization bill. An OMB paper accompanying the veto message labeled several cuts Congress had made in the defense budget as "injurious to national security" and recommended that the cuts be restored. It turned out, as the press duly reported, that some of the cuts had been agreed to by administration officials in the Department of Defense. Others were not cuts at all; funds had simply been shifted from one part of the defense budget to another. In still other instances, cuts were in reality deferrals of authorizations which Congress promised to approve if needed later.[18] The enumeration of OMB mistakes indicated that the staff people who had prepared the paper were simply unfamiliar with the routine communications between the Defense Department and Congress. Their unfamiliarity served to erode the credibility of a president who was attempting simultaneously to hold the federal budget in check and to increase necessary defense spending. The flawed veto message suggested the White House was not fully competent in attending to either goal.

Presidents want to exercise full command: over the subordinate officials of the executive branch and over the information needed to make decisions. They want to establish the rules and control the players in policy-making games of all levels. As government has grown in complexity, obstacles to the exercise of command have proliferated, and as middle and low games have become more remote from the Oval Office, recent presidents have sought to offset the erosion of their control over their administrations by enforcing on subordinate executives binding agreements of loyalty and by installing elaborate reporting and clearance systems designed to meet the needs of the growing ranks of budget examiners, management specialists, and special assistants who have been deployed to defend presidential prerogatives.

The result, however, has been to sever the presidential office from its natural root system in the executive branch. Presidents determined to command and impatient with subordinate bureaucracies have sought to create an alternate root system extending through the Executive Office of the President, in particular through OMB and the DPS staff, and the Office of Legislative Liaison directly to Congress, external interest groups, the press, and other sources of political support. These roots are shallow, however, and ultimately inadequate to sustain the president in the design and pursuit of a successful program for his administration. The Executive Office of the President can never be made large enough to fully substitute for the resources of information, experienced personnel, and contacts with reality to be found in executive departments and agencies.

The importance of the resources of the executive branch in achieving governmental competence is accelerating. The pace and significance of change in the immediate working environment of governmental organizations in recent years have been dramatic.[19] These changes include, for example, the increasing volume of legislation and administrative regulations; the greater turnover in Congress, reducing the number of experienced senior members; the great increase in the number and competence of congressional staffs; the weakening role of political parties as instruments for ensuring member discipline and cohesion, and the concomitant decline in the authority of the Speaker of the House and the power of many committee chairmen; the greater number and complexity of the issues before Congress (100 recorded votes per session in the early 1960s, 700 recorded votes in 1971);[20] the advent of the congressional budget process; the expanded role of the GAO; the new ethics rules; and the steadily growing use of the tax code to achieve programmatic objectives.

Of equal significance are the more esoteric changes in procedures, practices, and personalities that have altered the context of legislation and program administration: the increased number of oversight hearings (700–800 per session for both the House and the Senate, up from 300–400 twenty years earlier); the increased use of the suspension calendar and of the "modified open rule" on tax bills in the House; the increased number of subcommittees, including the addition of subcommittees to the House

Ways and Means Committee (and the increased number of members on that committee, from twenty-four to thirty-seven in 1974); the opening of legislative mark-up sessions to the public, with the attendant reduction in member dependence on professional committee staffs and increased reliance on their personal aides; the shift in power over Democratic Committee appointments from the Democratic members of the House Ways and Means Committee to the Democratic Policy and Steering Committee; changing relationships between committee chairmen and the ranking minority members; the increased use of recorded votes; increasing resort to the legislative veto (295 legislative veto provisions in force in 1975, over half of which had been enacted since 1968);[21] the appointment to committee chairmanships of younger members, who are less bound by party loyalty and led more by their own instincts.

The significance of such changes in the public management environment can be seen in the defeat of President Carter's proposal to control rising hospital costs. The proposal had to be approved by four different legislative subcommittees, each with different views about the proposal and each with younger members who were not susceptible to party or parent committee discipline. David Stockman, for example, was a freshman Republican in the House from Michigan at the time and the author of a much-quoted and respected critique of congressional behavior on domestic programs that coined the term "social pork barrel."[22] Of Carter's cost control bill, he said, "My real design was to offer amendments to dramatize and point out that the whole approach was defective. I wanted to allow it to sink of its own weight."[23] On the other side was Congressman Andrew Maguire, a second-term Democrat from New Jersey with a Harvard Ph.D. He had recruited a cadre of staff specialists and the aid of no-cost fellows from the Robert Wood Johnson Foundation to help him. According to reports, "Joe Onek, a presidential aide on hospital cost matters . . . went to have lunch with Maguire one day and ended up in something akin to a seminar. Maguire took his experts along to lunch."[24] With respect to HEW's role, an HEW health adviser said:

[HEW Secretary] Joe [Califano] took on the hospitals in a personal way. I think he assumed the people of the United States felt the same way. But this was an issue that had to be negotiated and compromised. Joe seemed unable to compromise or unwilling to do it himself or to delegate it out. The real compromises as we went along were the work of the Congressional people.[25]

The result was that the president and his HEW secretary failed to get anything like the cost controls they wanted. They had been badly outplayed in the middle and low games by, among other people, young congressmen and their aides who would not have been in the game a few years earlier. The significance of such changes for an administration's legislative and managerial prospects is likely to be accurately detected first by the permanent government, by the specialized agencies and bureaucracies, by the players in the low game. For the president and his program, therefore, it is important that the Executive Office establish effective working relationships with the departments and agencies through both formal and informal mechanisms. The objective of these relationships should not be to dominate communications, to place a presidential transmitter in every subordinate bureau, as Richard Nixon tried to do. Nor should it be to delegate sensitive political issues to subordinates with divided loyalties, thus placing the president at risk. Rather, it should be to maintain contact with the governmental system—to receive as well as transmit—to build up interdependence and trust far down in the executive structure, and to maintain the president's capacity to play and influence the middle and low games likely to determine the fate of his policies.

The president's overriding goal as chief executive of the government must be to convert political executives who may first appear in his office as representatives of competing and partisan bureaucratic interests into members of a united administration. The most difficult aspect of this task is to establish himself, together with his most trusted White House advisers, on a common wavelength with his political executives and to become a working member of his own administration. Don K. Price has stated the need succinctly:

For political accountability as well as for effective management we must try to reverse the tendency by which the President seeks (or is obliged by Congressional pressure) to build his Executive Office into a command post controlling the details of executive business. As he does so Congressional committees are therefore tempted to try to cut down his flexible discretionary control over his staff agencies and over the Cabinet and Cabinet committees. Each of these two tendencies is accentuated by the other—a vicious circle that has diminished the utility of the Executive Office and the public accountability of the executive departments.[26]

How well the president achieves this management goal depends in large measure on how he organizes his advisory process. Every president faces this task. Moreover, every president designs a different advisory system depending on such personality variables as his cognitive style, sense of efficacy, and orientation toward conflict.[27] It is generally recognized that a policy making system must be adaptable to presidential style and preferences. Lyndon Johnson, for example, had no formal system, preferring to give general instructions to his key White House aides, then support them in their efforts, which often completely bypassed cabinet officers, to weld together an administration position. Richard Nixon employed a rather elaborate formal system, especially in foreign policy, that operated through hierarchically organized coordination mechanisms strictly orchestrated by his White House staff. Gerald Ford, according to his OMB Director James T. Lynn, "recognized that people don't put all of their thinking down on paper. He loved to get a good debate going, to get the views and nuances he had not gotten in the memos. It really was a very collegial style of decisionmaking."[28] Jimmy Carter's system has been described as founded on

a paradox at the highest level of the administration: a President who simultaneously seeks to retain policy decisions—large and small—for himself while following through on his promise to give his Cabinet a large policy-making role. . . . Decentralization of power to the Cabinet and the White House staff, combined with final decision-making authority in the Oval Office itself, has left the Administration with a multitude of semi-autonomous fiefdoms, quarreling bitterly among themselves and speaking with different voices to the public.[29]

Perhaps more than any other, however, the Carter administration's experience demonstrates that a conscious effort must be made to design a disciplined policy-making system with the president's needs in mind. More than any recent president, Carter made a good-faith attempt to make cabinet government a reality. In the process he demonstrated that, at least in its more literal interpretations, it is a fundamentally unworkable notion.

But too much has been made of the need to adapt policy-making systems to the operating style of the president. Not enough attention has been paid to the desirability of the president's adapting his style to the needs of his administration as a whole, that is, to the needs of his political executives that grow out of the multiple roles they must play. This is even more difficult to achieve at the highest level of government because of the balkanization of the executive branch, which makes it virtually impossible to delegate any major issue to the exclusive jurisdiction of a single department. The trick is to obtain sufficient collegiality among the executives of the individual agencies with a stake in an issue so that they can put their specialized political and programmatic perspectives in the service of the president without dissolving into hostile, narrow-minded factions. This is an achievable goal, but only if the president is determined to create the conditions necessary for collegiality to flourish. He is most likely to do so by taking the time to work through policy problems with his political executives, to establish working relationships of substance with them on issues all regard as important. By the questions he asks and the quality of the answers he insists upon, he is establishing performance criteria for his political executives. Political executives who must demonstrate reasonableness and competence to the president personally perform differently than executives whose main contact with the president is through staff memoranda that are screened by White House staff advisers. Presidents who work personally with political executives find that they receive advice of higher quality than if they rely on briefing books prepared by their staffs to educate themselves on the substance of issues.

An equally overlooked ingredient of effective presidential management is the encouragement and support the White House gives to political executives' efforts to manage their own departments. It is to little avail if the president and his staff establish good working relationships with executives who are unable to maintain close contact with their own organizations or to develop the ability to direct their activities. By controlling the timing, content, and purpose of policy discussions, the president and his principal assistants can provide powerful incentives to senior executives to assume effective leadership positions in the departments. If the White House seeks merely to coerce subordinate agencies into strict obedience to an arbitrary command and control system, they may destroy even the possibility of effective departmental management.

A case in point occurred during the Nixon administration. In an attempt to translate Richard Nixon's theme of a New Federalism into political reality at HEW, Secretary Elliot Richardson forwarded a major departmental reform proposal to the White House in 1972.[30] He had used the rationale incorporated in this proposal in fashioning his budget request to OMB. Even though that request was within OMB's ceiling, OMB followed its traditional practice of assembling the diverse views and approaches of its various budget examiners, modifying them somewhat, ensuring their conformity with the overall ceiling, and forwarding them to the department as its budget allowance.[31] The effect was to undercut the newly developed rationale on dozens of issues that were in no sense presidential.

Recognizing the importance of an effective advisory process, the Carter administration conducted a review of Executive Office decision-making processes only a few months into his term.[32] The basis for the review was a set of case studies on how specific policy decisions were reached. One of these studies, "The Case of the Missing Shoe Import Option," revealed that one policy option finally chosen by the president—an Orderly Marketing Agreement with Korea and Taiwan covering imported nonrubber footwear—had been included in early staff papers, then disappeared without a trace, and was not included in the final staff paper sent to the president by his special trade representative. The option reemerged at a meeting with the president during which a politically sensitive White House staff aide argued its merits. The president endorsed it, noting that he wished he had gotten the advice earlier, but this unleashed a last-minute blizzard of memos from the affected agencies advocating other courses of action. Among the conclusions drawn from the study were (1) the necessity for a structured domestic policy review process similar to one employed by the NSC; and (2) "a strong, permanent government expertise exists and is there to be used." A senior aide remarked that "we don't have to duplicate the rest of the government here at the White House; we only have to be smart enough and humble enough to draw on it."

Had this advice been incorporated into presidential and executive office routines for communicating with subordinate officials, many of the policy mistakes of the Carter administration might have been averted.

Choosing Executives

Presidents can further the cause of governmental competence in another way. Choosing the right people is obviously crucial to improving executive performance in government. But what are the traits, characteristics, or attributes of senior executives who can fulfill the role inherent in their offices? For the most part, appointments have been based on the president's desire for loyalty, on the need to maintain relationships with important constituencies or to acquire specific political skills such as influencing Congress, or on the desire to appoint individuals who are prestigious or who symbolize an administration's political intentions. While the criteria for appointments include the executive, intellectual, and personal capacities needed for effective performance of specific jobs, these criteria all too frequently count for less in the making of the final choice than the others.

Yet, as Lewis A. Dexter has observed, "The most important instrument with which the leader has to work is himself—his own personality and the impression which he creates on other people."[33] George P. Schultz and Kenneth W. Dam, veterans of high-level service in the Executive Office of the President, argue:

The exact organizational form of the coordination mechanism is usually far less important than is commonly supposed, especially when the interests of large departmental bureaucracies are at stake. . . . what count more than the structure of the coordinating mechanism are the personal qualities of the key officials and their ability to work together. . . . Team spirit may be regarded by academics and pundits as a hackneyed concept; but nothing is more important for effective policy-making, especially in difficult periods.[34]

The president has a vital stake in the personal qualities of the people he appoints and in their individual capacities to carry out their responsibilities. Because these responsibilities are unique, he is well advised to go beyond their professional and political credentials to seek individuals who are likely to be personally well matched to the roles they will play.

Studies of leadership and decision making have sought to identify the characteristic traits of leaders, such as intelligence, achievement, and dependability. Earlier studies of leadership traits demonstrated the difficulty of identifying a stable and reliable set of such traits. Recent work has sought to identify personality and motivational traits associated with leadership effectiveness in formal organizations, especially at the highest levels. E. E. Ghiselli, for example, identifies traits especially related to managerial success, including supervisory ability, need for occupational achievement, need for self-actualization, decisiveness, and lack of need for job security.[35]

Another trait likely to be important to performance as a manager and decision maker is an individual's cognitive style. Relatively recent developments in cognitive psychology suggest the appropriateness of viewing the human mind as an information-processing system.[36] Individuals differ widely in the types and complexity of the structures—beliefs, images, or other models and ideas about reality—they use to process information and in the ways in which they create, modify, or validate these structures, that is, learn. But all individuals need such mental constructs in order to make sense of what otherwise would be an overwhelming amount of information, and they are of great significance in decision making. James L. McKenney and Peter G. W. Keen have developed what they call a "model of cognitive style."[37] Their idea is that people differ fundamentally both in how they process and in how they evaluate information. With respect to processing, *preceptive* individuals test incoming sensory data against preformed concepts, whereas *receptive* thinkers focus more on the details and are more inductive in interpreting them. With respect to evaluation, *intuitive* thinkers employ trial-and-error methods and respond to cues in ways they are not always able to verbalize; *systematic* thinkers structure and analyze information using explicit methods or algorithms. The authors' central argument is that

decisionmaking is above all situational and, therefore, includes problem finding. The manager scans his environment and organizes what he perceives. His efforts are as much geared to clarifying his values and intents as to dealing with predefined problems.[38]

McKenney and Keen further postulate that thinkers of a particular type are better suited to some management contexts than to others. For example, intuitive thinkers may have trouble mastering details that must be understood in methodical sequences, but they may perform well when information is lacking, problems are unstructured, and uncertainties are dominant. Thus some exceedingly bright officials are intuitive and preceptive, reacting with impatience to carefully structured, systematic staff work, appearing to shoot from the hip, quickly and restlessly tossing out ideas and proposals, and making up their minds in a seemingly unsystematic way. Their solutions nonetheless may be good ones, even inspired ones, considering the complexity and pressure of many decision situations. Good middle game players, who use their intuitive abilities to discover compromises, may do poorly in low games, where more systematic thinking is needed; likewise, good low game players may perform poorly in middle games.

It is also important to recognize that incoming information is likely to be processed in a way that fulfills a decision maker's emotional needs, for example, the need for continuity of beliefs, for simplicity, and for certainty.[39] A decision maker may ignore factors or events of obvious importance, be unwilling to consider opposing arguments or views, or shift ground repeatedly in maintaining commitment to a course of action that is consistent with ingrained beliefs or images of reality. Unanticipated problems, complex trade-offs, and evidence inconsistent with a chosen course of action may go unrecognized or literally unrecorded in the decision maker's mind. These tendencies may serve certain executives well, as when they persevere in the face of numerous distractions to reach a solution that works; alternatively, they may lead to outcomes that are self-destructive because of the decision maker's inability to change his or her views or alter incorrect beliefs.

Though elusive, attributes such as personality, emotional makeup, and cognitive style can be crucial to an executive's performance. That this is so is suggested by an often-voiced critique of President Jimmy Carter. Columnist Joseph Kraft observed, for example, that "Carter and his advisers seem far less acute than most men of experience in detecting implicit contradictions, in seeing the tension (which characterizes most serious problems) between one good claim and another good claim." Thus they choose the right course of action on each separate issue, then allow events to impose the trade-offs.[40] Columnists Rowland Evans and Robert Novak have said of Carter, "Comfortable in the role of engineer, he carefully considers both sides. But he resists the final stage of decision-making, preferring to live with contradictory alternatives."[41] Said former Congressman John Brademas:

Carter tended to think comprehensively and rationally, not that we think irrationally, but Carter tended to say, "Okay, what's the problem? Let's analyze it, look at the pros and cons, what's best for the country?" Then he'd say, "We're going to have a comprehensive this and a comprehensive that." We don't operate that way. We're piecemeal incrementalists.[42]

By way of contrast to a cognitive style in which interrelationships are ignored, Elliot Richardson became well known among his associates for his elaborate doodles, created with blue felt-tipped pens during meetings and lengthy conversations. "You can see the way he thinks even in doodles," said long-time Richardson aide Richard Darman. "Nothing is left loose, everything connects when it's done like a well-wrought synthesis. Elliot's always struggling to see the interrelationship between things in any issue."[43] One of Richardson's objections to the MBO process was that "no attempt was made to relate the objectives to each other, much less to make them mutually reinforcing."[44]

An assessment of executive leadership at the Department of Agriculture under Secretary Bob Bergland suggests the cumulative effects on organizational performance that can flow from the personal shortcomings of top executives. Though praised and admired by many associates and representatives of agricultural interests, Bergland was also described as "over his head," away from his office a great deal, and capable of making three serious misstatements during a one-hour press briefing (though friends explained that he was tired following a long trip). The deputy secretary post was left vacant for six months, so much of the day-to-day direction of departmental activities during one period was supplied by the director of economics, policy analysis, and budget. That official was described as having aggressively accumulated authority but also as being an individual who "would be overworked if he had just two pieces of paper on his desk —that's how exhaustively he goes into things."[45] Another official, an assistant secretary who was a rival for internal authority in the department, was described as excessively stiff and aloof. Said a Washington businessman involved in agriculture, this assistant secretary "receives calls from 4 to 4:30—as if he were the pope."[46] The result of such deficiencies in personal skill and operating style was an impression among many, including Congress and the press, that the department was in disarray, slow to act, lacking a "strong profile."

Expecting the electorate to choose among presidential candidates on the basis of the subtleties of intellectual and managerial capacities is unrealistic. Far more should be expected, however, in the case of political executive appointments. Does this mean that candidates for such jobs should be submitted to a battery of tests and a psychological evaluation? This would clearly be impractical. Nor is there an ideal administrative personality against which candidates for senior positions can be measured. If there are proven common qualities, they may reduce to simple factors such as successful executive experience in a government organization and some familiarity with the substantive domain of the agency.

Upon being elected governor of Minnesota in 1976, however, Albert Quie made an attempt to incorporate leadership qualities and cognitive style into his appointment process. In asking candidates for positions as agency heads to fill out a nine-page form, he was seeking evidence of specific skills, interests, and problem-solving ability more than information on educational background and employment history. Valued attributes included willingness to take management risks, ability to create order out of chaos, and capacity to think on one's feet. Depending on self-assessments for such information has its shortcomings, but the idea that such dimensions should be seriously evaluated in the recruitment process is an idea whose time has been long in coming.

Being an Executive

When all else fails, as it often will, what can political executives do to help themselves? Against the pull of centrifugal forces, how should they do their jobs? If the system is not the solution but taking the time to manage is, then how should this time be spent?

When Neil Goldschmidt, Charles Duncan, and Moon Landrieu assumed their cabinet posts in September 1979, Mark Green, director of Congress Watch, offered them the following advice:

. . . if you want to leave something behind besides your official portraits, . . . develop a theme. Take a stand at the start. . . . Reach into, and motivate, the bureaucracy. . . . Develop a constituency. . . . unless the Cabinet official cultivates a supportive constituency, he will lack the roots to survive the first gusts of criticism and controversy. . . . Talk to your critics—but have your press office answer them.[47]

These are valuable suggestions. Executives can do much to help themselves toward effective performance by being purposeful and open.

These admonitions echo the body of studies, heavily influenced by the human relations school, that has sought to identify the behavior of effective leaders. The Ohio leadership studies, for example, conclude that two types of leader behavior are important:

. . . the leader's behavior in delineating the relationship between himself and members of the work group and in endeavoring to establish well-defined patterns of organization, channels of communication, and methods of procedure . . . [and] behavior indicative of friendship, mutual trust, respect, and warmth in the relationship between the leader and the members of his staff.[48]

Frequency and clarity of communications and respect for subordinates are, then, to be endorsed as ingredients in effective leadership, though they could hardly be characterized as sufficient conditions for executive success. If political executives choose to remain aloof, to play exclusively in the middle and high games, they will find that they exercise little or no influence on operations and therefore have a substantially weakened role in shaping what government actually does. "To get control of policy," as Herbert Kaufman puts it, "it is necessary to get control of administration."[49]

What, then, are the techniques of departmental leadership and management that would enable the political executive to "get control of administration"?[50] How can this be done in a manner consistent with the political executive's multiple roles?

In the early 1970s, top executives at HEW and at the Department of the Interior devised and relied on an approach to departmental management that was quite successful in enabling them to fulfill the various demands of their multipart roles. Though the approach took on certain aspects of a management system, it differed critically from earlier system reforms in that decision making was recognized as essentially political. Whatever the substance of an issue faced by agency heads, they must know who else will participate in determining the final outcome, what the views of these persons are, what their own relative power is, how important the outcome is to achieving their goals and therefore the types of compromises that might be considered, and how practical are the various strategies and tactics that might be pursued in this complex setting.

According to this approach, political executives should view themselves as having several objectives.

- Rather than having to react to events in an ad hoc fashion, executives must be able to base their direction of departmental activities on the President's priorities and theirs. To the extent that the president and departmental executives can establish a specific sense of direction or even a general framework of purpose, there must be a way to use it to guide departmental management.
- The executive and his or her staff must be able to spend most of their time on matters of greatest importance to them rather than be consumed by numerous minor issues that can just as well be delegated to subordinates.
- Due process in departmental decision making must be fostered by ensuring that subordinates with a stake in an issue have their say, thus minimizing distrust and anxiety within the organization.
- The substantive quality of decisions should be maintained at a high level by ensuring that, within the time available, careful analysis is done and relied upon, the relevant evidence is gathered and presented, alternate approaches are considered, and arguments over the validity of the analysis are heard.
- Separate departmental management activities must be coordinated so that the work load for program managers does not peak unreasonably and the number of different, conflicting, or duplicative directives is minimized.
- Decision-making processes must be kept as uncomplicated and free of burdensome paperwork as possible. Deadlines should be few but fully enforced. Reports, plans, studies, and other written communications required of subordinates should be limited to those that will be read and acted upon by top executives. Face-to-face communication and follow-up should be frequent.

The spirit of this management approach is expressed by Robert W. Fri, who, based on his federal executive experience, admonishes federal managers to

keep it simple. . . . It takes time to learn a complex system, and time is just what top federal managers don't have. . . . To be useful to top federal managers, . . . any system of management must be simple, easy to learn, and quickly responsive to a new manager's needs.[51]

Relatively straightforward management procedures can be instituted which are consistent with sustained pursuit of these objectives. These procedures can involve such devices as a "master calendar," a series of dates by which specific activities in policy planning, budget and legislative development, and program implementation are to occur; a "planning guidance" document, which lays out the assumptions, constraints, priorities, and issues that the department head wants each subordinate agency and bureau to consider in developing its annual policy, budget, and legislative proposals; agency plans, which address the questions raised in the planning guidance document and state what the agency intends to do and why; "issues papers" and an "overview memorandum," which describe the issues and alternatives facing the department as a whole and place bureau and agency proposals in an overall departmental context; "planning conferences," meetings at which departmental officials use the overview memorandum as a basis for face-to-face discussions of departmental affairs; "decision memoranda," which record the senior executive's decisions; and an "appeals process," through which subordinate officials can appeal an unfavorable decision.

To be effective, however, these mechanisms must be designed and used appropriately. Planning guidance documents, overview memoranda, and issues papers should be developed by teams drawn from all parts of the senior executive's staff. Though the planning office or its equivalent usually is assigned the lead, this office should not be allowed to "own" the planning process. Rather, responsibilities for reviewing bureau submissions, developing the issue agenda, and performing the necessary analysis should be shared by advisory staffs with different perspectives and primary responsibilities. The requirement that these staffs work together benefits both them and the senior officials who depend on their effectiveness as a team.

Moreover, the main planning documents should not be produced in secret by a group from the political executive's office. It is far better that initial drafts of such documents be reviewed by subordinate executives and their staffs, and revised as appropriate, before they are submitted to the political executive, thus creating a general spirit of cooperation between headquarters and subordinate organizations. The establishment, through such planning mechanisms, of a minimal set of rules and milestones reduces much of the apparent arbitrariness that commonly characterizes bureaucratic decision making. The willingness of the senior executive to tip his or her hand on policy and program alternatives removes some of the fear of secrecy and much of the uncertainty that can poison relationships between program (line) and staff officials and between political appointees and career civil servants. Though such deliberations will not be entirely free from distortions motivated by self-interest, bureau officials involved in front-line politics on a daily basis can be counted on to voice their real concerns in the course of these exchanges and thus keep senior officials in contact with their environment. The senior executive's meetings —though they need not necessarily be large—must include representatives of divergent views so that underlying issues can surface and be discussed.

While this kind of approach offers subordinate agencies better access to the decision-making process, clearer guidance as to what is expected, and reduced paperwork, it also exacts sacrifices. In the interests of departmental teamwork, many agency officials will have to yield autonomy in policy matters. They will have to discipline themselves to respect the master calendar and forego opportunities to "trap the secretary in the elevator" to wheedle favorable decisions from him or her. Top officials will have to spend time preparing to present and be cross-examined on their ideas, proposals, and priorities.

To those officials who enjoy riding in elevators and are good at the free-wheeling, brokering style of winning a concession, a process such as this is admittedly burdensome—"too bureaucratic." To those who take their multipart role seriously, however, the self-discipline is essential. The establishment of an overall context in which specific decisions can be made, the establishment and enforcement of due process in decision making, the reduction of paperwork, the use of systematic analysis in making major decisions, the coordination of different agency management processes, and the attempt to spell out the future implications of current decisions make sense to most agency managers and their staffs. They respond by giving better advice and assistance to a department's top management, and this response leads to better overall performance of the department.

Will help for the political executive come from any other quarter? It is unlikely that Congress will voluntarily come to the rescue of the weakened executive. Members of Congress and the several hundred committees and subcommittees will never accept the view that the president as chief executive has plenary authority over administration. Indeed, neither in practice nor in law is the executive function centralized in the Executive Office of the President or in the political executive offices.[52] In addition to continued congressional committee oversight, the line of command and supervision from the president down through his department heads to every employee, in the words of the first Hoover Commission,

has been worn away by administrative practices, by political pressures, and by detailed statutory provisions. Statutory powers often have been vested in subordinate officers in such a way as to deny authority to the President or a departmental head.[53]

A viable concept of public management must accommodate the tendency, originating in Congress, to force political accountability to the top while simultaneously pulling substantial policy-making activity toward the bottom of the executive hierarchy, where low games are played. Further changes *can* occur in legislative oversight institutions and activities; Congress has as much to gain from bringing order and coherence to its operations as the president does to his. But it is unlikely that these changes would eliminate many of the statutory grants of authority to subordinate officials or procedural constraints on executive discretion. There is no realistic prospect for greater consistency or coherence in congressional control of administration. Nor could the president usefully attempt to wrest such power from Congress. Congressional control of administration is quicksand for the White House and the cabinet. The more they struggle to escape its pull, the more surely they will be caught.

It is the perspective of this book that improvements in governmental competence will depend on those officials with the volition to exercise the necessary self-discipline and take the time to manage. Political executives can do much to help themselves move toward better management performance. A heavy burden is borne by the president as well. By his willingness to enter into relationships of mutual influence with his subordinates, and his encouragement to these subordinates to do the same within their organizations, he can create the kinds of communications that will maintain his connections with the realities that shape his program. He should not fear to do so.

REFERENCES

Chapter 1

1. *Washington Post,* July 15, 1980, p. A15.
2. James L. Sundquist, "The Crisis of Competence in Government," in Joseph A. Pechman, ed., *Setting National Priorities: Agenda for the 1980's* (Washington D.C.: Brookings Institution, 1980), p. 531.
3. For an analysis along similar lines, see Frederick J. Lawton, "The Role of the Administrator in the Federal Government," *Public Administration Review* 14:2 (Spring 1954): 112–18.
4. The Constitution also gave the House of Representatives the exclusive power to originate all legislation involving the raising of revenues, and practice has since conferred on the House the prerogative of originating spending legislation as well.
5. See Yeheskel Hasenfeld and Richard A. English, eds., *Human Service Organizations* (Ann Arbor: Univ. of Michigan Pr., 1974), pp. 1–23.
6. See Theodore J. Lowi, "American Business, Public Policy, Case Studies, and Political Theory," *World Politics* 16:4 (July 1964): 677–715, and "Four Systems of Policy, Politics, and Choice," *Public Administration Review* 32:4 (July/August 1972). 298–310. For a critique, see Lewis A. Froman, Jr., "The Categorization of Policy Contents," in Austin Ranney, ed., *Political Science and Public Policy* (Chicago: Markham, 1968), chap. 3.
7. The first federal grants to the states were in the form of land, primarily to support the development of public education. In 1837 Congress distributed a Treasury surplus to the states in the form of unrestricted cash grants. V. O. Key, Jr., *The Administration of Federal Grants to States* (Washington, D.C.: Public Administration Service, 1937). See also Paul H. Douglas, "The Development of a System of Federal Grants-in-Aid," *Political Science Quarterly* 35:1 (1920): 255–71, 522–44. For a case study, see Martha Derthick, *The Influence of Federal Grants: Public Assistance in Massachusetts* (Cambridge: Harvard Univ. Pr., 1970).
8. The President's Committee on Administrative Management (The Brownlow Committee), *Report of the Committee with Studies of Administrative Management in the Federal Government* (Washington, D.C.: U.S. Government Printing Office, 1937), p. 3.
9. Commission on Organization of the Executive Branch of Government, *The Hoover Commission Report* (New York: McGraw-Hill, 1949), p. 4.
10. For the history of the civil service, see Paul P. Van Riper, *History of the United States Civil Service* (Evanston, Illinois: Row, Peterson, 1958); *History of the Civil Service Merit Systems of the United States and Selected Papers,* compiled by the Congressional Research Service for the Subcommittee on Manpower and Civil Service of the House Committee on Post Office and Civil Service, Committee Print 94–29, 94 Cong., 2nd Sess. (Washington, D.C.: U.S. Government Printing Office, 1976); U.S. Civil Service Commission, *Biography of an Ideal: A History of the Federal Civil Service* (Washington, D.C.: U.S. Government Printing Office, 1974).
11. Leonard D. White, *The Republican Era, 1869–1901,* (New York: Macmillan, 1958) p. 319. Political scientists, including Woodrow Wilson, had been discussing the issue in the professional literature since 1887.
12. See also Richard E. Neustadt, "Politicians and Bureaucrats," in *American Assembly: Congress and America's Future,* 2nd ed. (Englewood Cliffs: Prentice-Hall, 1973), pp. 118–40.
13. See Walter Gellhorn and Clark Byse, *Administrative Law* (Brooklyn: Foundation Pr., 1958), pp. 166–95; Joseph P. Harris, *Congressional Control of Administration* (Washington, D.C.: Brookings Institution, 1964), pp. 249–78.
14. A valuable source of historical background is Harris, *Congressional Control of Administration.*

15. Harris, *Congressional Control,* p. 20.

16. Elliot L. Richardson, *The Creative Balance* (New York: Holt, Rinehart & Winston, 1976), p. 59.

17. Ibid., p. 58.

18. Ibid., p. 62.

19. For a brief informative account of the "emergent Congress," see Frederick C. Mosher, *The GAO: The Quest for Accountability in American Government* (Boulder, Colo.: Westview Pr., 1979), pp. 260–70.

20. Alan L. Otten, "Oversight," *Wall Street Journal,* March 6, 1975, p. 12. Quoted by William A. Niskanen, "Bureaucrats and Politicians," *Journal of Law & Economics* 18:3 (December 1975): 627.

21. Mosher, *The GAO,* p. 304.

22. The most comprehensive assessment of the GAO is that of Mosher. See also Harvey C. Mansfield, *The Comptroller General: A Study of the Law and Practice of Financial Administration* (New Haven: Yale University Press, 1939); W. F. Willoughby, *The Legal Status and Functions of the General Accounting Office* (Baltimore: Johns Hopkins, 1977); Darrell Hevener Smith, *The General Accounting Office: Its History, Activities and Organization* (Institute for Government Research, 1927); Harris, *Congressional Control of Administration,* pp. 135–52; General Accounting Office, *Improving Management for More Effective Government* (Washington, D.C.: U.S. Government Printing Office, 1971); General Accounting Office, *Evaluating Governmental Performance: Changes and Challenges for GAO* (Washington, D.C.: U.S. Government Printing Office, 1975).

23. Mosher, *The GAO,* p. 302.

24. Richard B. Stewart, "The Reformation of American Administrative Law," *Harvard Law Review* 88:8 (June 1973): 1667–1813.

25. Stewart, "American Administrative Law," 1670.

26. Abram Chayes, "The Role of the Judge in Public Law Litigation," *Harvard Law Review* 89:7 (May 1976): 1304. See also Donald L. Horowitz, *The Courts and Social Policy* (Washington, D.C.: Brookings Institution, 1977).

27. U.S. 45 CFR 121 and Appendices.

28. Hearing before the Select Subcommittee on Education of the Committee on Education and Labor, House of Representatives, 93rd Cong., 2nd sess., on H.R. 70, "Financial Assistance for Improved Educational Services for Handicapped Children," March 6, 7, 18, and 22, 1974, p. 101. See also U.S. Department of Health, Education, and Welfare, Office of Education, *Progress Toward a Free Appropriate Public Education,* A Report to Congress on the Implementation of Public Law 94–142: The Education for All Handicapped Children Act: January 1979.

29. The example provides a striking confirmation of the phenomenon Madison so clearly foresaw in *The Federalist.* "Its constitutional powers being at once more extensive, and less susceptible of precise limits," he wrote, "[the legislative department] can, with the greater facility, mask, under complicated and indirect measures, the encroachments which it makes on the coordinate departments." (*The Federalist,* no. 48, p. 323.) Indeed, warned Madison, in a representative democracy, where executive power is carefully limited, it is the "enterprising ambition" of the legislature against which the people ought to "exhaust all their precautions." Mr. Madison, meet Congressman Brademas.

Chapter 2

1. Details of this episode are described in "Nondegradation, the Courts, and the Clean Air Act," John F. Kennedy School of Government, Harvard University, Case No. C95-77-164.

2. A critical analysis of the court's decision in this case and its policy implications is found in Richard B. Stewart, "Judicial Review of EPA Decisions," *Iowa Law Review* 62:713 (1977): 740–50.

3. 45 CFR 233.70(a)(1). The regulation helpfully points out that no eye examination is necessary when both eyes are missing.

4. See Lance Liebman, "The Definition of Disability in Social Security and Supplemental Security Income: Drawing the Bounds of Social Welfare Estates," *Harvard Law Review* 89:5 (March 1976): 833–67.

5. Ibid., 843.

References

6. James W. Singer, "It Isn't Easy to Cure the Ailments of the Disability Insurance Program," *National Journal* 10:18 (May 6, 1978): 717.

7. These data are from the transcript of a talk given by Joseph A. Califano, Jr., at the John F. Kennedy School of Government, Harvard University, October 18, 1979.

8. Liebman, "Definition of Disability," 845.

9. Peter H. Schuck, "The Graying of Civil Rights Law: The Age Discrimination Act of 1975" *Yale Law Journal* 89:27 (1979): 30.

10. Rochelle L. Stanfield, "Age Discrimination Regs—They're Turning the Rule Makers Gray," *National Journal* 10:51–52 (December 30, 1978): 2066.

11. Schuck, "Civil Rights Law," 93.

12. Ibid., 1372.

13. Ibid., 2067.

14. Ibid., 2068.

15. Gordon Chase, "Implementing a Human Services Program: How Hard Will It Be?" *Public Policy* 27:4 (Fall 1979): 391.

16. John K. Iglehart, "Medical Technology—Is It Really Worth What It Costs?" *National Journal* 9:36 (September 3, 1977), p. 1372.

17. Quoted in Iglehart, "Medical Technology," p. 1373.

18. Christopher J. Zook, Francis D. Moore, and Richard J. Zeckhauser, "Policy Towards High Cost Users of Medical Care" (unpublished paper, January 29, 1980), p. 8.

19. Cf. Herbert Kaufman, *Red Tape: Its Origins, Uses, and Abuses* (Washington, D.C.: Brookings Institution, 1977). A survey and critique of academic theories of bureaucratization are found in John Markoff, "Governmental Bureaucratization: General Processes and an Anomalous Case," *Comparative Studies in Society and History* 17:4 (October 1975): 479–503.

20. Charles Peters, "Can Anything Be Done about the Federal Bureaucracy?" *Washington Post* magazine, October 1, 1978, p. 14.

21. Louis C. Gawthrop, *Bureaucratic Behavior in the Executive Branch: An Analysis of Organizational Change* (New York: Free Press, 1969), p. 2.

22. Walter Gellhorn, *When Americans Complain: Governmental Grievance Procedures* (Cambridge: Harvard Univ. Pr., 1966), p. 15.

23. Daniel A. Wren, *The Evolution of Management Thought* (New York: Ronald Pr., 1972), pp. 488–89.

24. Quoted by Daniel A. Wren from "Who Sunk the Yellow Submarine?" *Psychology Today* (November 1972): 120.

25. Quoted by Tana Pesso, "Local Welfare Offices: Managing the Intake Process," *Public Policy* 26:2 (Spring 1978): 305–30, from which this discussion is taken.

26. Ibid., 321.

27. Quoted in the *Washington Post,* December 14, 1978, p. A6. OMB Director McIntyre told reporters after the Carter speech containing these remarks, according to the Associated Press account, that no new auditors or investigators would be hired, and some might actually be lost.

28. Joseph A. Califano, Jr., transcript of a talk given at the John F. Kennedy School of Government, Harvard University, October 18, 1979.

29. Joanne Omang, "Students Denied Grants as 'Cheaters' ," *Washington Post,* January 12, 1979, p. A11.

30. 41 USC 501.

31. Taken from U.S. Office of Management and Budget, *Managing Federal Assistance in the 1980's, Working Papers, D. Evaluation of Pub. L. 95-224,* for comment draft, August 1979.

32. Gellhorn, *When Americans Complain,* p. 11.

33. Joanne Omang and R. R. Reid, "Nuclear Plant Operators Misread Data in Accident," *Washington Post,* May 18, 1979, p. A8.

34. Kaufman, *Red Tape,* p. 29.

35. Richard M. Pious, *The American Presidency* (New York: Basic Books, 1979), p. 221.

36. Daniel Katz et al., *Bureaucratic Encounters: A Pilot Study in the Evaluation of Government Services* (Ann Arbor: Institute for Social Research, Univ. of Michigan Pr., 1975), p. 198.

37. Quoted by Reinhard Bendix, "Who Are the Government Bureaucrats?" in Alvin W. Gouldner, ed., *Studies in Leadership: Leadership in Democratic Action,* rev. ed. (New York: Russell and Russell, 1965), p. 340.

References

38. Elliot L. Richardson, *The Creative Balance* (New York: Holt, Rinehart & Winston, 1976), p. 168.

39. The following account is from "The Carter Administration and Welfare Reform: Sequel," John F. Kennedy School of Government, Harvard University, Case No. C95-79-2415, prepared by David Whitman under the supervision of the author.

40. Ibid. (Italics added.)

41. Ibid. (Italics added.)

42. Charles Peters, "More Dollars and More Dollars and, etc.," *New York Times,* May 15, 1978, p. 35.

43. Henry Aaron, "Welfare Reform: Why Cost Estimates Increased," *New York Times,* May 24, 1978, p. A22.

44. "The Carter Administration," p. 16.

Chapter 3

1. *National Journal* 10:39 (September 30, 1978), p. 1570. At the same time, Henry Aaron, Califano's assistant secretary for planning and evaluation, also left the department. Appointed on the strength of his reputation as one of the country's leading policy analysts and most perceptive students of welfare and human resources policies, Aaron reportedly failed to establish a mutually satisfactory working relationship with Califano. For Aaron's role in welfare reform under Califano, see. . .

2. John K. Inglehart, "New Strategy For Medicare and Medicaid?" *National Journal* 10:12 (March 25, 1978): 472.

3. Ibid.

4. Quoted by Victor Cohn, "Medicare 'Reformer' Fired; Don't Shake Fast Enough," *Washington Post,* September 23, 1978, p. A3.

5. Ibid.

6. Richard Corrigan, "The Man Who's Done It All," *National Journal* 9:5 (January 29, 1977): 181.

7. "An Energy Chief Running Out of Gas?," *U.S. News and World Report* (July 16, 1979): 25.

8. "Horrible Conglomeration," *Time,* July 23, 1979, p. 29.

9. An account of Solomon's appointment and tenure at GSA is found in Bruce Adams and Kathryn Kavanagh-Baran, *Promise and Performance: Carter Builds a New Administration* (Lexington, Mass.: Lexington Books, 1979), pp. 141–53.

10. Ibid., p. 147.

11. Myra MacPherson, "The 'Freeze' For Jay Solomon," *Washington Post,* February 2, 1979, p. D4.

12. Thomas O'Toole, "Sawhill Saw Handwriting on the Wall," *Washington Post,* November 4, 1974, p. A9.

13. For one of the exceptional cases, in Mayor John Lindsay's administration of New York City, see Arthur H. Spiegel III, "How Outsiders Overhauled a Public Agency," *Harvard Business Review* (January/February 1975), reprinted in Phillip E. Present, ed., *People and Public Administration: Case Studies and Perspectives* (Pacific Palisades, Calif.: Palisades Pub., 1979), pp. 25–36.

14. Dick Kirschten, "I Lead Three Lives—The Eliot Cutler Energy Show," *National Journal* (October 27, 1979): 1807.

15. Quoted in Rowland Evans and Robert Novak, *Washington Post,* December 3, 1972, p. B7.

16. Doris Kearns, *Lyndon Johnson and the American Dream,* (New York: Harper & Row, 1976), p. 184.

17. George E. Reedy, *The Twilight of the Presidency* (New York: New American Library, 1970), p. 78.

18. Timothy B. Clark, "The Power Vacuum Outside The Oval Office," *National Journal* 11:8 (February 24, 1979): 297.

19. Joel Havemann, "The Cabinet Band—Trying To Follow Carter's Baton," *National Journal* 9:29 (July 16, 1977): 1109.

20. Quoted in Richard M. Pious, *The American Presidency* (New York: Basic Books, 1979) p. 238.

References

21. Louis Brownlow, *The President and the Presidency* (Chicago: Public Administration Service, 1949), p. 100.

22. Kearns, *Lyndon Johnson,* p. 253.

23. Jack Nelson, "Cabinet and Aides Get Word: Toe Carter Line," *Boston Globe,* April 21, 1978, p. 27.

24. Richard P. Nathan, *The Plot that Failed: Nixon and the Administrative Presidency* (New York: Wiley, 1975), pp. 39–40.

25. Quoted by Elizabeth Drew, "Phase: Engagement with the Special Interest State," *The New Yorker,* (February 27, 1978): 67.

26. Patrick Anderson, *The President's Men.* (Garden City: Doubleday, 1968), p. 446. For an account of how Califano functioned, see pp. 425–49.

27. Nathan, *Plot that Failed,* p. 48.

28. Richard E. Cohen and Rochelle L. Stanfield, "Transportation's Brock Adams—Learning How to Get Along," *National Journal* 9:30 (July 23, 1977): 1154.

29. Dan Morgan, "Bergland and White House Wrangle Over Farm Relief," *Washington Post,* April 9, 1978, p. A14.

30. Joseph W. Bartlett and Douglas N. Jones, "Managing a Cabinet Agency: Problems of Performance at Commerce," *Public Administration Review* 34:1 (January/February 1974): 63.

31. Joseph A. Califano, Jr., *A Presidential Nation* (New York: Norton, 1975), p. 49.

32. Kirschten, "I Lead Three Lives," 1805.

33. Ibid., 1805.

34. Rowland Evans and Robert Novak, *Washington Post,* March 24, 1978.

35. Morgan, "White House Wrangle," A14.

36. *Plot that Failed,* p. 49.

37. Henry A. Kissinger, *The White House Years* (Boston: Little, Brown, 1979), p. 23.

38. Sally Quinn, "Zbigniew Brzezinski: Insights, Infights, Kissinger and Competition," *Washington Post,* December 21, 1979, p. C1.

39. Edward Walsh, "Presidential Directive Against Bias Proves Puzzling To Authors, Recipients," *Washington Post,* June 17, 1977, p. A2.

40. See Gordon T. Yamada, "Improving Management Effectiveness in the Federal Government," *Public Administration Review* 32:6 (November/December 1972): 764–70.

41. William D. Ruckelshaus and the Environmental Protection Agency," John F. Kennedy School of Government, Harvard University, Case No. C16-74-027, pp. 14–15.

42. Rochelle L. Stanfield, "The Battle of the Bulge in H.U.D.'s 1979 Budget," *National Journal* 10:1 (January 7, 1978): 16.

43. Robert Wood, "When Government Works," *Public Interest,* 18 (Winter 1970): 42.

44. Wood, "When Government Works," 42–43.

45. Linda E. Demkovich, "The Rewards and Frustrations of the Federal Bureaucracy," *National Journal* 11:24 (June 16, 1979): 998.

46. Clark, "Power Vacuum," 297.

47. Grant McConnell, *Private Power and American Democracy* (New York: A. A. Knopf, 1967), p. 339. Hugh Heclo regards the concept of iron triangle as "disastrously incomplete." (Hugh Heclo, "Issue Networks and the Executive Establishment," in Anthony King, ed., *The New Political System* (Washington, D.C.: The American Enterprise Institute for Public Policy Research, 1978), p. 88. The reality, he believes, is that policy making and administration are in the hands of "issue networks" comprising varying numbers of policy specialists in and out of government who interact with one another on some aspect or problem of public policy.

48. Frederick V. Malek, *Washington's Hidden Tragedy* (New York: Free Press, 1978), p. 173.

49. McGeorge Bundy, *The Strength of Government* (Cambridge: Harvard Univ. Pr., 1968), p. 37.

50. John C. Whitaker, *Striking a Balance: Environment and Natural Resources Policy in the Nixon–Ford Years* (Washington, D.C.: American Enterprise Institute for Public Policy Research, 1976), p. 45. (Italics added.)

51. Suzanne H. Woolsey, "Time to Melt Down the Iron Triangle," *Washington Post,* May 6, 1980, p. A22.

52. Theodore Sorensen, *Kennedy* (New York: Harper & Row, 1965), pp. 301–2.

53. Arthur M. Schlesinger, Jr., *A Thousand Days* (Boston: Houghton Mifflin, 1965), pp. 568–69.

54. Dan H. Fenn, Jr., "Finding Where the Power Lies in Government," *Harvard Business Review* 57:5 (September/October 1979): 149.

55. Michael, Maccoby, Margaret M. and Robert Duckles, *Bringing Out the Best,* Final Report of the Project to Improve Work and Management in the Department of Commerce 1977–1979, John F. Kennedy School of Government, Harvard University, March 1980, p. 2.

56. Hugh Heclo, *A Government of Strangers: Executive Politics in Washington* (Washington D.C.: Brookings Institution, 1977), p. 238.

57. U.S. Congress, House Subcommittee on Manpower and Civil Service, Committee on Post Office and Civil Service, "Violations and Abuses of Merit Principles in Federal Employment" (Washington, D.C.: U.S. Government Printing Office, 1976).

58. Stephen Hess, *Organizing the Presidency* (Washington, D.C.: Brookings Institution, 1976), p. 133.

59. Quoted by Ronald J. Ostrow "Bell Learning How to Outfox Bureaucrats," the *Los Angeles Times,* November 7, 1977, p. 18.

60. Quoted in the *National Journal* Dom Bonafede, "A Day in the Life of a Cabinet Secretary," 11:19 (May 12, 1979): 792.

61. Richard Corrigan, "Bad Reviews for Schlesinger's Longest-Running Energy Show," *National Journal* 11:11 (March 17, 1979): 425.

62. Herman L. Weiss, "Why Business and Government Exchange Executives," *Harvard Business Review* 52:4 (July/August 1974): 132.

63. Elliot L. Richardson, *Responsibility and Responsiveness (II)* (Washington, D.C.: U.S. Department of Health, Education and Welfare, January 18, 1973), p. 6.

64. Kathy Sawyer, "Learning to Fit in the Cabinet," *Boston Sunday Globe,* October 28, 1979, p. 64.

65. Heclo, *Government of Strangers,* pp. 172–73.

66. Ibid., p. 172.

67. Clark, "Power Vacuum," 296.

68. Richard Fenno, *The President's Cabinet* (Cambridge: Harvard Univ. Pr., 1966) p. 132.

69. Califano, *Presidential Nation,* p. 22.

70. Hobart Rowen, "Kreps: Introspective Farewell," *Washington Post,* November 3, 1979, p. A-1.

71. Whitaker, *Striking a Balance,* p. 47.

72. A complete account of these events is contained in "The Carter Administration and Welfare Reform," President and Fellows of Harvard College, John F. Kennedy School of Government, Harvard University, Case No. C15-79-238-C15-79-241, 1979.

73. Califano, *Presidential Nation,* p. 31.

74. Havemann, "Cabinet Band," 1106.

75. W. Lloyd Warner et al., *The American Federal Executive* (New Haven: Yale Univ. Pr., 1963), pp. 241–42.

76. In addition to the references cited, analyses of the relationships between executive agencies and the press are found in Bernard Cohe, *The Press and Foreign Policy* (Princeton: Princeton Univ. Pr., 1963); Dan Nimmo, *Newsgathering in Washington* (New York: Atherton Pr., 1964); James Reston, *The Artillery of the Press* (New York: Harper & Row, 1967); and William L. Rivers, *The Opinionmakers* (Boston: Beacon Pr., 1965).

77. Jack Anderson, "Gasohol Project Moves, but Slowly," *Washington Post,* March 7, 1979, p. C16.

78. *Newsweek* called the *National Journal* "Washington's Required Reading." *Newsweek* 94:22 (November 26, 1979): 99–100.

79. Joel Havermann, "It's Not What You Know, But . . . ," *National Journal,* 10:2 (January 14, 1978): 66.

80. James Fallows, "The Press and Its Impact on Public Policy," in Charles Peters and James Fallows, editors, *The System* (New York: Praeger Pub., 1976), p. 112.

81. Ibid., p. 134.

82. Douglas Cater, *The Fourth Branch of Government* (Boston: Houghton Mifflin, 1959), p. 7.

83. "Carter's Cabinet, How It Rates," *U.S. News and World Report,* 85:15 (October 16, 1978): 20ff.

84. Fallows, *The System,* pp. 112–13.

85. Cater, *The Fourth Branch,* p. 2.

86. Bartlett and Jones, "Managing A Cabinet Agency," p. 62.

References

87. Kissinger, *The White House Years*, p. 21.
88. Quoted in Malek, *Washington's Hidden Tragedy*, pp. 44–45.
89. Ibid., p. 45.
90. Quoted by Carl C. Croft, "Morton Assessed 'Most Photogenic,'" *The Washington Post*, August 13, 1972, p. A8.
91. Hobart Rowen, "Kreps: Intropective Farewell," *The Washington Post*, November 3, 1979, p. A4.
92. John McDonald, "The Businessman in Government," *Fortune* 50:1 (July 1954): 70.
93. Kilpatrick *et al.*, *The Image of the Federal Service*, (Washington, D.C.: Brookings Institution, 1964), p. 238. See also Franklin P. Kilpatrick, Milton C. Cummings, Jr., and M. Kent Jennings, *Source Book on a Study of Occupational Values and the Image of the Federal Service* (Washington, D.C.: Brookings Institution, 1964), Chapter 13, pp. 360–96.
94. Leonard Sayles, *Mangerial Behavior*, (New York: McGraw-Hill, 1964) p. 2.
95. Stu Henigson, "A Different Style at Energy," *Boston Globe*, April 8, 1980, p. 2.
96. Ibid.

Chapter 4

1. Frederick V. Malek, *Washington's Hidden Tragedy*, (New York: Free Press, 1978) p. 24.
2. Quoted in Joel Havemann, "Can Carter Chop Through the Civil Service System?" *National Journal* 9:17 (April 23, 1977): 617.
3. Graham T. Allison, *Essence of Decision*, (Boston: Little, Brown, 1971) pp. 67–100.
4. Frederick C. Mosher, *Program Budgeting* (Chicago: Public Administration Service, 1954), pp. 37–42.
5. Jesse Burkhead and Jerry Miner, *Public Expenditure* (Chicago: Aldine-Atherton, 1971), pp. 177–85.
6. See Charles L. Schultze, *The Politics and Economics of Public Spending* (Washington, D.C.: Brookings Institution, 1968), pp. 15–34, and Allen Schick, "The Road to PPB: The Stages of Budget Reform," *Public Administration Review* 26:4 (December 1966): 243–58.
7. Aaron Wildavsky, *The Politics of the Budgetary Process* (Boston: Little, Brown, 1979), p. 203.
8. For a brief historical background to MBO in the public sector, see Frank P. Sherwood and William J. Page, Jr., "MBO and Public Management," in Fred A. Kramer, ed., *Contemporary Approaches to Public Budgeting* (Cambridge: Winthrop Pub., 1979), pp. 130–37.
9. Rodney H. Brady, "MBO Goes to Work in the Public Sector," *Harvard Business Review* 51:2 (March/April 1973): 65; Robert W. Fri, "How to Manage the Government for Results: The Rise of MBO," *Organizational Dynamics* 2:4 (Spring 1974): 19–33.
10. Brady reprinted in Phillip E. Present, ed., *People and Public Administration: Case Studies and Perspectives* (Pacific Palisades, Calif.: Palisades Pub., 1979), pp. 224–38.
11. Sherwood and Page, "MBO and Public Management," p. 134.
12. Ibid.
13. Richard Rose, *Managing Presidential Objectives* (New York: Free Press, 1976), pp. 75–76.
14. Ibid., p. 78.
15. Ibid., p. 78.
16. Ibid., p. 94.
17. Richard Rose, "Implementation and Evaporation: The Record of MBO," *Public Administration Review* 37:1 (January/February 1977): 68.
18. Rose, *Managing Presidential Objectives*, pp. 66, 115.
19. Ibid., p. 81.
20. Ibid., pp. 120–21.
21. Rose, "Implementation and Evaporation," 70.
22. Sherwood and Page, "MBO and Public Management," 139.
23. Quoted in Joel Havemann, "Taking up the Tools to Tame the Bureaucracy," *National Journal* (April 2, 1977): 514.
24. Quoted in Aaron Wildavsky and Arthur Hammond, "Comprehensive Versus Incremental Budgeting in the Department of Agriculture," in Fremont J. Lynden and Ernest G. Miller, eds., *Planning Programming Budgeting* (Chicago: Markham, 1967), p. 143.
25. Wildavsky and Hammond, "Comprehensive Versus Incremental Budgeting," 157.

References

26. Wildavsky, *The Politics of the Budgetary Process,* p. 213.

27. See Graeme M. Taylor, "Introduction to Zero-Base Budgeting," *Bureaucrat* 6:1 (Spring 1977): 33–55.

28. A. E. Buck, *The Budget in Governments of Today* (New York: Macmillan, 1934), p. 172, cited by James D. Suzier and Ray L. Brown, "Where Does Zero Base Budgeting Work?" *Harvard Business Review,* 55:6 (November/December 1977): 76.

29. For a further description of the ZBB process, see Taylor, "Zero Base Budgeting"; Peter A. Phyrr, *Zero-Base Budgeting: A Practical Management Tool for Evaluating Expenses* (New York: Wiley, 1973); and "Zero-Base Approach to Government Budgeting," *Public Administration Review* 37:1 (January/February 1977): 1–8.

30. For elaboration of the criticisms of ZBB, see Robert N. Anthony, "Zero Base Budgeting Is a Fraud," *Wall Street Journal,* April 27, 1977, pp. 177–79; and Allen Schick, "The Road from ZBB," *Public Administration Review* 38:2 (March/April 1978): 177–79.

31. See Havemann, "Taking Up the Tools," p. 517.

32. Regina Herzlinger, "Zero-Base Budgeting in the Federal Government: A Case Study," *Sloan Management Review* (Winter 1979): 9.

33. Herzlinger, "Zero-Base Budgeting," 8.

34. Wildavsky, *The Politics of the Budgetary Process,* p. 214.

35. See Aaron Wildavsky, "A Budget for All Seasons? What the Traditional Budget Lacks," *Public Administration Review* 38:6 (Nov./Dec. 1978): 501–9.

36. See Robert W. Hartman, "Budget Prospects and Process," in Joseph A. Pechman, Jr., ed., *Setting National Priorities: Agenda for the 1980's* (Washington, D.C.: Brookings Institution, 1980), pp. 384–85.

37. Harold Seidman, *Politics, Position, and Power,* (New York: Oxford Univ. Pr., 1970) p. 3.

38. Kaufman, "Reflections on Administrative Reorganization," in Pechman, ed., *Setting National Priorities: Agenda for the 1980's* (Washington, D.C.: Brookings Institution, 1980) pp. 391–92.

39. Seidman, *Politics, Position, and Power,* p. 3. Basic references on reorganization are: Frederick C. Mosher, ed., *Governmental Reorganization: Cases and Commentary* (Indianapolis): Bobbs-Merrill, 1967). The President's Committee on Administrative Management, Louis Brownlow, Chairman, *Report of the Committee,* 74th Cong., 2nd Sess. (Washington, D.C.: U.S. Government Printing Office, 1937); *Commission on the Organization of the Government for the Conduct of Foreign Policy, Appendix O: Making Organizational Change Effective: Case Studies of Attempted Reform in Foreign Affairs* (Washington, D.C.: National Academy of Public Administration, June 1975); Herbert Emmerich, *Essays on Federal Reorganization* (University, Ala.: Univ. of Alabama Pr., 1950); Herbert Emmerich, *Federal Reorganization and Administrative Management* (University, Ala.: Univ. of Alabama Pr., 1971); Herbert Kaufman, *Are Government Organizations Immortal?* (Washington, D.C.: Brookings Institution, 1976); President's Council on Executive Organization (Ash Council). *Papers Relating to the President's Departmental Reorganization Program: A Reference Compilation* (Washington, D.C.: Superintendent of Documents, March 1971); Martin Landau, "Redundancy, Rationality, and the Problem of Duplication and Overlap," *Public Administration Review* 29:4 (July/August 1969): 346–58; Harvey C. Mansfield, "Federal Executive Reorganization: Thirty Years of Experience," *Public Administration Review* 29:4 (July/August 1969): 332–45; Rufus E. Miles, Jr., "Consideration for a President Bent on Reorganization," *Public Administration Review* 37:2 (March/April 1977): 155–62; Clifford L. Berg, "Lapse of Reorganization Authority," *Public Administration Review* 35:2 (March/April 1975): 195–200; Harvey C. Mansfield, "Reorganizing the Federal Executive Branch: The Limits of Institutionalization," *Law and Contemporary Problems* 35:3 (Summer 1970): 461–95; Commission on Organization of the Executive Branch of Government (Hoover Commission), *General Management of the Executive Branch: A Report to Congress* (Washington, D.C.: U.S. Government Printing Office, February 1949); Herbert Kaufman, "Reflections on Administrative Reorganization," 391–418.

40. Social Security Administration, *Commissioner's Bulletin,* No. 3, January 5, 1979. (Mimeographed.)

41. Kaufman, "Reflections on Administrative Reorganization," p. 396.

42. Seidman, *Politics, Position, and Power,* p. 103.

43. Chris Black, "Q&A with Richard Pettigrew," *Boston Sunday Globe,* July 23, 1978, p. 2.

44. Ed Walsh, "White House Casting a Colder Eye on Re-Organization Plans," *Washington Post,* December 6, 1978, p. A2.

45. Ibid.

References

46. *Public Papers of the Presidents of the United States, Jimmy Carter,* Book I (Washington, D.C.: U.S. Government Printing Office, 1977), p. 258.

47. Executive Order 12083, September 27, 1978, *Public Papers of the Presidents of the United States, Jimmy Carter* Book II (Washington, D.C.: U.S. Government Printing Office, 1978), p. 1637.

48. Much of this account is from Wolf Von Eckardt, "Federal Follies—The Mismanaging of Historic Preservation," *Washington Post,* December 1, 1979, p. B1.

49. Theodore Levitt, "Management and the 'Post-Industrial' Society," *Public Interest* 44 (Summer 1976): 92.

50. Michael Maccoby, Margaret M. and Robert Duckles, *Bringing Out the Best,* Final Report of the Project to Improve Work and Management in the Department of Commerce, 1977–1979, John F. Kennedy School of Government, Harvard University, March 1980, Chapter I, p. 6.

51. For a useful survey of the development of earlier leadership studies, see Warren Bennis, *Changing Organizations* (New York: McGraw-Hill, 1966), pp. 64–78, and Daniel A. Wren, *The Evolution of Management Thought,* (New York: Ronald Pr., 1972) parts III and IV. The classic literature includes: F. J. Roethlisberger and W. J. Dickson, *Management and the Worker* (Cambridge: Harvard Univ. Pr., 1939), which reported the findings of the Hawthorne experiments; Elton Mayo, *The Social Problems of an Industrial Civilization* (Cambridge: Harvard Univ. Pr., 1941); and Stuart Chase, *Men at Work* (New York: Harcourt, Brace & World, 1941). For criticism of the Hawthorne experiments, see H. A. Landsberger, *Hawthorne Revisited* (Ithaca: Cornell Univ. Pr., 1958), and Alex Carey, "The Hawthorne Studies: A Practical Criticism," *American Sociological Review* 32:3 (June 1967): 413–416.

52. See, for example, Eugene E. Jennings, *An Anatomy of Leadership: Princes, Heroes, and Supermen* (New York: McGraw-Hill, 1960), pp. 180–85; the writings of William H. Whyte, Jr.: "Group Think," *Fortune* (March 1952): 114–17, *The Organization Man* (New York: Doubleday, 1956), and "The Social Engineers," *Fortune* (January 1952): 88–93; Erich Fromm, "Man Is Not a Thing," *Saturday Review* (March 16, 1957): 9–11; Malcolm McNair, "Thinking Ahead: What Price Human Relations?" *Harvard Business Review* 35:2 (March/April 1957): 15–23; Robert N. McMurry, "The Case for Benevolent Autocracy," *Harvard Business Review* 36:1 (January/February 1958): 82–90.

53. Jennings, *Anatomy of Leadership,* p. 186.

54. See, for example, Abraham Maslow, *Motivation and Personality* (New York: Harper & Row, 1954); Chris Argyris, *Personality and Organization: The Conflict Between the System and the Individual* (New York: Harper & Row, 1957); Douglas McGregor, *The Human Side of Enterprise* (New York: McGraw-Hill, 1960).

55. Victor Thompson, *Without Sympathy or Enthusiasm* (University, Ala.: Univ. of Alabama Pr., 1975), p. 26.

56. Donald Warwick, quoted in David Berg, ed., *Failures in Organization Development and Change* (New York: Wiley, 1977), p. 141.

57. Maccoby et al., *Bringing Out the Best,* Chapter 2, p. 5.

58. Maccoby et al., *Bringing Out the Best,* Chapter 5, p. 3.

59. Michael Crozier, *The Bureaucratic Phenomenon* (Chicago: Univ. of Chicago Pr., 1964), p. 208.

60. U.S. Office of the White House Press Secretary, "Text of Address by the President to the National Press Club," March 2, 1978. (Mimeographed.)

61. Background for the Carter plan is contained in the U.S. Presidential Reorganization Project, Personnel Management Project, vol. 1, *Final Staff Report* (Washington, D.C.: U.S. Government Printing Office, 1977).

62. "Management implies continuity. The circulation of managerial personnel is no less desirable. The development of such personnel in recent years has offered concrete evidence both of the feasibility of the practice and of its value. In the majority of cases, careers have involved experience in more than one department, and in a few instances transfers have taken place after general managerial rank has been attained. An incidental advantage of a reasonable degree of circulation in managerial posts will be found in the fact that it facilitates adjustments of personalities which are occasionally desirable in the course of shifting political leadership.

"To praise such circulation of personnel, with its incidental opportunities for adjustment, weakens not at all the assumption that the sine qua non of the departmental system lies in the essential permanence of its corps of managers." Brownlow Committee, p. 268.

63. Robert Angle and Martha Walters, "Carter: More Inept Reform." *Nashua Telegraph,* May 18, 1978, p. 4.

64. U.S. Office of the White House Press Secretary, "Address by the President, March 2, 1978."

65. E. E. Lawler, *Pay and Organizational Effectiveness: A Psychological View* (New York: McGraw-Hill, 1971), summarized in Barry Bozeman, *Public Management and Policy Analysis* (New York: St. Martin's, 1979), p. 199.

66. Douglas McGregor, "An Uneasy Look at Performance Appraisal," *Harvard Business Review* 50:5 (Sept./Oct. 1972): 133–38.

67. Timothy B. Clark, "Senior Executive Service—Reform From the Top," *National Journal* 10:39 (September 30, 1978): 1545.

68. Haynes Johnson, "Morale," *Washington Post,* May 24, 1978, p. A3.

69. Bernard Rosen, "A New Mandate for Accountability in the National Government," *Bureaucrat* 8:1 (Spring 1979): 3.

70. Quoted in Frederick C. Thayer, "The President's Management 'Reforms': Theory X Triumphant," *Public Administration Review,* July/August 1978, p. 313.

71. See, for example, Frederick C. Thayer, "The President's Management 'Reforms.' Theory X Triumphant," *Public Administration Review* 38:4 (July/August 1978): 309–14; and Maccoby et al., *Bringing Out the Best,* chapter 1.

72. Kaufman, "Reflections on Administrative Reorganization," 416.

73. Marvin Bernstein, "The Presidency and Management Improvement," *Law and Contemporary Problems* 35:3 (1970): 55.

Chapter 5

1. Leonard D. White, *The Federalists,* (New York: Macmillan, 1958) p. 471.

2. Harold F. Williamson, *Growth of the American Economy* (Englewood Cliffs, N.J.: Prentice-Hall, 1951), p. 609; Herman E. Kooss and Peter F. Drucker, "How We Got Here: Fifty Years of Structural Change in the Business System and the Business School, 1918–1968," in Peter F. Drucker, ed., *Preparing Tomorrow's Business Leaders Today* (Englewood Cliffs, N.J.: Prentice-Hall, 1969), pp. 9–10.

3. Alfred D. Chandler, Jr., "The Structure of American Industry in the Twentieth Century: A Historical Overview," in Edward J. Perkins, ed., *Men and Organizations* (New York: Putnam, 1977), p. 31. For a more extended analysis, see Alfred D. Chandler, Jr., *The Visible Hand* (Cambridge: Belknap Press, 1977).

4. Chandler, *Visible Hand,* p. 466.

5. Ibid.

6. Michael A. Murray, "Comparing Public and Private Management: An Exploratory Essay," *Public Administration Review,* 35:4 (July/August 1975): 364–71.

7. Chandler, *Visible Hand,* pp. 34–35.

8. Peter F. Drucker, *Concept of the Corporation* (New York: Mentor Books, 1972), p. 108.

9. Ibid., p. 113.

10. Ibid., p. 110.

11. Leonard D. White, *The Republican Era, 1869–1901* (New York: Macmillan, 1958) p. 387.

12. Samuel P. Hays, *Conservation and the Gospel of Efficiency: The Progressive Conservation Movement, 1890–1920* (Cambridge: Harvard Univ. Pr., 1959), p. 125.

13. John Philip Hill, *Federal Executive* (Boston: Houghton Mifflin, 1916), pp. 6–7.

14. W. F. Short, *The Development of the National Administrative Organization of the United States* (Baltimore: Johns Hopkins, 1923), pp. 453–54.

15. Quoted in Leonard D. White, *Introduction to the Study of Public Administration* (New York: Macmillan, 1926), p. 19.

16. Martin H. Schiesl, *The Politics of Efficiency* (Berkeley: Univ. of California Pr., 1977), pp. 172–73.

17. Ibid., p. 176.

18. Ibid.

19. For an account of the most recent experience with applying business methods to the

problems of municipal government, see David Rogers, *Can Business Management Save the Cities?* (New York: Free Press, 1978).

20. Committee for Economic Development, *Improving Executive Management in the Federal Government* (New York: Committee for Economic Development, 1964), statement by Marvin Bower and Frederick R. Kappel, p. 74.

21. Richard P. Nathan, *The Plot that Failed: Nixon and the Administrative Presidency* (New York: Wiley, 1975), p. 38.

22. Jimmy Carter, *Why Not the Best?* (New York: Bantam Books, 1975), p. 175.

23. Quoted in Bruce Adams and Kathryn Kavanagh-Baran, *Promise and Performance: Carter Builds a New Administration* (Lexington, Mass.: Lexington Books, 1979), p. 141.

24. In their classical *Organizations* (New York: Wiley, 1958), pp. 12–30, James G. March and Herbert A. Simon draw a sharp distinction between the scientific management theorists, with their "machine model" of task organization, and administrative management theory, which, though based on a similar physiological view of the employee, is concerned with assigning tasks to departments within organizations.

25. Chester I. Barnard, *The Functions of the Executive* (Cambridge: Harvard Univ. Pr., 1950).

26. Max Weber, *The Theory of Social and Economic Organization,* trans. by A. M. Henderson and Talcott Parsons, edited and with an introduction by Talcott Parsons (Glencoe, Ill.: Free Press, 1947), pp. 330–34.

27. Ibid., p. 334.

28. Barry Bozeman, *Public Management and Policy Analysis* (New York: St. Martin's, 1979), pp. 95–96.

29. James Burnham, *The Managerial Revolution* (New York: John Day Co., 1941), p. 80.

30. Ibid., p. 150.

31. Leonard R. Sayles, *Leadership* (New York: McGraw-Hill, 1979), p. 2.

32. Kenneth R. Andrews, *The Concept of Corporate Strategy* (Homewood, Illinois: Dow Jones-Irwin, 1971), p. 7.

33. Robert B. Buchele, *The Management of Business and Public Organizations* (New York: McGraw-Hill, 1977), p. 282.

34. David Finn, *The Corporate Oligarch* (New York: Simon & Schuster, 1969), p. 18.

35. Buchele, *Business and Public Organizations,* pp. 282, 284.

36. Sayles, *Leadership,* p. 3.

37. Henry Mintzberg, *The Nature of Managerial Work* (New York: Harper & Row, 1973), p. 5.

38. Peter F. Drucker, *Technology, Management, and Society* (New York: Harper & Row, 1977), p. 38.

39. Mintzberg, *Managerial Work,* p. 4.

40. Buchele, *Business and Public Organizations,* p. 276. He calls attention to the diversity of business management practices depending on their size, their complexity, and their type. See pp. 54–62.

41. Harvard Business School Club of Washington, D.C., *Businessmen in Government: An Appraisal of Experience* (Washington, D.C., 1958), p. 32.

42. Peter F. Drucker, *The Practice of Management* (New York: Harper & Row, 1954), pp. 7–9. (Italics added.)

43. Paul H. Appleby, *Big Democracy* (New York: A. A. Knopf, 1945), pp. 1, 6–7.

44. Ibid., p. 4.

45. White, *Public Administration,* p. 17.

46. Ibid., p. 18.

47. Ibid. In his general discussion, White draws extensively on an early analysis of public and business administration by Josiah C. Stamp, "The Contrast Between the Administration of Business and Public Affairs," *Journal of Public Administration* 1:3 (July 1923): 158–71.

48. White, *Public Administration,* p. 19.

49. Redfield, in White, *Public Administration,* p. 19.

50. Marver Bernstein, *The Job of the Federal Executive* (Washington, D.C.: Brookings Institution, 1958), p. 37.

51. A summary of these kinds of propositions based on an extensive survey of the literature that directly addresses this question is found in Hal G. Rainey, Robert W. Backoff, and Charles H. Levine, "Comparing Public and Private Organizations," *Public Administration Review* 36:2 (March/April 1976): 233–44.

References

52. Peter Woll's *American Bureaucracy* (New York: Norton, 1977), for example, discusses the evolution and character of American governmental organizations without drawing any distinctions from nongovernmental organizations.

53. Louis C. Gawthorp, *Bureaucratic Behavior in the Executive Branch: An Analysis of Organizational Change* (New York: Free Press, 1969).

54. Ibid., p. 249.

55. Peter M. Blau and W. Richard Scott, *Formal Organizations, A Comparative Approach* (London: Routledge & Kegan Paul, 1963), pp. 43, 45–57.

56. W. Lloyd Warner et al., *The American Federal Executive* (New Haven: Yale Univ. Pr., 1963); W. Lloyd Warner and James C. Abegglen, *Occupational Mobility in American Business and Industry, 1928–1952* (Minneapolis: Univ. of Minnesota Pr., 1954), and their *Big Business Leaders in America* (New York: Harper & Row, 1955).

57. Warner et al., *American Federal Executive,* p. 22.

58. *Newsweek,* June 18, 1979, p. 75. For elaboration on this point, see Richard G. Darman and Laurence E. Lynn, Jr., "The 'Business–Government Problem': Inherent Difficulties and Emerging Solutions," in John T. Dunlop, ed., *Business and Government* (Cambridge: Harvard Business School, 1980).

59. James R. Rawls, Robert A. Ullrich, and Oscar Tivis Nelson, Jr., "A Comparison of Managers Entering or Reentering the Profit and Nonprofit Sectors," *Academy of Management Journal* 18:3 (September 1975): 616–23.

60. Ibid. 621.

61. Bruce Buchanan II, "Government Managers, Business Executives, and Organizational Commitment," *Public Administration Review* 34:4 (July/August 1974): 339–47. See also Bruce Buchanan II, "Red Tape and the Service Ethic, Some Unexpected Differences Between Public and Private Managers," *Administration and Society* 6:4 (February 1975): 423–44.

62. Buchanan, "Government Managers," 339.

63. R. P. Rhinehart et al., "Comparative Study of Need Satisfaction in Governmental and Business Hierarchies," *Journal of Applied Psychology* 53:3 (June 1969): 230–35.

64. Franklin P. Kilpatrick, Milton C. Cummings, Jr., and M. Kent Jennings, *The Image of the Federal Service* (Washington, D.C.: Brookings Institution, 1964), p. 162.

65. Ibid., p. 164.

66. In 1936, E. Pendleton Herring, in his *Federal Commissioners: A Study of Their Careers and Qualifications* (Cambridge: Harvard Univ. Pr., 1936), noted that the few individuals with broad business experience who served on regulatory commissions tended to leave after their work was done. He concluded (p. 31): "When the task is fresh and challenging it is attractive to the men of imagination and enterprise who are exploring and developing their specialty outside government. In the heavy daily task of administering the law, there is little to hold such men."

67. See John J. Corson, *Executives for the Federal Service* (New York: Columbia Univ. Pr., 1952).

68. Quoted in Felix A. Nigro and Lloyd G. Nigro, *Modern Public Administration.* 4th ed. (New York: Harper & Row, 1977), p. 15.

69. Quoted in John McDonald, "The Businessman in Government," *Fortune* 50:1 (July 1954): 69.

70. Bernstein, *The Job of the Federal Executive,* p. 31.

71. Ibid., p. 36.

72. Bernstein, pp. 200–201, from *Colliers* (April 2, 1954), p. 31.

73. Bernstein, *The Job of the Federal Executive,* p. 207.

74. Ibid., p. 212.

75. Ibid.

76. Ibid., pp. 215, 216.

77. Federick V. Malek, *Washington's Hidden Tragedy* (New York: Free Press, 1978), p. 19.

78. Frederick V. Malek, "Mr. Executive Goes to Washington," *Harvard Business Review* 50:5 (September/October 1972): 64–65.

79. Ibid., 68.

80. Malek, *Washington's Hidden Tragedy,* pp. 44–45, 55.

81. Ibid., p. 55.

82. Herman Nickel, "Candid Reflections of a Business man in Washington," *Fortune* 99:2 (January 29, 1979): 36–49.

83. Cf. Edward C. Banfield, "Corruption as a Feature of Governmental Organization," *Journal of Law and Economics* 18:3 (December 1975): 591–99.

84. Barnard, *Functions of the Executive,* p. 93.

85. Kooss and Drucker, "How We Got Here," p. 13.

86. Marilyn Bender, *At The Top* (New York: Doubleday, 1975), p. 49.

87. An exception is Dun and Bradstreet ratings of the credit worthiness of state and municipal governments.

88. Burnham, *Managerial Revolution* p. 106. See also Peter M. Blau and W. Richard Scott, *Formal Organizations* (San Francisco: Chandler, 1962), p. 43.

89. Dick Kirschten, "Interior Seeks a Balance Between Environmentalist and Indian Claims," *National Journal* 9:48 (November 26, 1977): 1841.

90. Richard E. Cohen and Rochelle L. Stanfield, "Transportation's Brock Adams—Learning How to Get Along," *National Journal* 9:30 (July 23, 1977): 1154.

91. Otto Lerbinger and Nathaniel H. Sperber, *Key to the Executive Head* (Reading, Mass.: Addison-Wesley, 1975), p. 1.

92. Drucker, *Technology, Management, and Society,* p. 94.

93. Harry Levinson, *The Exceptional Executive: A Psychological Conception* (New York: New American Library, 1971), p. 117.

94. See John Quarles, *Federal Regulation of New Industrial Plants: A Survey of Environmental Regulations Affecting the Siting and Construction of New Industrial Plants and Plant Expansions* (New Plants Report, P.O. Box 998, Ben Franklin Station, Washington, D.C.).

95. Quoted by T. Mitchell Ford, "Changing Ground Rules for the CEO," *S.A.M. Advanced Management Journal* 44:4 (Autumn 1979): 42.

96. Quoted By Bruce Adams, "The Limitations of Muddling Through: Does Anyone in Washington Really Think Anymore?" *Public Administration Review* 39:6 (November/December 1979): 547.

97. Quoted by Phyllis Theroux in *New York Times Magazine,* June 8, 1980, p. 98.

98. Quoted by Adams, "Muddling Through," 546.

99. Kenneth Andrews, *The Concept of Corporate Strategy* (Homewood, Ill.: Dow Jones-Irwin, 1971), p. 228.

100. Chris Argyris, "The CEO's Behavior: Key to Organizational Development," *Harvard Business Review* 51:2 (March/April 1973): 56.

101. Ibid.

102. Sayles, *Leadership,* pp. 216, 217.

103. Elliot L. Richardson, *The Creative Balance* (New York: Holt, Rinehart & Winston, 1976), p. 159.

104. Quoted in Martha Derthick, *Policymaking for Social Security* (Washington, D.C.: Brookings Institution, 1979), p. 79.

105. David Finn, *The Corporate Oligarch* (New York: Simon & Schuster, 1969), p. 15.

106. Chris Argyris, *Behind the Front Page* (San Francisco: Jossey-Bass, 1974).

107. Donald N. Frey, "Bell & Howell's Long Struggle," *New York Times,* December 13, 1979, p. D2.

108. N.R. Kleinfield, "Inside Bell's Executive Suite," *New York Times,* January 2, 1979, p. D2.

109. "International Paper Tries Managing for the Long Run," *Business Week* (July 28, 1980): 102.

110. Philip J. Holts, "David Brinkley's Journal," *Washington Post/Potomac,* January 27, 1974, p. 20.

111. Frey, "Bell & Howell's Long Struggle," p. D2.

112. Walter Kiechel, III, "Tom Vanderslice Scales the Heights at G.E.," *Fortune* (July 30, 1979): 80.

113. Kleinfield, "Inside Bell's Executive Suite," p. D2.

114. Joseph L. Bower, "Effective Public Management," *Harvard Business Review* 55:2 (March/April 1977): 131–40.

115. Address given by Joseph A. Califano at Harvard University, Oct. 18, 1979.

116. Harold Seidman, *Politics, Position and Power,* (New York: Oxford Univ. Pr., 1970), p. 50.

117. *The Federalist,* No. 51, p. 337.

118. Quoted by Graham T. Allison, Jr., "Public and Private Management: Are They Fundamentally Alike in All Unimportant Respects," in U.S. Office of Personnel Management, *Setting*

References

Public Management Research Agendas: Integrating the Sponsor, Producer, and User (OPM Document 127-53-1, February 1980), p. 27.

119. Quoted by Bender in *At the Top*, p. 9.

120. Theodore Levitt, "Management and the 'Post-Industrial' Society," *Public Interest* 44 (Summer 1976): 74.

Chapter 6

1. *Congressional Weekly*, December 19, 1973, p. 17.

2. Details of this case are described in *Maximum Allowable Cost (MAC)*, John F. Kennedy School of Government, Harvard University, Case no. C14–80–282.

3. The important literature in the pluralist tradition includes Arthur Bentley, *The Process of Government* (Chicago: Univ. of Chicago Pr., 1908); E. Pendleton Herring, *Public Administration and the Public Interest* (New York: McGraw-Hill, 1936); David Truman, *The Governmental Process* (New York: A. A. Knopf, 1951); Robert A. Dahl, *A Preface to Democratic Theory* (Chicago: Univ. of Chicago Pr., 1956), *Who Governs?* (New Haven: Yale Univ. Pr., 1961), and *Pluralist Democracy in the United States* (Chicago: Rand McNally, 1967); Earl Latham, *The Group Basis of Politics* (New York: Octagon Books, 1965).

4. Kenneth Prewitt and Alan Stone, *The Ruling Elites* (New York: Harper & Row, 1973), p. 114.

5. Steven Lukes, *Power: A Radical View* (London and New York: Macmillan, 1974), p. 15.

6. Prewitt and Stone, *Ruling Elites*, p. 116.

7. Earl Latham, "The Group Basis of Politics: Notes for a Theory," *American Political Science Review* 46:2 (June 1952): 376–97.

8. Other groups were also involved: the National Association of Chain Drug Stores, Inc., the National Wholesale Druggists' Association, and the National Association of Pharmaceutical Manufacturers.

9. Prewitt and Stone, *Ruling Elites*, p. 2.

10. The important literature in the elitist tradition includes Gaetano Mosca, *The Ruling Class* (New York: McGraw-Hill, 1939), a work originally published in Italian in 1896; Robert Michels, *Political Parties: A Sociological Study of the Oligarchical Tendencies of Modern Democracy* (New York: Collier, 1962), first published in Germany in 1911; Robert S. Lynd, *Middletown* (New York: Harcourt Brace Jovanovich, 1929) and *Middletown in Transition* (New York: Harcourt Brace Jovanovich, 1937); Floyd Hunter, *The Community Power Structure* (Chapel Hill: Univ. of North Carolina Pr., 1953); C. Wright Mills, *The Power Elite* (New York: Oxford Univ. Pr., 1956); Peter Bachrach and Morton Baratz, *Power and Poverty: Theory and Practice* (New York: Oxford Univ. Pr. 1970); E. E. Schattschneider, *The Semi-Sovereign People* (New York: Holt, Rinehart & Winston, 1960).

11. Mills, *Power Elite*, p. 9.

12. Prewitt and Stone, *Ruling Elites*, p. 13.

13. Ibid., p. 17.

14. Justifications for the use of a game metaphor in this kind of analysis are found in Graham T. Allison, "Conceptual Models and the Cuban Missile Crisis," *American Political Science Review* 63:3 (September 1969): 708; Eugene Bardach, *The Implementation Game: What Happens After a Bill Becomes a Law* (Cambridge: MIT Press, 1977), pp. 55–58; Norton Long, "The Local Community as an Ecology of Games," *American Sociological Review* 64:5 (November 1968): 251–61; Michael Maccoby, *The Gamesman: Winning and Losing the Career Game*, (New York: Simon & Schuster, 1976), pp. 100ff. See also Herman Hesse, *The Glass Bead Game (Magister Ludi)* (New York: Holt, Rinehart & Winston, 1969), and Erich Berne, *Games People Play* (New York: Ballantine Books, 1973), who defines games as incidents between people that "tend to follow definite patterns which are amenable to sorting and classification," with the sequence "circumscribed by unspoken rules and regulations" (p. 17).

15. This and the following possibilities are discussed by Leonard Sayles in *Leadership* (New York: McGraw-Hill, 1979), pp. 211–19.

16. Richard E. Neustadt, *Presidential Power*, (New York: New American Library, 1964), p. 105.

References

17. Emmette S. Redford, *American Government and the Economy* (New York: Macmillan, 1965), pp. 58ff, and his *Democracy in the Administrative States*, (New York: Oxford Univ. Pr., 1969), chaps. 4 and 5, pp. 83–131. Cf. Yehezkel Dror, *Venture in Policy Sciences: Concepts and Applications* (New York: American Elsevier, 1971).

18. Charles E. Summer, *Strategic Behavior in Business and Government* (Boston: Little, Brown, 1980), p. 61.

19. Mills, *Power Elite*, p. 244.

20. Daniel A. Dreyfus, "The Limitations of Policy Research in Congressional Decision Making," in Carol H. Weiss, ed., *Using Social Research in Public Policy Making* (Lexington, Mass.: Lexington Books, 1977), p. 100.

21. The high game is similar to Redford's "macropolitics," which he defines as "the politics that arises when the community at large and the leaders of the government as a whole are brought into the discussion and determination of issues. The distinguishing factor is the breadth of involvement." *Democracy in the Administrative State*, p. 107. However, as to the actual functions performed in the macropolitical system, Redford cites seven, only one of which, crisis resolution, is associated with the high game as defined here. The rest are what are called later middle and low game functions.

High game issues and participants are also akin to the activities and members of Mills's "power elite," which comprises occupants of the "strategic command posts of the social structure" who are in a position to "make decisions having major consequences" (p. 4).

22. Mills, *Power Elite*, p. 245.

23. Redford's characterization of his idea of subsystem policies, that is, the politics of particular areas of program specialization, is included in what we have termed the middle game.

24. Cf. Gabriel A. Almond, *The American People and Foreign Policy* (New York: Praeger, 1960), p. 143: "Under circumstances of peace or of only moderate international tension, most of the daily decisions of diplomacy and foreign policy are 'remote.' They involve little known peoples in far-away countries, or highly technical problems such as boundary settlements, international trade, and the complex issues of foreign loans and foreign economies. They are, indeed, the stuff out of which war and peace, victory and defeat, are made. But foreign policy is a tapestry of infinite complexity, and even the expert can only hope to achieve familiarity with a part of its intricate designs."

25. Quoted in Peter H. Schuck, "The Graying of Civil Rights Law: The Age Discrimination Act of 1975," *The Yale Law Journal* 89:27 (1979): 45.

26. Rochelle L. Stanfield, "Issues Come Before Politics Says the New Transportation Secretary," *National Journal* 11:51–2 (December 22, 1979): 2146.

27. See Timothy C. Clark, "The Gentian Violet Case—or How One Firm Learned to Hate the FDA," *National Journal* 10:25 (January 24, 1978): 1010–15.

28. Francis E. Rourke, *Bureaucracy, Politics, and Public Policy* (Boston: Little, Brown, 1969), p. 41.

29. Eliot Marshall, "Psychotherapy Faces Test of Worth," *Science* 207:4 (January 1980): 35.

30. Carl J. Freidrich, "Public Policy and the Nature of Administrative Responsibility," in Alan Altschuler, ed., *The Politics of the Federal Bureaucracy* (New York: Dodd, Mead, 1968): 334–35.

31. Herbert Kaufman, "Reflections on Administrative Reorganization," in Joseph A. Pechman, ed., *Setting National Priorities: The 1978 Budget* (Washington, D.C.: Brookings Institution, 1977), p. 400. See also Luther Gulick, "Politics, Administration, and the 'New Deal'," *Annals of the American Academy of Political and Social Science* 169 (September 1933): 62.

Chapter 7

1. The President's Committee on Administrative Management, Louis Brownlow, Chairman, *Report of the Committee*, 74th Cong., 2nd sess. (Washington, D.C., U.S. Government Printing Office, 1937), p. 2.

References

2. Richard E. Neustadt, *Presidential Power* (New York: New American Library, 1964), pp. 107, 110.

3. Brownlow Committee Report, p. 5.

4. McGeorge Bundy, *The Strength of Government* (Cambridge: Harvard Univ. Pr., 1968), pp. 38–39.

5. Richard M. Pious, *The American Presidency* (New York: Basic Books, 1979), p. 212.

6. Leadership and management studies have not investigated this phenomenon. Though they distinguish between problems of attaining and of maintaining leadership, they seldom touch systematically on how an outsider can become a real leader of an organization.

7. Harlan Cleveland, *The Future Executive* (New York: Harper & Row, 1972) p. 13.

8. Michael Maccoby et al., *Bringing Out the Best,* Final Report of the Project to Improve Work and Management in the Department of Commerce, 1977–1979, John F. Kennedy School of Government, Harvard University, March 1980, pp. 1–21.

9. Paul R. Lawrence and Jay W. Lorsch, *Organization and Environment: Managing Differentiation and Integration* (Cambridge: Division of Research, Graduate School of Business Administration, Harvard University, 1967), p. 2.

10. Ibid., p. 243.

11. Ibid., p. 245.

12. For a detailed if somewhat dated account of such offices, see Arnold J. Meltsner, *Policy Analysts in the Bureaucracy* (Berkeley: Univ. of California Pr., 1976), pp. 173–77.

13. Ibid., p. 220.

14. Neal R. Peirce, "The Democratic Nominee—'If I Were President . . .'," *National Journal* 8:29 (July 17, 1976): 993–94.

15. Charles Schultze, *The Politics and Economics of Public Spending* (Washington, D.C.: Brookings Institution, 1968), p. 102.

16. Quoted by Martin Schram, "For Carter One Crisis May Solve Another," *Washington Post,* December 2, 1979, p. A6.

17. Jack Nelson, "Cabinet Aides Get Word: Toe Carter Line," *Boston Globe,* April 21, 1978, p. 1.

18. Walter Pincus, "Carter Called Mistaken on Some Points in Veto Message" *Washington Post,* September 1, 1978, p. A2.

19. See Lester M. Salamon, "The Presidency and Domestic Policy I, The Changing Context: Interdependence, Third-Party Government, and the Democratic Distemper. A paper prepared for "Managing the Federal Government: The Role of the President," a panel meeting of the National Academy of Public Administration, April 10–11, 1980, Washington, D.C.

20. Steven Roberts, "Many Members of House Retiring as Pressures Outweigh Rewards," *New York Times,* March 27, 1978, p. 1.

21. Lawrence Dodd and Richard L. Schott, *Congress and the Administrative State* (New York: Wiley, 1979), pp. 231–32.

22. David A. Stockman, "The Social Pork Barrel," *The Public Interest,* 39 (Spring 1975): 3–30.

23. Ward Sinclair, "Administration's Bill Loses Out as Rules on Hill Have Changed," *Washington Post,* November 14, 1978, p. A4.

24. Ibid.

25. Quoted by Ward Sinclair, "HEW Lobbying Faulted," *Washington Post,* November 13, 1978, p. A1.

26. Don K. Price, "The Institutional Presidency and the Unwritten Constitution." A paper presented for discussion at a roundtable at the White Burkett Miller Center of Public Affairs, University of Virginia, March 1980, p. 22.

27. For an excellent discussion of presidential management styles and models, see Alexander L. George, *Presidential Decisionmaking in Foreign Policy: The Effective Use of Information and Advice* (Boulder, Colo.: Westview Press, 1980), part 2.

28. Timothy B. Clark, "The Power Vacuum Outside the Oval Office," *National Journal* 11:8 (February 24, 1979): 298.

29. Ibid., p. 296.

30. Laurence E. Lynn, Jr., and John M. Seidl, "Policy Analysis at HEW: The Story of the Mega-Proposal," *Policy Analysis* 1:2 (Spring 1975): 232–73.

References

31. Ibid. 267.

32. David S. Broder, "The Case of the Missing Shoe Import Option," *Washington Post,* July 23, 1977, p. 4.

33. Lewis A. Dexter, "Some Strategic Considerations in Innovating Leadership," in Alvin W. Gouldner, ed., *Studies in Leadership; Leadership in Action* (New York: Russell & Russell, 1960), p. 592.

34. George P. Schultz and Kenneth W. Dam, *Economic Policy Beyond the Headlines* (New York: W.W. Norton, 1977), p. 159.

35. See, for example, the following works by E. E. Ghiselli; *Explorations in Management Talent,* (Pacific Palisades, Calif.: Goodyear, 1971); "Differentiation of Individuals in Terms of Their Predictability," *Journal of Applied Psychology* 40:6 (December 1956): 374–77; "Traits Differentiating Management Personnel," *Personnel Psychology* 12:4 (December 1959): 535–44; "The Validity of Management Traits Related to Occupational Level," *Personnel Psychology* 16:2 (May 1963): 109–12. See also M. D. Dunnette, "Predictors of Executive Success," in F. R. Wickert and D. E. McFarland, eds., *Measuring Executive Effectiveness* (New York: Appleton-Century-Crofts, 1967), pp. 7–48; A. K. Korman, "Organizational Achievement, Aggression, and Creativity," *Organization Behavior and Human Performance* 6:5 (September 1971): 539–613; Allan Nash, "Vocational Interests of Effective Managers," *Personal Psychology* 18:1 (February 1965): 21–38. Cited by Barry Bozeman, *Public Management and Policy Analysis* (New York: St. Martin's Pr., 1979), p. 206, n. 14, p. 207, n. 15.

36. "Recent developments in cognitive balance and dissonance theories, attribution theory, attitude theory, social learning theory, and personality theory are moving or already have moved each of them into an information-processing framework." George, *Presidential Decisionmaking in Foreign Policy,* pp. 55–56.

37. James L. McKenney and Peter G. W. Keen, "How Managers' Minds Work," *Harvard Business Review* 52:3 (May/June 1974): 79–90.

38. Ibid., p. 81.

39. John D. Steinbruner, *The Cybernetic Theory of Decision: New Dimensions of Political Analysis* (Princeton: Princeton Univ. Pr., 1974). See also Robert F. Coulam, *Illusions of Choice: The F-111 and the Problem of Weapons Acquisition Reform* (Princeton: Princeton Univ. Pr., 1977). George notes that a "shift has occurred away from the fundamental premise of earlier cognitive balance theories that viewed man as a 'consistency seeker' to the different premise of recent attribution theory (and other psychological theories as well), which views man as a 'problem solver.'" George, *Presidential Decisionmaking in Foreign Policy,* p. 56.

40. Joseph Kraft, "Colliding Moral Decisions," *Washington Post,* June 20, 1978, p. A11.

41. Rowland Evans and Robert Novak, "The 'Divided' President," *Washington Post,* June 14, 1978, p. A27.

42. Paul Clancy and Shirley Elder, "The Speaker and the President So Near and Yet So Far" *Boston Globe* magazine, April 27, 1980, pp. 50–51.

43. Heidi Sinick, "Cooling Off with Elliot Richardson," *Washington Post Potomac,* February 17, 1974, p. 14.

44. Elliot L. Richardson, Preface *Policy Analysis* 1:2 (Spring 1975): 224.

45. Dan Morgan, "Trying to Lead the USDA Through the Thicket of Politics," *Washington Post,* July 5, 1978, p. A8.

46. Ibid.

47. Mark Green, "Open Letter to Cabinet Newcomers: How to Make a Difference and Avoid Instant Obscurity," *Washington Post,* September 23, 1979, p. C8.

48. Quoted in Bozeman, *Public Management and Policy Analysis* p. 208. The study quoted is R. M. Stogdill and A. E. Coons, eds., *Leader Behavior: Its Description and Measurement* (Columbus: Bureau of Business Research, Ohio State University, 1957). See also Daniel Katz, Nathan Macoby, and Nancy Mosse, *Productivity, Supervision, and Morale in an Office Situation* (Ann Arbor: Survey Research Center, University of Michigan, 1950).

49. Herbert Kaufman, "Reflections on Administrative Reorganization," in Joseph A. Pechman, ed., *Setting National Priorities: The 1978 Budget* (Washington, D.C.: Brookings Institution, 1977), p. 400.

50. The following is based on ideas contained in Laurence E. Lynn, Jr., and John M. Seidl,

References

" 'Bottom-Line' Management for Public Agencies," *Harvard Business Review* 55:1 (January/February 1977): 144–53.

51. Robert W. Fri, "How to Manage the Government for Results: The Rise of MBO," *Organizational Dynamics* 2:4 (Spring 1974): 19–33.

52. Stephen Hess, *Organizing the Presidency* (Washington, D.C.: Brookings Institution, 1976), p. 10.

53. Commission on Organization of the Executive Branch of Government, *The Hoover Commission Report* (New York: McGraw-Hill, 1949), p. 5.

INDEX

Index